AIDS CRISIS IN AMERICA

A Reference Handbook
Second Edition

Other Titles in ABC-CLIO's
CONTEMPORARY
WORLD ISSUES
Series

Abortion, Second Edition, Marie Costa
American Homelessness, Second Edition, Mary Ellen Hombs
Drug Abuse in Society, Geraldine Woods
Euthanasia, Martha Gorman and Carolyn Roberts
Feminism, Judith Harlan
Gay and Lesbian Rights, David E. Newton
Human Rights, Second Edition, Nina Redman and Lucille Whalen
Religion in the Schools, James John Jurinski
The Religious Right, Glenn H. Utter and John W. Storey
Victims' Rights, Leigh Glenn
Welfare Reform, Mary Ellen Hombs

Books in the Contemporary World Issues series address vital issues in today's society such as terrorism, sexual harassment, homelessness, human rights, gambling, animal rights, and air pollution. Written by professional writers, scholars, and nonacademic experts, these books are authoritative, clearly written, up-to-date, and objective. They provide a good starting point for research by high school and college students, scholars, and general readers, as well as by legislators, businesspeople, activists, and others.

Each book, carefully organized and easy to use, contains an overview of the subject; a detailed chronology; biographical sketches; facts and data and/or documents and other primary-source material; a directory of organizations and agencies; annotated lists of print and nonprint resources; a glossary; and an index.

Readers of books in the Contemporary World Issues series will find the information they need in order to better understand the social, political, environmental, and economic issues facing the world today.

AIDS CRISIS
IN AMERICA

A Reference Handbook
Second Edition

Eric K. Lerner and
Mary Ellen Hombs

**CONTEMPORARY
WORLD ISSUES**

ABC-CLIO

Santa Barbara, California
Denver, Colorado
Oxford, England

Library of Congress Cataloging-in-Publication Data
Lerner, Eric K.
    AIDS crisis in America : a reference handbook / Eric K. Lerner and Mary Ellen Hombs.—2nd ed.
        p. cm.—(Contemporary world issues)
    Previously published: AIDS crisis in America / Mary Ellen Hombs. Santa Barbara, Calif. : ABC-CLIO, 1992.
    Includes bibliographical references and index.
    ISBN 1-57607-070-0 (alk. paper)
    1. AIDS (Disease)—United States—Epidemiology.   2. AIDS (Disease)—Government policy—United States. 3. AIDS (Disease)—United States—Bibliography.   I. Hombs, Mary Ellen.   II. Hombs, Mary Ellen. AIDS crisis in America.   III. Title.   IV. Series.
    RA44.A25H655   1998
    362.1'969792'00973—dc21   98-25764
                                                                              CIP

04 03 02 01 00 99 98   10 9 8 7 6 5 4 3 2 1

ABC-CLIO, Inc.
130 Cremona Drive, P.O. Box 1911
Santa Barbara, California 93116-1911

This book is printed on acid-free paper ♾ .

Manufactured in the United States of America

In memory of
Earl Erick Lerner

Contents

List of Tables, xiii
Preface, xv

1 Introduction, 1
    AIDS: The Beginning of an
        Epidemic, 1
    Background, 3
    The Basic Science of AIDS, 5
    Medical Treatment of HIV, 9
    Demographics of HIV, 11
    Community Response to
        AIDS, 12
    The Government Response to
        HIV/AIDS, 15
    Systems of Care in the United
        States, 21
    The Role of People with AIDS
        in Shaping Public Policy, 25
    The Role of Business, 27
    The Impact of Combination
        Therapy, 30
    Ramifications for the Future, 32
    Notes, 35

2 Chronology, 39

3 Biographical Sketches, 81

4 Facts and Statistics, 95
    Centers for Disease Control Surveillance Case
        Definition, 95
    Opportunistic Infections, 97
    HIV Testing, 103
        Privacy and Testing, 104
        Testing Centers, 104
    Development of an AIDS Vaccine, 104
    The World Situation, 106
        Sub-Saharan Africa, 108
        Asia, 111
        Latin America, 113
        The Caribbean, 114
        Eastern Europe and Central Asia (Russia), 115
        Western Europe, Australia, and New Zealand, 115
    AIDS in the United States, 116
        U.S. Government Funding for AIDS Research and
            Treatment, 116
        The Rise and Decline of AIDS Mortality during the
            Epidemic, 116
        AIDS in Individual States, 119
        Needle Exchange in the States, 130
    HIV/AIDS in Specific U.S. Populations, 132
        Men Who Have Sex with Other Men, 132
        Women, 137
        Children, 144
        Adolescents, 148
        The Elderly, 149
        African Americans, 152
        Hispanics, 154
        Native Americans, 156
        Hemophiliacs, 157
        Injection Drug Users, 158
        Prisoners, 160
        Health Care Workers, 161

HIV/AIDS and American Public Opinion, 162
Notes, 162

5 Documents and Reports, 169

The Onset of the Epidemic in the
United States, 169
Opportunistic Infections, 170
Naming the Disease, 175
Blood and Blood Products, 176
Perinatal Transmission, 179
Transmission among Heterosexuals and Prison
Inmates, 179
Risk Reduction, 180
Government Responses to the Epidemic, 182
The Surgeon General's Report, 182
Presidential Advisory Council on HIV/AIDS
Resolution on Needle Exchange Programs, 189
Firsthand Perspectives on the Epidemic, 190
People with AIDS (PWAs) Take a Stand, 190
Women and HIV/AIDS, 192
Injection Drug Users, 193
Homeless People with HIV/AIDS, 194
Hemophiliacs, 196
The Impact of HIV/AIDS on Other Aspects of
Society, 198
HIV/AIDS and the Correctional System, 198
HIV/AIDS and the Workplace, 204
Notes, 205

6 HIV/AIDS and the Law, 207

Significant Legislation since 1982, 207
Legal Aspects of HIV/AIDS, 210
Discrimination, 210
Criminal Prosecution for HIV Transmission, 211
Legal Considerations for HIV-Infected Persons, 214
Selected Cases, 217
Americans with Disabilities Act Cases, 217
Biting, 222
Employment and Workplace Issues, 222

HIV and Health Care Professionals, 225
HIV-Positive Children and Their Rights, 225
HIV Status and the Right to a Fair Trial, 227
Housing, 227
Parental Rights, 227
Rape and Attempted Murder, 228
Sentencing and the Impact of Seropositive
    Status, 228
Sexual Acts by HIV-Positive Individuals Who Do
    Not Divulge Their Status, 229
Social Security Appeals, 229
Testing and Confidentiality, 230
Notes, 232

7 Government Agencies, Organizations, and
    Hot Lines, 235
Federal Agencies, 235
National Nonprofit Organizations, 238
PWA Organizations in Canada and the United
    States by Province and State, 247
    Canada, 248
    United States, 248
State AIDS Hot Lines, 251
Patient Assistance Programs, 255

8 Reference Materials, 259
Print Materials, 260
    Reference Books, 260
    Newsletters and Pamphlets, 265
    Anthologies, 275
    Personal Accounts, 278
    Photographic Works, 282
Nonprint Materials, 283
    Films and Videos, 283
    CD-Roms, 289
    Websites, 292

Glossary, 295
Index, 315
About the Authors, 325

Tables

4.1 Regional HIV/AIDS Statistics and Features, December 1997, 107

4.2 U.S. AIDS Cases by Age Group, Exposure Category, and Sex, July 1995– June 1997, 117

4.3 U.S. Government AIDS Expenditures, Fiscal Years 1996–1998, 119

4.4 U.S. AIDS Cases, Case Fatality Rates, and Deaths, 1981–June 1997, 120

4.5 U.S. AIDS Cases and Annual Rates per 100,000 Population, by State, July 1995–June 1997, 121

4.6 Persons Reported to be Living with HIV and AIDS by State and Age Group, through June 1997, 122

4.7 Fiscal Year 1997 ADAP Funding by State and Source, 125

4.8 Estimated State ADAP Client Income Levels Based on Federal Poverty Guidelines, 127

4.9 U.S. Male Adult and Adolescent AIDS Cases by Exposure Category and Race/Ethnicity, July 1996–June 1997, 133

4.10 U.S. Female Adult and Adolescent AIDS Cases by Exposure Category and Race/Ethnicity, July 1996–June 1997, 139

4.11 U.S. Pediatric AIDS Cases by Exposure Category and Race/Ethnicity, July 1996–June 1997, 146

4.12 U.S. AIDS Cases in Adolescents and Adults under Age 25, by Sex and Exposure Category, July 1995–June 1997, 150

Preface

Offering a comprehensive picture of the history, significance, and future of HIV/AIDS in this country is a formidable task, even though so much has already been written on the subject of HIV/AIDS and its impact in the United States. Yet it seems that now in light of recent treatment advances, Americans have developed a sense of complacency in dealing with the epidemic. They seem to think that the crisis is over, but nothing can be further from the truth. Current statistics indicate that a large number of people fail treatment on the new multidrug cocktail combinations for a variety of reasons, including naturally occurring resistance, adverse side effects, and individual failure to comply with complex dosing regimens. Furthermore, not every HIV-infected individual accesses these therapies. In 1997, researchers from the Columbia School of Public Health conducted a study of 700 HIV-infected New Yorkers. They found that of white patients, 33 percent took protease inhibitors, while only 12 percent of African American patients did.[1] Another concern is that those who have developed resistance to the newest therapies will transmit drug-resistant strains of HIV, which may be even more pernicious (similar to multidrug resistant tuberculosis, which arose in urban

America in the wake of AIDS). The evidence suggests that HIV/AIDS is going to thrive in the United States for some time and continue to be a killer of Americans in the prime of life.

This book offers a variety of resources in the hope that every individual can find a way to connect with this important problem and presents readable information that does not evade the blunt impact of the facts since 1981. It will be obvious from reading this material that the reality of HIV/AIDS is very close to home for most Americans. The epidemic of HIV/AIDS in our nation now reaches into every kind of community: urban and suburban, small cities, rural areas. All sorts of institutions have responded to it, some unwillingly: schools, religious communities, hospitals, offices, and industries. As a result, students at every level, their teachers, writers, and the concerned public have sought further information about the causes of HIV/AIDS and its solutions. Countless school papers and research projects have been undertaken. For all those individuals who come into closest contact with HIV/AIDS—whether they be health care workers, teachers, religious leaders, volunteers, or those touched on a personal level—there is a need to access accurate information presented in a straightforward manner. The goal for this book is to provide a basis for understanding and the means with which to further investigate.

Chapter 1 is an introductory essay designed to give an overview of the history and challenges posed by AIDS. Chapters 2 and 3 include a survey of key events and players in the history of the epidemic and a time line of significant activity. Chapter 4 provides a quick reference to facts and statistics on the epidemic. Tables and overviews of important facts are provided to show how HIV/AIDS affects populations of the world, the nation, the states, and special groups. Chapter 5 examines the U.S. epidemic through documents and reports from original sources. These are presented first historically, through excerpts from government reports, and then according to groups of people and social institutions affected by HIV/AIDS. Legal aspects of HIV, including federal legislation, the U.S. Supreme Court decision on the application of the Americans with Disabilities Act to asymptomatic HIV-positive individuals, discrimination, criminal prosecutions for HIV-transmission, and legal considerations for HIV-infected individuals are covered in Chapter 6. The chapter concludes with a selection of legal cases revolving around HIV. Because HIV/AIDS represents such a complex problem, there are many professional and voluntary organizations, as well as government agencies, involved in studying it and addressing it. Chapter 7 provides a selective listing of these groups and offers sources for further pursuit of specialized interests and opportunities for personal involvement. Chapter 8 presents an extensive reference bibliography that includes print, audiovisual, and Internet resources.

Acknowledgments

No one attempting to write about this topic could do so honestly without acknowledging the excellent documentary work done by many others affected by the epidemic, or the countless volunteers and professionals who endured my endless questions. I have tried to list all of them in Chapters 7 and 8. I hope that many more people will be encouraged to appreciate their dedication. I would especially like to thank Lee Hardy, AIDS Research Information Center, Inc., for his encouragement and vast resource of knowledge; my mother, Patricia Lerner, for her unfailing support; Baba Raul Canizares, for his nurturing, insight, and guidance; Narayan Ramos for standing up for me; and, perhaps most of all, my eleda, Obatala Ajaguna, for whatever quality in myself that enabled me to see this project through; my spiritual mother, Yemaya Olokun for her protection; and to Olodumare, all ancestors and orishas (Mo juba.)

Notes

1. Leroy Whitfield. 1997. "Black Plague." *Positively Aware* 8.5: 42.

Introduction 1

AIDS: The Beginning of an Epidemic

First, a couple of snapshots from early in the history of AIDS in the United States:

1982. Baltimore, Maryland. A young man bides time in a dimly lit gay bar. He reads the local gay paper, which features a story about six gay men hospitalized with either a rare form of pneumonia or a cancer previously seen only in elderly Mediterranean men. Immediately, his mind flashes back to a Japanese science fiction movie called *The Mysterians* that he saw as a child in which an alien race unleashed a fatal virus that decimated the human race. At one point the alien leader, who looked like a precursor to Darth Vader, announced on every television in the world: "Resistance is futile—surrender all hope." People fell dead in the street, covered with spots like medieval plague victims. That movie kept an eight-year-old boy up for weeks. Now he can't remember how it ended, but he feels he's back living those childhood nightmares. A former partner comes over to him, but his face has the drawn look of a sick person. The young man mumbles some words and walks away.

1

Later in 1982. New York, New York. Representatives of the gay community are gathered to discuss police brutality against the community. Larry Kramer starts shouting about the mounting number of gay men dying—a topic the organizers did not wish to include on the agenda. "How can we just stand around here when we are dying in droves?" he asks. There is a chilled silence in the room after he speaks. Many lower their eyes and quietly wring their hands.

1983. New York, New York. A reporter enters an urban hospital to interview a gay man afflicted with AIDS who claims he is being abused by the hospital staff. The patient charges that the nurses won't change his bed pan or answer his calls; frequently, they make fun of him in his presence as though he isn't there. The reporter is accompanied by the man's caseworker from the Gay Men's Health Crisis organization. The two men must suit up in surgical gloves, mask, and gown to pay a visit. The patient is in his early forties. His skin has the texture of suede and hangs loosely from his torso, which is exposed by an undone gown, and from his face. A web of tubes is fused to his arms and nose. His pupils are dilated, making his eyes appear even more sunken. Yet, he speaks gently, not even saying harsh things about the nurses who seem determined not to care for him. At one point, he reflects that he still feels desire, then he pauses as if he realizes such a thing is impossible. On their way out, the caseworker tells the reporter about another case. The patient was comatose. When the caseworker walked in to visit, a nurse was measuring the circumference of his anus to settle a lottery among the staff. Three years later, the reporter reads the caseworker's obituary in the *New York Times*.

Even in these early years of the epidemic, gay men were not alone in experiencing the devastation of AIDS. In 1987, Randy Shilts wrote in *And the Band Played On*:

> Unsettling news came from every borough. Haitians were showing up at Brooklyn hospitals with toxoplasmosis. A number of them also contracted Pneumocystis, implying a connection with GRID [Gay Related Immune Deficiency]. The Haitians adamantly insisted they were heterosexual.
>
> There were also more junkies coming down with gay pneumonia in the Bronx. At the Albert Einstein College of Medicine, Dr. Arye Rubinstein was trying in vain to get his colleagues to believe that the sick babies he was seeing were also victims of GRID.[1]

Background

The human immune system disorder now known as Acquired Immune Deficiency Syndrome, or AIDS, was first identified in the United States in 1981, when physicians in New York City and San Francisco were confronted with the mysterious deaths of a growing number of young men who had illnesses usually held in check by the body's natural defenses. By the end of 1996, over 379,258 American men, women, and children lost their lives to AIDS according to the Centers for Disease Control (CDC). According to UNAIDS, the figure worldwide then stood at 11.7 million deaths.

A period of delay between HIV infection and the onset of related illness makes it difficult to fully assess the impact HIV will have, regardless of current prevention efforts. Currently, only 29 states report HIV infections; that group does not include the three states with the greatest number of AIDS cases. Thus, any CDC estimate of total cases in the United States is a guess.

Since 1996 there has been a decline in the number of both AIDS deaths and new AIDS cases in the United States because of recent advances in therapy. This decline has been achieved with the use of a class of drugs known as protease inhibitors in combination with at least two other antiretroviral medications. Not all infected people can take advantage of these drugs, however. A recent study shows that one-third of white Americans with AIDS use a protease inhibitor as part of their treatment, whereas only 12 percent of black Americans do.[2] More than 50 percent of AIDS sufferers in the United States today are either black or Hispanic.[3] Furthermore, whereas historically AIDS has infected predominantly gay men, more than 50 percent of current infections in the United States stem from injection drug use.[4] Heterosexual transmission is increasingly prevalent.[5] The fastest-growing group of people newly exposed to HIV is Americans over age 55.[6] The epidemic is taking on the mutable character of HIV itself, which is highly variable and can change in response to exposure to drugs.[7]

Worldwide, UNAIDS estimates that 31.6 million people are living with the HIV infection—virtually 1 percent of the adult population in the prime of life.[8] Approximately 8.2 million orphans have been created by the pandemic, and 16,000 new infections occur daily.[9] Treatment with the latest therapies is beyond the means of 90 percent of infected people, and an effective preventive or therapeutic vaccine may be decades away.[10]

The situation in sub-Saharan Africa has attracted special attention, since nearly two-thirds of people with AIDS live there.[11] In fact, scientists have traced the first case of AIDS to a Bantu man from the Congo who died in 1959.

The plague in Africa may seem remote to citizens of the United States. But today, the holy in Gongohoue, Benin, gather local villagers together at a feast for Sakpata (a.k.a. Babalu-aiye), a spirit associated with pestilence, during which they hand out condoms and share information about how to prevent AIDS.[12] Also today, a priest in Tampa, Florida, takes the lit end of a cigar in his mouth and cleanses a young female AIDS sufferer with a stream of smoke in the name of Babalu-aiye in a rite of healing repeated in barrios throughout the United States. This juxtaposition reminds us that the same spirit of pestilence ravaging bodies on distant continents also resides in our midst. We are all human beings who aspire either to avoid affliction or be healed.

Worldwide, heterosexual transmissions account for more than 70 percent of infections.[13] As previously noted, heterosexual transmissions are increasing rapidly as a mode of infection in the United States, but HIV/AIDS continues to be seen as primarily a disease of gay men and intravenous (IV) drug users, the first groups infected in the country.[14] Although AIDS is now known to result from HIV, a retrovirus, the U.S. epidemic has been fueled as much by the social factors of political disenfranchisement, homophobia, racism, and sexism as by any infectious agent.

This book will document the biological mechanisms through which HIV infects people and the complex issues the virus raises for the greater society. The stigma of AIDS compounds existing problems of prejudice and social inequity. The burdens faced by communities already struggling with discrimination, poverty, a lack of health care, and drug addiction have increased incrementally in the wake of this disease. The vast numbers of HIV/AIDS cases in these communities have provoked fear and contempt among the politically powerful rather than mobilize them to develop adequate resources for essential medical research and necessary systems of care.

Certainly, significant improvements in the provision of care to infected populations have been made in recent years, but efforts have been inadequate to the challenge. Many of the afflicted go without treatment, and no consistent strategy for prevention has been developed on a national level.[15]

It remains to be seen how society will adjust as the epidemic continues to evolve dynamically in response to changing treatment options and the composition of infected populations. What will happen as those who have developed resistance to protease inhibitors infect others with a drug-resistant virus? Will new strains be more deadly and more contagious than previous ones? Will an increase in longevity among those infected overwhelm the Medicaid and Social Security systems on which so many Americans rely for medical care and maintenance? These questions will challenge future leaders on the issue of HIV/AIDS.

Meanwhile, HIV has entrenched itself as part of America's social landscape. Nearly everyone knows someone who has been infected. The tremendous cost in young lives lost has had a devastating effect on individuals, families, and society in general. Many persons from infected communities—particularly the gay community—have transformed their grief and loss into an unparalleled response of activism, creating new organizations and new approaches to providing medical care and support services.

HIV has also insinuated itself into institutions, such as businesses. Anti-HIV/AIDS drugs represent a great source of profit for the pharmaceutical industry, and those drugs are likely to be in demand for some time. Other industries have grown up around the epidemic. Many institutions, such as medical care facilities, have had to make continual adjustments throughout the course of the epidemic.

Ultimately, the AIDS epidemic forces all institutions of American society to establish new policies—whether it is the military, which bans HIV-positive people from enlisting, or a Philadelphia church that posts a sign indicating that those with HIV are not welcome to worship there. Young people today will need to determine future public policy.

The Basic Science of AIDS

In 1998, the mystery of the early infections discussed previously has been explained as Acquired Immune Deficiency Syndrome, which results from infection with HIV. Transmission of the virus occurs through exchange of body fluids, most typically as a result of vaginal or anal intercourse; exchange of blood products, as occurs when sharing syringes or through the direct infusion of blood products; and congenital or perinatal exchange transmission between a mother and her fetus or newborn child.

HIV is a retrovirus—a type of primitive virus unknown in humans until very recently that is much smaller and less complex in structure than a normal virus. A retrovirus's inner core consists only of a partial strand of ribonucleic acid (RNA), which carries genetic information for retroviruses, as opposed to that of deoxyribonucleic acid (DNA), which is the autoreproducing agent for many viruses. Its simpler structure, however, does not make it easier to attack medically; in fact, these very simple viruses overcome normal immune defenses. The structure of the HIV retrovirus is an RNA core protected by an inner capsid of structural proteins surrounded by an outer envelope composed of simple glycoproteins and a liposome-based shell. The outer envelope is made up largely of materials taken from human cell membranes. The immune system has a difficult time telling the difference between HIV and normal human cells, which is one reason HIV defeats the body's immune defenses. The outer envelope glycoproteins are used by the virus to attach itself to T4 cells, the main target of HIV.[16] HIV then attacks the cells of the immune system, thus compromising the body's ability to fight off disease. A patient becomes subject to a host of opportunistic infections that are present in most people's bodies but require a weakened immune system to flourish.

It can take from a few months to many years for HIV to damage the immune system. Initial entry to T4 cells and macrophages is gained through the bloodstream. An initial immune response is mounted, which recent studies show may be characterized by fever, joint pain, and night sweats.[17] HIV proliferates to a high level in the blood, and the body mounts an immune response to the infection and usually develops antibodies within six months.[18] These antibodies are detected by the Enzyme-Linked-Immuno-Sorbent Assay (ELISA) and Western Blot tests, typically used to identify HIV infection. The antibodies do not eliminate all of the virus, which multiplies and causes gradual damage to the immune function as it kills T4 cells and causes macrophages to function improperly. The damage may be detected by a decline in the number of T4 cells. A T4 cell count of 1,000 is considered normal; under 200 indicates a severe compromise of the immune system. The appearance of frequent, unusual, or severe infections indicates that the immune system is not operating properly.[19]

This resulting dysfunction of the immune system is recognized as AIDS, a term that describes the syndrome of certain opportunistic infections resulting from immune deficiency that has been acquired. AIDS itself is not a disease; it is an acronym used to describe a number of illnesses that appear in someone whose immune system has been weakened by HIV infection. The first stage of the HIV spectrum is described as asymptomatic HIV infection, meaning infection is present without symptoms. A person may be seropositive, meaning he or she has tested positive for HIV antibodies but has no visible symptoms and may remain healthy for a number of years. Several long-term studies of gay men with HIV infection have shown that HIV is a progressive infection that leads to serious illness in a majority of people in 8 to 12 years.[20]

It is important to note that children born with HIV disease do not have acquired immune deficiency but rather a primary immune deficiency. Therefore, the presentation of symptoms and opportunistic infections is very different for that group.[21]

As the immune system is gradually damaged, the person becomes symptomatic or HIV ill, experiencing a variety of symptoms that may include lymphadenopathy (chronically swollen lymph nodes), weight loss, fatigue, diarrhea, night sweats, thrush (oral candidiasis, a white plaque coating the tongue), severe skin conditions, and other problems.[22] Women have experienced chronic vaginitis, pelvic inflammatory disease, cervical cancer, and chronic sexually transmitted diseases.[23]

With the body's defenses substantially impaired, the HIV-infected person becomes unusually vulnerable to serious infectious illnesses such as tuberculosis, endocarditis (an infection of the heart's lining), meningitis, and bacterial pneumonias. These infections also affect the general population, but they occur far more frequently and are potentially fatal in HIV-infected persons.[24]

Persons with severe immune deficiency, indicated by a T cell count of 50 or less, may succumb to one or more opportunistic infections such as *Pneumocystis carinii* pneumonia (PCP) or Kaposi's sarcoma. Many people with serious immune suppression also develop one of a number of related organic mental disorders such as cognitive impairment (language or movement disorders) known as AIDS dementia complex.[25]

The course of illness after the appearance of HIV-related symptoms varies greatly from person to person, depending on access to medical care, psychological and social stability, nutrition, drug and alcohol use, availability of appropriate housing and support services, and other factors that affect health. The progression of HIV infection in children, who have immature immune systems, is likely to be much more rapid than that in adults, although some children have a long, relatively stable course.[26]

The federal CDC definition of AIDS was developed as an official surveillance tool using specific diagnostic criteria to enable the medical community to track the spread of HIV illness.[27] The

CDC initially defined AIDS as HIV infection plus a history of one of a number of opportunistic infections that are extremely rare and unquestionably related to immune deficiency. That definition was increasingly criticized, however, because it excluded other serious infections known to be intimately associated with HIV infection, such as pulmonary tuberculosis and bacterial pneumonias. Moreover, because it was based on HIV-related manifestations in gay white men, the group studied the most early in the epidemic, CDC's initial definition of AIDS excluded significant numbers of women, persons of color, and persons who had contracted HIV through IV drug use.[28] Despite the rapid changes in our understanding of the HIV/AIDS epidemic and the communities affected, CDC's definition of AIDS was not revised between 1987 and 1992.

Although it has been generally acknowledged that the initial CDC definition of AIDS included only a small portion of the spectrum of HIV patients, statistics based on the definition were widely used to allocate funding and set research priorities. Federal disability entitlements, Medicaid, and a variety of other benefits were also tied to the definition. Up until 1992, many patients died without ever reaching a CDC diagnosis. Under mounting pressure to expand the definition, CDC announced in August 1991 that it would implement a new surveillance definition of AIDS by early 1992 that would include all individuals with extremely low T4 cell counts (below 200); however, it did not do so until 1993. The CDC has since revised the number of recorded AIDS deaths for the period before that date.

To summarize, in *Medical Management of HIV Infection*, John Bartlett analyzes the progression of HIV disease in the following stages:

- Viral transmission
- Primary HIV infection
- Seroconversion
- Clinical latent period with or without persistent generalized lymphadenopathy (swollen glands) (PGL)
- Early symptomatic HIV infection (previously known as AIDS-Related Complex [ARC] and more recently referred to as B symptoms according to the 1992 CDC classification)
- AIDS indicator condition according to the 1987 CDC criteria and revised 1993 CDC criteria that include a CD4 cell count of 200/mm or less

• Advanced HIV infection characterized by a CD4 cell count of 50/mm or less[29]

Medical Treatment of HIV

In 1996, *Time* magazine named medical researcher David Ho its Man of the Year for "helping lift a death sentence—for a few years at least, and perhaps longer—on tens of thousands of AIDS sufferers, and for pioneering the treatment that might, just might lead to a cure [for HIV/AIDS]."[30] This belief was based on the extraordinary finding that a class of drugs known as protease inhibitors used in combination with two existing anti-HIV drugs could reduce the amount of virus in an HIV-infected person's blood to undetectable levels and spur at least a partial regeneration of the immune system. *Time* acknowledged in its accolade that this course of treatment is well beyond the means of 90 percent of AIDS sufferers worldwide, including many in the United States, because of its extraordinary cost of up to $20,000 per year.[31]

In light of this recent advance, the impact of which is discussed in more detail later in this chapter, it may be difficult to fathom how dark the situation appeared before the discovery. Little more than twenty years ago, in 1977, an overwhelming sense of frustration gripped the medical professionals treating Grethe Rask—arguably the first Western European to die of AIDS —for an unknown disease probably of tropical origin. Those professionals could not solve the mysteries of her case. The disease could be some common tropical culprit they had overlooked. The doctors pleaded with Rask to undergo more tests.

> The virulent microbes that were haunting her body were not revealed by the bombardment of tests she endured in her last days. On December 12, 1977, Rask died at age forty-seven.
>
> An autopsy revealed that Rask's lungs were filled with millions of organisms known as *Pneumocystis carinii*; the organisms had caused a rare pneumonia that had caused her to slowly suffocate. The diagnosis raised more questions than answers: No one died of *Pneumocystis*.[32]

In the twenty years between Rask's death and the advent of combination therapy, many strategies were tried, but few yielded meaningful long-term results for HIV sufferers. Benchmarks in the medical treatment of HIV disease include:

- May 1983—Luc Montagnier team at the Pasteur Institute in Paris identifies a retrovirus (later known as HIV in the United States) as the cause of AIDS
- March 1985—The U.S. Food and Drug Administration (FDA) approves the first HIV antibody test
- March 1987—Zidovudine® (AZT) is approved by the FDA as the first anti-HIV drug
- 1988—The Salk Immunogen Vaccine, a therapeutic vaccine for those infected with HIV, enters human trials and shows some promising results over the next four years, although large-scale trials and development have yet to be done
- June 1989—Aerosolized pentamidine is approved by the FDA for the treatment and prophylaxis of *Pneumocystis carinii* pneumonia, the leading cause of death for people with AIDS
- November 1995—The FDA announces that the drug 3TC (Zerit) used in combination with AZT is the preferred first line of treatment in primary HIV care because the two drugs together deter HIV from developing resistance

In the six-year gap between the approval of pentamidine and the endorsement of the 3TC/AZT combination, few prospects existed for developing an effective medical response to HIV disease. The pessimism throughout the medical research community was so strong that the 1994 International Conference on AIDS was postponed for a year because so few advances had been made at the previous year's conference.

Through the mid-1990s, the lack of available treatments meant there was little advantage to learning whether one was infected with HIV. The stigma and discrimination associated with such infection caused many to decide not to seek testing. The benefits of knowing one's HIV status have changed, however, with the development of combination therapy that may indefinitely delay the onset of HIV-related illness through early intervention, and most health care professionals believe access to the new therapy creates an incentive for testing. Unfortunately, as mentioned previously, such treatment remains largely unavailable for many poor persons who have little or no access to health care.

Demographics of HIV

Initially, in the early 1980s, the demographics of the AIDS epidemic were defined by "the 'Four H's' of the disease risk groups—homosexuals, heroin addicts, hemophiliacs, and Haitians."[33] Since none of these groups was a part of the social mainstream, it was easy for society to overlook their suffering or to create bizarre explanations for it. For instance, it was theorized that gay men destroyed their immune systems through their voracious sexual appetites and that Haitians afflicted themselves through blood contact in religious rituals.[34] Hemophiliacs were thus stigmatized by this association with outsider groups. And medical professionals feared for their own welfare because the groups at risk for AIDS were those susceptible to hepatitis—as were medical professionals.[35]

In April 1985, more than a year after it was recognized that AIDS is caused by the HIV retrovirus, the CDC removed Haitian immigrants from the list of groups especially at risk for infection. Although this move underscored the realization within the health community that HIV is transmitted through people's behavior, it did not necessarily change the public perception that a group affiliation rather than a risk behavior makes one susceptible to HIV.

Although risk factors are useful in understanding the epidemiological patterns of the epidemic, they should not overwhelm the fact that it is human beings rather than ideas or behaviors that suffer from AIDS. As of June 1997, the Centers for Disease Control had recorded 612,078 reported cases of AIDS in the United States. The affected groups break down as follows:

- 84 percent adult/adolescent men
- 15 percent adult/adolescent women
- 1 percent children
- 43 percent African American
- 36 percent white
- 20 percent Hispanic

At nearly 49 percent of cases, men who have sex with men account for the largest exposure category, with injection drug users following at 26 percent. For cases diagnosed between June 1996 and July 1997, however, the percentage of cases involving men who have sex with men fell to 38 percent. The percentage of cases for men who have sex with men is significantly higher among whites (76 percent) than among blacks (38 percent) or Hispanics (44 percent). The percentage of cases for men who have sex with men compared with injection drug users is virtually equal among black men (38 percent and 36 percent, respectively) and is close for Hispanics (44 percent and 37 percent, respectively). Statistically significant percentages of total AIDS cases exist for men who have sex with other men and also use injection drugs—8 percent for whites, 8 percent for blacks, and 7 percent for Hispanics.

Among women, injection drug use has been the largest risk factor, accounting for 44 percent of infections overall, followed closely by heterosexual contact, which accounts for 39 percent of cases. Hispanic women were the most likely to have been infected through heterosexual contact, which accounted for 46 percent of infections among that group.

The percentages of blacks and Hispanics infected do not correspond with those groups' representation in the general population. As of 1997, blacks accounted for only 12 percent of the general population of the United States, yet they account for 43 percent of AIDS cases; for Hispanics the comparable figures are 11 percent and 20 percent.[36] The factors that contribute to this disparity are analyzed in Chapter 4, under HIV/AIDS in Specific Populations.

Community Response to AIDS

Most AIDS advocacy groups and service providers sprang from the middle-class, white, gay community, where the HIV/AIDS epidemic first emerged in the United States. With few or no government efforts to provide care, for the most part these community-based organizations were privately funded and aided by thousands of volunteers who have served tirelessly and compassionately. As more drug users, persons of color, and women became affected with HIV, existing AIDS organizations were challenged to meet their needs as well. With the advent of the Ryan White Comprehensive AIDS Resource Emergency (CARE) Act in 1990, many organizations turned to the government for funding. Today, those organizations generally cannot limit the types of persons they care for if they are to compete successfully for government funding. For instance, as of July 1998, nearly 40 percent of the clients served by the Gay Men's Health Crisis in New York City were neither gay nor bisexual; the breakdown of clientele follows:

- Total number of active HIV-infected clients—6,532
- Male—80.1 percent
- Female—19.9 percent
- White (non-Latino/a)—34.1 percent
- Black (non-Latino/a)—30.3 percent
- Latino/a (all races)—30.8 percent
- Asian/Pacific Islander—1.3 percent
- Native American—0.4 percent
- Race/ethnicity undisclosed—0.9 percent
- Gay/lesbian/bisexual—60.7 percent
- Heterosexual—35.3 percent
- Sexual orientation undisclosed—3.8 percent[37]

The Whitman-Walker Clinic in Washington, D.C., historically a gay and lesbian health care service provider, also illustrates the evolution of community organizations. The clinic's
clientele changed as it sought to meet the demands of the epidemic and became increasingly entrenched in ethnic minority
communities. The clinic began in 1973 as a volunteer-run organization to provide health care to Washington, D.C.'s gay and lesbian community. By 1983, the clinic had started to emphasize
AIDS-related services; for example, it sponsored a major AIDS
forum on April 4, 1983, that was attended by over 1,000 people.
Today, the clinic is a major agency with an annual operating budget of $20 million and 220 full-time staff members. Its services
reach two of every three people living with AIDS in Washington,
D.C. Through its Robert N. Schwartz Housing Services, the clinic
provides shelter to 75 clients—71 percent of whom are African
Americans and 15 percent Latino—who would otherwise be
homeless. Whitman-Walker implements the D.C. Needle Exchange program, which exchanges between 8,000 and 10,000 needles a week.[38]

AIDS service providers do not need multimillion dollar
budgets to be effective. The AIDS Research Information Center
(ARIC) is a case in point. It operates out of a donated single-
room office and is run entirely by volunteers. When Executive
Director Lee-Angel Hardy was diagnosed with AIDS in 1990, he
committed himself to finding out all he could about AIDS medications and communicating that information to others who
were infected with HIV. ARIC's motto is "patient empowerment
through information," and the organization is a major Internet
resource and telephone hot line that provides free information
on treatment of HIV and its attendant opportunistic infections to

thousands of HIV-positive clients and their care providers. The organization produces one of the most comprehensive references available on AIDS medicines, *ARIC's Encyclopedic AIDS Medical Glossary*, a 500-page reference book containing more than 3,000 well-researched definitions of medical terms and extensive appendixes. The organization relies on a desktop printer and a photocopier without a sheet feed for most of its publishing activities.

Indeed, the AIDS epidemic has fostered creativity, resourcefulness, and compassion in many groups and individuals. Hair salons have become community education centers. Pet enthusiasts have rallied to ensure that people with AIDS have constant companionship and love by giving them the support needed to keep their dogs and cats. Individuals have turned their kitchens into bakeries for local "meals on wheels" programs that serve homebound people with AIDS (PWAs).

In spite of these demonstrations of commitment, however, the AIDS epidemic has increasingly tapped social resources as it spreads to ever widening populations. Affected communities must develop their own service organizations. African American and Hispanic communities face obstacles in their efforts to deal with the HIV/AIDS epidemic, which is just one of many pressing priorities in communities already disproportionately affected by massive unemployment, poverty, violence, and drug addiction. As mentioned previously, these communities, which have been blamed for, and discriminated against because of, these serious social problems, have been understandably afraid of the added stigma of AIDS.[39]

Some individuals living with HIV and AIDS have made a significant impact on public perception by giving a human face to the disease. Actor Rock Hudson's death from AIDS in 1985 brought the first significant media attention to the issue and caused the first public reaction by President Ronald Reagan, who knew Hudson personally. The education efforts of HIV-infected teenager Ryan White between 1983 and 1990 and the public statements of Kimberly Bergalis in 1991, a Florida woman who allegedly became infected by her dentist, have had a significant impact on legislative debate on HIV/AIDS issues. The 1991 announcement by basketball star Earvin "Magic" Johnson about his HIV infection constituted a new level of acknowledgment of risk. Johnson's popularity humanized the epidemic for many people who had never known someone living with HIV or AIDS.

For the most part, however, society has pervasively denied that a terrible toll is being taken by HIV—the loss of over a quarter million lives during the 1990s alone—and has exhibited a lack of compassion for persons with AIDS and their loved ones. This apathy, in turn, has resulted in a lack of the political will needed to commit adequate resources to both medical research and the care of persons with HIV-related illness and a lack of attention to and openness about crucial education and prevention messages.

The Government Response to HIV/AIDS

The HIV/AIDS epidemic, now well into its second decade, has tested government's ability to provide leadership in formulating an appropriate public response to the crisis. During the administrations of Ronald Reagan and George Bush, prejudices and fears about AIDS shaped the public debate and response to the epidemic, which may have sapped officials' political will to devise responsible and compassionate public policies.

Throughout the late 1980s, an ominous silence existed on the federal level, as Presidents Reagan and Bush rarely mentioned the epidemic. There was much study of AIDS and little action: The recommendations of the 1988 *Report of the Presidential Commission on the HIV Epidemic* were ignored, and President Bush did not respond to the 1991 report of the National Commission on AIDS, even though both reports decried the lack of national leadership on AIDS policy.[40]

In 1990, the U.S. Congress enacted the first federal legislation directed at providing care for persons with AIDS and HIV. The Ryan White CARE Act provides for emergency funding for prevention, health services, and health care in communities hardest hit by AIDS, and the AIDS Housing Opportunities Act promotes housing options for homeless persons with HIV-related illness. Both programs, however, were funded at low levels. There has been little or no clear direction in federal policy regarding HIV/AIDS research, prevention, and care.

Although the inclusion of persons with HIV among those protected by the 1990 Americans with Disabilities Act was a significant step, many federal programs still actively discriminate against persons with HIV/AIDS. HIV testing is required by the military and is a condition of employment in the State Department, and nonresidents may be denied entry to the United States or legalization of their immigration status if they are HIV positive.

In some cases, federal policies have actually hampered the

efforts of other groups. For example, the federal government has placed limitations on explicit safe sex and drug use information in federally funded education materials.[41]

When Bill Clinton was elected president in 1992, hopes were high within the AIDS activist community that his administration would provide much-needed assistance. In fact, Clinton's commitment to developing a national health care policy had revolutionary implications for the health care delivery system in the United States as a whole. The Presidential Advisory Council analyzed the impact of the failure to implement a national health care policy on HIV-infected Americans:

> The Administration's proposal for universal health insurance would have ensured [an adequate standard of] care for most HIV-infected Americans. Unfortunately, Congress rejected that proposal. As a result, we are left with a piecemeal system of health care in which many do not have access to basic primary medical care or the promising new combination drug therapies, which offer them the best chance for long-term survival. Medicaid, upon which more than 50 percent of people with AIDS rely for health care, and the Ryan White CARE Act are the existing programs through which most HIV/AIDS care is provided.[42]

The Clinton administration did make significant strides toward improving the situation for people with AIDS. It is useful to examine the accomplishments and failures of the Clinton administration from two perspectives: that of the administration itself (as described in Clinton's *National AIDS Strategy* 1997) and that of the Presidential Advisory Council on AIDS. Whereas the Clinton administration's strategy rightfully credits Clinton with making progress, his advisory panel has been both complimentary and critical.

The Clinton administration makes its own case in the *National AIDS Strategy 1997*, a document that states the administration's goals and accomplishments. The goals for the national effort to end the HIV/AIDS epidemic are:

- To develop more effective treatments, a preventive vaccine to protect the uninfected, and a cure for those currently infected through strong, continuing support for HIV-related research

- To reduce the number of new HIV infections in adults and children in the United States until the number of new infections reaches zero by providing strong, continuing support for effective HIV prevention efforts
- To ensure that all people living with HIV have access to services—ranging from health care to housing and supportive services—that are affordable, of high quality, and responsive to their needs
- To ensure that all people living with HIV are not subject to discrimination
- To provide strong, continuing support for international efforts to address the HIV epidemic
- To ensure that research advances are translated into improved HIV prevention programs and to enhance care for HIV-positive persons.[43]

In noting the Clinton administration's successes in the fight against AIDS, the strategy cites the huge increase in federal spending for HIV-related care and services—from $193 million in 1986 to $3.8 billion in 1996.[44] Funding for the Ryan White CARE Act increased by 158 percent between FY1993 and FY1996 and was extended through the year 2001. Support for housing programs for PWAs increased by 96 percent in the same period, and National Institutes of Health (NIH) HIV prevention funding increased by 24 percent. Federal assistance to state AIDS drug assistance programs to purchase AIDS drugs for uninsured HIV-infected citizens rose by 221 percent between FY1995 and FY1997.[45]

The strategy continues:

> The National Institutes of Health Revitalization Act of 1993 provided the Office of AIDS Research with enhanced authority to develop and implement an annual AIDS research plan and budget. Approval of AIDS drugs by the Food and Drug Administration has been further accelerated. A community-based AIDS prevention planning process has empowered local communities to target resources toward innovative AIDS prevention programs. Eligibility for Social Security disability benefits for people with AIDS has been simplified, and Federal laws prohibiting discrimination against people living with HIV and AIDS have been vigorously enforced.[46]

Furthermore, several significant medical research achievements occurred under the Clinton administration, according to the *National AIDS Strategy 1997*, including:

- Gaining FDA approval of 16 new HIV-related drugs, 8 new indications, and 3 new diagnostics for HIV and related conditions, developed through public- and private-sector efforts, since January 1993
- Supporting research that led to the finding that the use of AZT during pregnancy, childbirth, and the first six weeks of life can reduce the transmission of HIV from mother to child by two-thirds
- Approving in record time a promising new class of AIDS drugs known as protease inhibitors
- Launching a four-year $100 million research effort to develop effective topical microbicides
- Developing the first Federal Plan for Biomedical Research on HIV and AIDS to improve coordination of HIV-related research
- Facilitating the creation of the Forum for Collaborative HIV Research to identify opportunities for clinical effectiveness research to improve care for HIV-positive individuals.[47]

Clinton's record on AIDS is far more impressive than that of the Republicans who came before him. But much remains to be done to accomplish the goals the administration has outlined. One of the most astute critics of Clinton's record has been the Advisory Council he appointed. The council's *Second Progress Report* on December 7, 1997, although recognizing genuine accomplishments, also voiced some sharp criticisms. The report was particularly critical of Clinton's second term, stating that:

> Progress in the federal response to AIDS has stalled in recent months, contributing to a sense of diminished priority for AIDS issues. We are concerned that ONAP [Office of National AIDS Policy] has not been provided with adequate staff or appropriate status within the White House structure needed to make it most effective. When the future funding of the AIDS Drug Assistance Program (ADAP) was at risk earlier this year, AIDS advocates were forced to look to Congress, not the White House, for leadership. In May, the Vice President announced a 30-day expedited Administration re-

view of the feasibility of expanding Medicaid to cover all indigent HIV-infected individuals; however, many months have passed, no pilot project has been put in place, and the Administration continues to send mixed and conflicting signals regarding its pursuit of the objective of expanding Medicaid coverage. The combination of these actions raises serious questions about the current priority of AIDS issues for the Administration.

In one crucial area of the federal response to AIDS —the national effort to prevent HIV transmission— the Administration, like its predecessors, has failed to lay out a coherent strategic plan of action.[48]

The report is particularly critical of the Clinton administration's position on needle exchange. It strongly criticizes Secretary of Health and Human Services Donna Shalala for not lifting the ban on federal funds to support needle exchange in spite of evidence that needle exchange could dramatically reduce the spread of HIV (see Chapter 4, under Needle Exchange in the States, for a detailed analysis of this issue). In March 1998, the Advisory Council issued a no-confidence statement on the Clinton administration's commitment to reducing the spread of HIV based on this ban (the full text of this statement is given in Chapter 5). Overall, the administration's commitment to prevention issues failed to meet with the council's approval.

More than 16 years after the epidemic was first recognized, the United States still has not laid out a coherent, effective national strategy to prevent HIV transmission. Experts estimate that more than 40,000 Americans will have become infected with HIV this year alone. Despite a wealth of knowledge regarding the elements of an effective HIV prevention strategy, there is little evidence that the nation has made significant progress in reducing the number of new infections. In recent years, the Administration has failed to provide bold leadership. The federal investment in HIV prevention is disproportionately small compared to the amount of the epidemic's annual price tag in medical care and lost productivity, let alone in human suffering and loss of life.

Moreover, the Administration often fails to make optimum use of its limited investment in HIV prevention.

It has maintained outdated restrictions on the ability of some federally funded HIV prevention programs, especially those targeting school-age youth, to provide explicit and appropriate information to those at greatest risk. As a result, many HIV prevention educators must censor themselves with an eye to retaining their funding rather than providing the most effective prevention message possible.[49]

The council expressed concern over the administration's handling of other key issues, including funding for HIV, treatment, care, and housing services; the expansion of Medicaid coverage to asymptomatic individuals; reduction of the cost of new therapies; the monitoring of access to new therapies and related medical care in private managed health care systems; the Indian Health Service's lack of a coherent HIV prevention strategy and culturally sensitive case management guidelines for HIV-infected Native Americans; and a national dialogue on how to provide HIV care. This last issue has strong ramifications for future administrations. The council elaborated:

Last December, the Council recommended a national dialogue on how, over the long term, the federal government should structure and pay for medical and support services for people with HIV/AIDS. Currently, Medicaid, the Ryan White CARE Act, and other ancillary funding sources are providing critically needed support for sustaining a comprehensive continuum of HIV care. However, the impact of new drug therapies on the clinical course and potential new manifestations of HIV disease must inevitably result in modification of the existing provision of services and will require additional funding. Despite significant effort to promote a formal, structured, national policy dialogue, progress has stalled. At the same time, the changing nature of the epidemic has sparked a new sense of urgency for such dialogue, which, in many cases, has already begun at the local level. A comprehensive review of HIV service delivery and funding mechanisms at the federal, state, and community levels must be undertaken at the earliest possible date, with active participation by all affected parties.[50]

Systems of Care in the United States

In the wake of the Clinton administration's failure to implement a universal health care policy, HIV-infected Americans have no reliable umbrella access to care. Many federal programs for AIDS care are administered through the Ryan White CARE Act, which was signed into law on April 18, 1990, and was reauthorized for another five years in May 1996. The act is administered through the Health Resources and Services Administration and serves as the primary funding source for many local AIDS service providers throughout the country.

According to the *National AIDS Strategy 1997,* the Ryan White CARE Act delivers funds through competitive grants under the following titles:

- Titles I and II of the CARE Act provide funds for outpatient care, support services, insurance continuations, community-based care, and case management; funds are given to cities and states primarily on a formula basis. Title II also provides drug reimbursement funding for persons living with HIV/AIDS under the AIDS Drug Assistance Program (ADAP).
- Title IIIb of the CARE Act provides early intervention services such as counseling and testing, medical care, and educational services for medically underserved persons with the goal of reducing HIV-related illness.
- Title IV seeks to increase the availability of research, care, and services for women, infants, children, and youth in a community-based, family-centered system of care.
- Title V provides reimbursement for dental care for low-income persons living with HIV and AIDS, funds Special Programs of National Significance (SPNS), and supports AIDS Education and Training Centers that provide up-to-date HIV-related training for health care professionals.[51]

By far the greatest single cost to the federal government related to the AIDS epidemic is that of Medicaid. According to the Human Rights Campaign Fund, 53 percent of Americans living with AIDS rely on Medicaid for their health care coverage; this figure includes 90 percent of the children who have AIDS.[52] Since both the president and Congress are committed to balancing the budget by the year 2002, Medicaid funding may be subject to change. Some discussion of placing a cap on Medicaid benefits has taken place, but advocates for people living with HIV/AIDS are generally opposed to such a cap. The Human Rights Campaign Fund, which lobbies Congress on issues of concern to the gay and lesbian communities, opposes Medicaid caps and argues that:

> President Clinton's budget proposal includes a plan to impose a per capita cap on Medicaid spending. The administration claims that a cap is needed to ensure that Medicaid costs are controlled. But the rate of growth in federal spending on Medicaid has slowed dramatically, from 15 percent annually from 1985 to 1995 to only 3.3 percent last year. This suggests costs are already moving in the right direction—without the potential harm a per capita cap would impose. Imposing a per capita cap would be devastating for thousands of men, women, and children living with AIDS—a "per capita cap" would cut annual Medicaid spending per beneficiary. When states are faced with picking up the bill for care after the capped federal Medicaid has been spent, they may respond by imposing restrictions on the care that beneficiaries need the most. People with AIDS may lose access to the very benefit that provides them with hope and renewed health—prescription drugs.[53]

The Clinton administration has tried repeatedly to allay the fears of people living with AIDS by reiterating its commitment to Medicaid in the *National AIDS Strategy 1997* and other forums. Much enthusiasm was generated among those afflicted with HIV/AIDS in 1997 when Vice President Al Gore announced that he was studying the possibility of extending Medicaid benefits to asymptomatic HIV-positive individuals. After a long delay, however, it was announced that the cost of such benefits was prohibitive, even though many AIDS advocates argued that the plan would effectively save money in the long run. John S. James provided an interesting analysis of the situation in January 1998:

> This proposal appears to have been initially rejected by the Clinton Administration as too expensive. The problem seems to be that it was developed with the expectation of being revenue neutral, that is, that it would save as much money as it costs. While it may

be revenue neutral in the long run, there would be a net expense at first. Since people with early HIV infection are treated, there is no immediate hospitalization savings to offset against the drug costs. (For those with advanced AIDS, treatment clearly does save money even in the short term.) In other diseases and public health programs, the customary calculation is cost per year of life saved. For early treatment of HIV, this cost is on the order of $10,000 (about the price of the drugs) since it now appears that HIV disease may be postponed indefinitely in many cases by effective early treatment. The cost per year of life saved is well within what is paid in other diseases, where $50,000 or even much more is often acceptable. (The revenue-neutral goal would appear to mean the cost per year of life saved must be $0. Or less.)[54]

Not every person with HIV/AIDS depends on Medicaid or Medicare. In 1996, the U.S. Congress demonstrated sensitivity to HIV-positive individuals' need for private insurance by passing the Health Insurance Portability and Accountability Act, Pub. L. 104-191, codified at 29 U.S.C. 1181. The act addresses key concerns of HIV-positive individuals over their rights to private insurance, including concerns over insurance when changing jobs or returning to work after a period of disability, exclusion for preexisting medical conditions, denial of coverage because of HIV status, and cancellation of coverage because of the cost of insuring someone with HIV. The specifics of this groundbreaking legislation include:

1. A one-year limit on the exclusion of preexisting conditions for which "medical advice, diagnosis, care, or treatment was recommended or received within the 6-month period" prior to employment.
2. Credit is given for previous coverage. As long as the individual had coverage (including private insurance, government plan, church plan, or COBRA [federally paid continuation of employee benefits plan] but excluding Medicare and Medicaid) for 18 months continuously until at least 63 days prior to the commencement of new coverage and has no other form of insurance coverage, insurers cannot deny individual coverage or impose restrictions based on preexisting conditions.

3. Group plans and insurers cannot restrict coverage or continuation of coverage based on receipt of health care or medical history of HIV.
4. Group plans and insurers cannot charge higher premiums based on an employee's "health status–related factor," including HIV.
5. Group plans and insurers can restrict and limit the amount, level, extent, and nature of benefits for similarly situated individuals, meaning that as long as the restrictions affect everyone equally, there can be caps on costs and limits or exclusions to types of coverage, such as prescriptions, even though such policies may more detrimentally affect someone who is HIV positive. Group coverage must be continued unless there has been nonpayment of premiums, fraud, or similar infractions. Thus, an insurer cannot deny renewal of a policy merely on the basis of excessively expensive or unique claims.

Although this plan may alleviate the concerns of some of those afflicted with HIV, a recent CDC report estimates that approximately 225,000 HIV-positive individuals in the United States have neither public nor private insurance.[55] These people are in an especially precarious situation. The hope offered by recent treatment advances may be as far removed for them as if they lived in the Third World.

One program that may provide relief for some of the uninsured (or underinsured) is the AIDS Drug Assistance Program, which grew out of the federally funded AZT Assistance Program and came into its own in 1987. Its purpose is to provide expensive AIDS medication to low-income people with HIV who have limited or no medical coverage. According to the National ADAP Monitoring Project of the National Alliance of State and Territorial AIDS Directors, the program often served originally as a step in an individual's path from private insurance coverage to ADAP to Medicaid. That pattern has changed because of medical advances. People with HIV/AIDS are living longer and maintaining better health. They may not become totally disabled and thereby qualify for Medicaid, which is based on disability. Therefore, the burden on ADAP has increased.[56] As of July 1997, 43,494 people with HIV/AIDS had used ADAP services, an increase of 39 percent since July 1996. National monthly ADAP expenditures rose 36 percent between January and July 1997.[57]

ADAP is administered differently in each of the fifty states. Thirty-six states supplement ADAP with their own funds. The majority of funding comes from six high-incidence states: California, Illinois, Louisiana, Massachusetts, New York, and Pennsylvania.[58] The Ryan White CARE Act constitutes $272.7 million (69.8 percent) of ADAP funds, whereas state funds total $118.1 million (or 30.2 percent).[59] (A detailed analysis of levels of ADAP funding and benefits is given in Chapter 4, under AIDS in Individual States.)

The Role of People with AIDS in Shaping Public Policy

The AIDS epidemic has altered the ways society views individuals with a terminal illness and the way those individuals see themselves. On March 24, 1987, hundreds of New Yorkers—many of them HIV positive—gathered under the banner of the AIDS Coalition to Unleash Power (ACT UP) and staged a major demonstration on Wall Street to protest what they perceived as profiteering from AIDS medications by pharmaceutical companies. The protest resulted in seventeen arrests. Shortly after the demonstration, the Food and Drug Administration announced that it would significantly shorten the drug approval process. This was the first major ACT UP protest and one of its earliest successes.

In the years that followed, people with AIDS were responsible for radically changing the way medical research is conducted in the United States, changing the course of the drug approval process, motivating pharmaceutical firms to institute compassionate use programs, and, most important, making it clear that patients were entitled to have a say in their treatment. The activities of organized groups like ACT UP have brought significant media attention to the AIDS crisis, attention the epidemic would not likely have received without those activities, although more recently the media has paid less attention to ACT UP in particular.

ACT UP has been criticized for both its tactics and its membership, which historically has consisted mostly of white gays and lesbians. Whatever one feels about the organization's tactics or the character of its membership, it is important to look at its results. Significant accomplishments can be attributed to the actions of AIDS activists, including:

- The 1993 expansion of the Centers for Disease Control Surveillance Case Definition of AIDS
- Burroughs Wellcome lowering the cost of AZT
- HIV-infected Haitians being released from the detention center in Guantanamo Bay
- The FDA expediting the drug approval process

Many other examples can be cited. On April 24, 1996, four members of ACT UP New York were arrested after staging a media photo opportunity during which they plastered signs on Stadtlanders Pharmacy's showcase store to denounce its policy of charging a 37 percent markup over the suggested retail price of the protease inhibitor Crixivan. In their view, that cost constituted an undue hardship for HIV-infected individuals who had to pay for the life-prolonging medication. Stadtlanders's Mail Order Pharmacy responded the next day by offering a 19.5 percent cash discount on the price of the drug.

Activism by the HIV infected is not defined solely by acts of civil disobedience. The October 1997 issue of *Poz* magazine profiled Hydeia Broadbent, a charismatic 13-year-old African American living with AIDS. Best known for her appearance at the 1996 Republican Convention, Broadbent travels around the United States making speeches and appearances to educate people about AIDS issues. As the *Poz* article illustrates, she is not reluctant to use a little subversion to get a message across:

> For a finale, Hydeia pulls some change from her pocket and asks the two boys to come to the stage. She shakes the coins in her tiny hands, then thrusts her closed fists forward. She beckons each of them to choose a hand, but offers this warning: "If you pick a hand with coins in it, you have AIDS." One boy picks the right hand, the other picks the left. But when Hydeia opens her fists, coins drop from both hands. The audience is baffled. "There," the speaker announces. "You both have AIDS. If you didn't want to have AIDS, you wouldn't have picked either hand. You had a choice. You could've chosen not to pick a hand, but you did it anyway just because I asked you to."[60]

Activism by PWAs is not always public. Consider this example:

Miguel, a gay Latino man in his late twenties, discovers he is

HIV positive when he goes to the doctor with a chronic fungal infection. Shortly after his diagnosis, he gives up his career as a beautician and volunteers at a local AIDS organization. Because he is bilingual, he is given a full-time job as a caseworker for the agency's few Hispanic clients. He begins a street outreach program to educate local prostitutes—both male and female—about HIV prevention. He secures a grant from the health department to cover his expenses. He teaches the prostitutes to become HIV educators and gives them small stipends from the grant. On any given night he may explain to a young hustler how to bleach his syringe or demonstrate to a transvestite how to use a female condom for protection when engaging in receptive anal sex with a client. By the time he was forced to retire because of advancing AIDS, Miguel had certified more than a dozen prostitutes as educators, one of whom assumed his agency job.

The Role of Business

Since the beginning of the epidemic, the United States has granted 2,918 patents for HIV/AIDS-related products, including prescription medicines and diagnostic tests.[61] The AIDS epidemic has created numerous opportunities to profit for those who cater to the needs of people living with HIV/AIDS, including the pharmaceutical industry, the viatical insurance trade, and businesses created for and by people living with HIV disease, among others.

One business to benefit from the AIDS crisis has been the pharmaceutical industry. In 1995 alone, sales of antiviral drugs for AIDS reached at least $1.3 billion.[62] The history of the development of AIDS medications includes episodes in which the issue of fair pricing has taken on a moral dimension. Whereas in a free market economy business is expected to seek a return on investment, the only standard for determining that level of profit is what market demand will bear. When the product is life-saving medication, ethical issues will inevitably be raised over pricing practices.

One of the examples most frequently cited by AIDS anti-profiteering activists is that of Burroughs Wellcome's pricing of AZT, developed as an experimental anticancer drug through government-funded research in 1964. That application did not prove useful, but in 1984 scientists from both Burroughs Wellcome and the National Cancer Institute discovered that AZT effectively blocked HIV replication in vitro. At the same time, the Orphan

Drug Act was passed by the U.S. Congress. The law was designed to encourage the pharmaceutical industry to develop medications for rare diseases by giving the industry financial incentives, including a seven-year lock on the market. This plan combined with other government incentives enabled Burroughs Wellcome to develop AZT for less that $100 million compared with the average cost of $125 million to develop a new drug.[63]

When AZT premiered on the market, it was the only drug that had a treatment benefit for people living with AIDS. At a cost of around $8,000 a year at the recommended dosage, AZT was one of the most expensive drugs in existence and was beyond the economic means of many people who were dying and had no other hope. By October 1989, it was estimated that half of the 42,000 people in the United States living with AIDS were taking AZT, 7,000 of whom could acquire the medication only through a limited $20 million U.S. government access program that was already running out of money.[64] AIDS activists, those who were dying, and even members of Congress exhibited anger at what they perceived as Burroughs Wellcome taking advantage of a situation. ACT UP organized demonstrations at the Stock Exchanges in London, New York, and San Francisco, chanting slogans such as "Be the first on your block to sell your Burroughs Wellcome stock." The House Subcommittee on Health and the Environment, led by Representative Henry Waxman, began an investigation into Burroughs Wellcome's pricing practices. There were hints from Senator Edward Kennedy's office that the venerable senator was exploring ways to nationalize AZT by invoking a law from World War I that allows the government to revoke exclusive patents in the interest of national security.

Burroughs Wellcome announced that it would cut the price of AZT by 20 percent, insisting it had been planning to do so for some time in spite of the fact that its timing coincided with increased public scrutiny. Rep. Waxman remarked that the move was a "good first step," but no further action was ever taken by either Burroughs Wellcome or the government. *Time* magazine published the following estimate of the cost of AZT: manufacturer's cost per capsule: 30 cents to 50 cents; wholesale price: $1.20; retail price: $1.30 to $1.50. Industry analyst Jo Walton of Shearson Lehman Hutton in London was quoted in *Time* as saying: "The average operating profit from all the sales of Burroughs Wellcome is 20 percent. Though they have a 30 percent operating profit margin on AZT, it's still within the bounds of the pharmaceutical industry."[65] Burroughs Wellcome never clarified its profit margin on AZT, although 1988 estimates ranged from a low of $25 million to a high of $100 million.[66]

As of April 1998, there are still no standards for drug pricing, and none of the major drug companies has disclosed its exact profits from the AIDS epidemic. In 1996, ACT UP Golden Gate did a survey of typical pharmacy costs for common anti-HIV therapies. The average costs ran from an absolute minimum of $13,000 a year to about $20,000 a year.[67] The survey also found substantial variations in pricing among pharmacies and made a compelling case for people who pay for their own prescriptions to request pricing information from several pharmacies.

The study also analyzed Abbott Laboratories' profits from Ritonavir (Norvir), one of the most effective protease inhibitors on the market. The analysis suggested that Abbott could earn a 110 percent annual return on its investment.[68] Abbott's pricing policies are not atypical for a company in the pharmaceutical industry, and it has incurred no charges of abuse such as those levied against Burroughs Wellcome.

In addition to pharmaceutical companies, viatical firms have also profited from the AIDS epidemic. A viatical settlement is one in which a consumer designates a company as the beneficiary of his or her life insurance policy in exchange for a lump-sum cash payment. The viatical firm then becomes the policy beneficiary, must pay the premiums, and receives the face value of the policy when the original policy holder dies. The April 1998 issue of *Poz*, a magazine for those who are HIV positive, featured at least nine color advertisements for viatical settlement firms. Such ads routinely appear in magazines that cater to gay and HIV-positive clients.

The February 2, 1996, CDC National AIDS Hotline Bulletin published guidelines from the Federal Trade Commission to specify factors a person with a terminal disease should consider when choosing a viatical company.

- Contact several viatical companies to be sure of the best value
- Check with state insurance regulators to ensure that the viatical company meets licensing requirements
- Resist high-pressure sales tactics
- Verify that the company has the payout money on hand and is not "shopping" the policy to a third party
- Ask about the company's policy for protecting the consumer's privacy

- Check the tax consequences of assigning the policy and implications for public assistance benefits
- Consult with a lawyer about probate estate considerations.[69]

Viatical settlements are now tax-exempt under the Health Insurance Portability and Accountability Act of 1996, Pub. L. 104–191, codified at 29 U.S.C. § 1181.

The Impact of Combination Therapy

The advent of combination therapy—a protease inhibitor, such as Ritonavir or Crixivan, used in conjunction with two other antiretroviral drugs, AZT with 3TC, for instance—has affected the treatment and prognosis for thousands living with HIV. In naming Aaron Diamond Foundation researcher David Ho as its Man of the Year for 1996, *Time* magazine explained the significance of this therapy:

> This year, for the first time, there is something that looks like hope. Early this summer AIDS patients taking therapeutic "cocktails" that combine protease inhibitors with other antiviral drugs began experiencing remarkable recoveries. Their viral loads fell. Their T-cell counts climbed. Their health improved—perhaps temporarily but often dramatically. Hospices and AIDS clinics across the U.S. began to empty.
>
> Then in July, David Ho reported on a most promising experiment. By administering the protease inhibitor cocktails to patients in the earliest stages of infection, his team seems to have come tantalizingly close to eliminating the virus from the blood and other body tissues.
>
> This is, as an AIDS expert puts it, hope with an asterisk. Even if Ho's treatment works, there is still no magic bullet for patients in late stages of the disease. The cost of the cocktails (up to $20,000 a year) puts them beyond the reach of all but the best-insured patients—and out of the question for the 90 percent who live in the developing world.[70]

The effectiveness of this treatment is supported by the following statistics:

- The CDC indicated that HIV-related mortality dropped 68 percent from 1995 to 1997[71]
- CMV (a herpes virus) and cryptosporidiosis (a parasitic infection) declined by 80 percent
- Kaposi's sarcoma and *Pneumocystis carinii* pneumonia declined by 70 percent
- Data from the Johns Hopkins Hospital revealed an overall 60 percent decline in the incidence of opportunistic infections[72]

Combination therapy has defined the goal for the treatment of HIV/AIDS. According to Dr. John G. Bartlett, head of infectious diseases at the Johns Hopkins Medical Institutions, the goal of treatment is to reduce the amount of HIV measurable in the blood to as low a level as possible—to no virus or less than 500 copies per milliliter (the threshold of detectability for many viral assay tests).[73]

Not everyone benefits from the new therapy, however, and some patients develop resistance to the cocktail. Dr. Steven Deeks recently presented data from the University of California at San Francisco's large public AIDS clinic at San Francisco General Hospital. He focused on the records of 136 HIV-infected patients who started on protease inhibitors in March 1996. Initially, most of those patients' viral loads were substantially reduced and in many cases were undetectable. But by September 1997, the virus had returned to detectable levels in 53 percent of the patients in the sample.[74] In the same Associated Press report, David Ho indicated that there could be a host of reasons the virus returned, including patients not taking their pills on time or actually missing doses. Deeks reiterated this point, saying "Compliance is critical. When we say compliance, we mean rigid adherence to over 20 pills a day."[75] The report also suggested that those who had previously been treated with many other drugs or who had severely compromised immune systems were also at risk of failure.[76]

Activist Stephen Gendin recently documented the situation of someone who has failed treatment—himself: "Now I'm screwed. Because I didn't understand how resistance works, I now know I was jumping from one suboptimal treatment to the next. Each time I made the virus stronger and reduced my future options. Today I've run through all the nucleoside analogues and three protease inhibitors. Nothing works for me."[77]

In addition to not constituting a viable treatment for everyone living with HIV, as mentioned previously the new treatment regimens carry substantial price tags that range from $15,000 to $20,000 per year and create economic burdens for systems of care. For instance, a decrease in the number of inpatients admitted for AIDS-related conditions and a resulting increase in the number of outpatients treated can create economic havoc. A recent Associated Press report provides some sobering statistics:

> Hospitals get far less reimbursement from either public or private insurance for outpatient care than for admitting the seriously ill—so outpatient AIDS clinics are in trouble. [At] St. Vincent's Hospital in New York [City], hospital admissions of seriously ill AIDS patients dropped from 110 a month in 1994 to 50 a month last year [1996], while the hospital doubled the people treated as outpatients to 2,000 a month. That saved insurers $2 million on hospital admissions. Yet even as outpatient services doubled, insurance payments for those services rose from just $110,000 a month in 1994 to $182,000 a month in 1996.[78]

Ramifications for the Future

The impact of triple combination therapy on hospital revenue is just one unanticipated consequence of the scope of the HIV/AIDS epidemic, but other factors are far more grave for people living with HIV. For instance, what happens to someone who has been receiving social security disability for the past four years but whose condition no longer meets the clinical standard of disability? Let us examine one situation.

Steve is a thirty-six-year-old, college-educated, white gay male. He was diagnosed HIV positive four and a half years ago; one year later he developed complications that led to a diagnosis of full-blown AIDS. At the time, he was employed as an administrative aide at the public library and made the transition to receiving social security disability through short-term disability coverage under his insurance plan. He believed he had only two or three years to live, so he "spent down" to meet the criteria for additional public assistance and transferred his assets to his sister.

Two years ago he began to receive combination therapy, covered under Medicaid. Now he feels as good as he did before becoming infected. His viral load remains less than 500 copies per milliliter, and his T cells are almost 500. In spite of this good news, he is terrified. He has read reports of what happens to people when their therapy is interrupted, and he can only obtain his medicines through public assistance. But he no longer meets the criteria for disability and knows it is only a matter of time before he is reevaluated. Steve has been out of the workforce for more than three years, and he knows a prospective employer will have no difficulty figuring out why. The laws and the entire situation are confusing. Steve just wants to live now that he's been given another chance to do so.

Steve's situation is all too familiar to thousands of people across the country who have benefited from the new treatments; however, he is one of the lucky ones. Many of those living with HIV/AIDS in the United States will never have access to appropriate medical treatment. A few examples include a homeless man people turn away from because *muluscom contagiosum* (a viral skin infection that can grow out of control in people with compromised immune systems) makes him appear like a leper, a freelance artist with no insurance who earns too much to qualify for public assistance but too little to pay for medicine, and a welfare mother who lives in a state that has a cap on access to protease inhibitors. Seemingly endless scenarios can be constructed that preclude someone living with HIV/AIDS from receiving adequate medical treatment in the United States. The tragedy is that in the real world, those scenarios translate into people made of flesh and bone and sparked with emotion, intellect, and perception. Who is to tell them they do not matter or that they matter only so many dollars worth?

The immediate question HIV/AIDS poses to citizens of the United States is how much those citizens value human life. If the current wave of combination therapy or the next treatment advance costs $15,000 per year per life maintained, does everyone in U.S. society have a right to receive that care if his or her condition requires it, or should only those who have the means to pay for treatment themselves be entitled to it? Or should a lottery system be used? The question is not going to go away. Given the history of AIDS activism, people with HIV/AIDS are unlikely to remain quiet if their right to live is sacrificed because of economics.

For those identified as most at risk by virtue of group affiliation, names reporting is another frightening prospect. Names reporting refers to the practice of state governments recording the names of all those who test HIV positive. By January 1998, 30 states had adopted the practice of names-based registry of HIV-positive residents. History has shown that the identification of marginalized people can lead to legal sanctions and violence against them as in the holocaust during World War II. Many behaviors that result in HIV infection are currently illegal. Injection drug use is treated as a criminal rather than a medical condition. Sodomy laws remain on the books in 19 states. Also, 27 states have specific laws regarding HIV infection, and the number is increasing.[79] Activists worry that individuals will choose not to be tested because of the fear of stigmatization, which will result in increases in both the numbers of HIV-infected individuals being identified at later stages of disease, and more transmissions overall (since fewer people will know their HIV-positive status.)

Regarding the issue of criminal prosecution for HIV transmission (or attempted transmission), if the current treatment trend holds, what will become of these cases? If society no longer assumes that HIV/AIDS is a fatal disease, what justification is there for holding a man in prison for thirty years because he did not tell his girlfriend he was HIV positive (or for imprisoning a retarded woman because she did not tell her alleged rapist she was seropositive)? There is no criminal penalty for exposing someone to herpes or to many other sexually transmitted diseases. (Recall that syphilis can be fatal if left untreated.) This is one more area of the social landscape that will shift as HIV/AIDS treatment changes.

Through June 1997, 374,656 people in the United States have died from AIDS. That number will continue to climb; the only question that remains is how high. Perhaps part of that answer lies within the U.S. political will to change, stagnate, or backslide.

The dead cannot forget or imagine. The Yoruba of West Africa and the diaspora have a saying "when a palm tree dies, the young leaves perish with it."[80] No young black man will ever learn how to slice a backhand from Arthur Ashe, nor can an aspiring gay writer have his first manuscript critiqued by Reinaldo Arenas. Many have died who could have shaped the character of the younger generation and inspired them to political thought or deed. The loss of so many lives to the AIDS epidemic is a loss for us all, but for the young people who will never know those who are gone the deaths leave a mysterious vacuum as the youths begin to explore the world and their nascent sense of self. If the devastation of AIDS is not to claim more lives among the generation now coming of age, if the seeds of life growing up now are to be ensured the chance to reach toward the sun without the taint of HIV infection obscuring their chances, the U.S. populace must address critical issues of social responsibility in the face of contagion.

Notes

1. Randy Shilts. 1987. *And the Band Played On: Politics, People and the AIDS Epidemic.* New York: St. Martin's Press, p. 124.

2. Leroy Whitfield. 1997. "Black Plague." *Positively Aware: The Journal of the Test Positive Aware Network,* September–October: 42.

3. American Association for World Health. 1997. *Give Children Hope in a World with AIDS.* Washington, D.C.: American Association for World Health, p. 11.

4. Centers for Disease Control. 1997. *HIV/AIDS Surveillance Report.* Atlanta: Centers for Disease Control, July.

5. Ibid.

6. Associated Press. 1998. "AIDS Rising Fastest among Those over 50," January 23.

7. Warner C. Greene. 1996. "AIDS and the Immune System," quoted in Lee Hardy, *ARIC's Encyclopedic AIDS Medical Glossary.* 2d Ed. Baltimore: AIDS Research Information Center, appendix III.

8. UNAIDS. 1997. *Report on the Global HIV/AIDS Epidemic.* HYPERLINK http://www.unaids.org_http://www.unaids.org_.

9. Ibid.

10. Ibid.

11. Andrew Purvis. 1996–1997. "The Global Epidemic." *Time,* December 31–January 6: 78.

12. Jane Steele. 1998. "Obaluaiye: The King Who Owns the Earth." *Oshun,* Winter: 3.

13. Purvis, "The Global Epidemic," p. 78.

14. Centers for Disease Control, *HIV/AIDS Surveillance Report.*

15. Presidential Advisory Council on AIDS. 1997. *Second Progress Report,* December 7. Washington , D.C.: The White House, pp. 1–14.

16. George Carter, contributing writer for *Poz.* 1997. Private communication. September 12.

17. Joann Loviglio. 1997. "Study: Symptoms Can Reveal HIV." Associated Press, December 16.

18. Lee Hardy. 1996. *ARIC's Encyclopedic AIDS Medical Glossary,* 2d ed. Baltimore: AIDS Research Information Center, p. 24.

19. Institute of Medicine, National Academy of Sciences. 1989. *Mobilizing against AIDS.* Washington, D.C.: National Academy Press, pp. 114–130.

20. George F. Lemph, et al. 1990. "Projections on AIDS Morbidity and

Mortality in San Francisco," *Journal of the American Medical Association* 263: 1497.

21. Eric Lerner. 1995. "Dr. Jack Lambert on HIV Infection in Children." *The DIRT on AIDS.* Baltimore: AIDS Research Information Center, vol. 1, issue 1, February, p. 1.

22. Alan R. Lifson, George W. Rutherford, and Harold W. Jaffe, "The Natural History of HIV Infection, 1363," Institute of Medicine, *Mobilizing against AIDS*, pp. 65–80.

23. New Jersey Women and AIDS Network. 1990. *Me First: Medical Manifestations of HIV in Women.* New Brunswick: New Jersey Women and AIDS Network.

24. Institute of Medicine, *Mobilizing against AIDS*, pp. 65–80.

25. Ibid.

26. Ibid., pp. 80–91.

27. Centers for Disease Control. 1987. "Revision of the CDC Surveillance Case Definition for Acquired Immunodeficient Syndrome." *Morbidity and Mortality Weekly Report* (MMWR).

28. David Barr. 1990. "What Is AIDS? Think Again." *New York Times*, December 1, p. A-25.

29. Dr. John G. Bartlett. 1997. *Medical Management of HIV Infection.* Baltimore: Johns Hopkins University School of Medicine, p. 1.

30. Phillip Elmer-DeWitt. 1996–1997. "Turning the Tide." *Time*, December 30–January 6: 55.

31. Ibid.

32. Shilts, *And the Band Play On*, p. 7.

33. Ibid., p. 20.

34. Ibid., pp. 222 and 135.

35. Ibid., p. 133.

36. American Association for World Health. *Give Children Hope*, p. 11.

37. Gay Men's Health Crisis. HYPERLINK http://www.aidsnyc.org/gmhc.

38. Whitman-Walker Clinic. 1998. *Whitman-Walker Clinic, Inc., Factsheet.* Washington, D.C.: Whitman-Walker Clinic, pp. 1–7.

39. Harlton L. Dalton. "AIDS in Blackface." *Daedalus* 118: 205.

40. Report of the Presidential Commission on the Human Immunodeficiency Virus Epidemic (1988), pp. 157–158; *America Living with AIDS*, Washington, D.C., National Commission on Acquired Immine Deficiency Syndrome (AIDS), pp. 111–119, 149.

41. *America Living with AIDS*, p. 21.

42. Presidential Advisory Council on AIDS. 1997. *Second Progress Report.* December 7, Washington, D.C., The White House, p. 6.

43. White House. 1997. *The National Aids Strategy,* Washington, D.C., The White House, p. 3.

44. Ibid., p. 19.

45. Ibid., p. 7.

46. Ibid.

47. Ibid., p. 15.

48. Presidential Advisory Council on AIDS, *Second Progress Report,* p. 1.

49. Ibid., pp. 3–4.

50. Ibid., p. 8.

51. White House, *The National AIDS Strategy,* p. 38.

52. http://www.hrc.org.

53. Ibid.

54. John James. 1998. *AIDS Treatment News* 286 (San Francisco), January 9.

55. A. K. Nakishima, J. F. Jones, P. L. Fleming, and J. R. Ward. 1997. "Who Will Pay for HIV Treatment? Health Insurance Status of the HIV-Infected Person." *Supplement to the HIV/AIDS Project Group.* Atlanta: Centers for Disease Control and Prevention. IDSA 35th Annual Meeting, San Francisco, California, September 13–16.

56. Arnold Doyle, Richard Jeffreys, and Joseph Kelly. 1998. *National ADAP Monitoring Project: Interim Technical Report, March 1998.* Washington, D.C.: National Alliance of State and Territorial AIDS Directors and AIDS Treatment Data Network, pp. 25–26.

57. Ibid., p. 12.

58. Ibid., p. 14.

59. Ibid.

60. Steve Friess. 1997. "She's Come a Long Way from Baby." *Poz,* October: 62.

61. U.S. Division of Patents. http://patents.cnidr.org/welcome.html.

62. Purvis, "The Global Epidemic" p. 78.

63. Christine Gorman. 1989. "How Much for a Reprieve from AIDS? Accused of Overcharging for AZT, Burroughs Wellcome Defends the Cost of the Drug but Cuts Its Price 20%." *Time,* October 2.

64. Ibid.

65. Ibid.

66. Ibid.

67. Stephen LeBlanc, Rob Sabados, and Don Howard. 1996. "Your Money or Your Life: ACT UP's Survey of Unconscionable AIDS Drug Pricing, Drug Pricing Survey Results." San Francisco: ACT UP Golden Gate, October, p. 3.

68. Ibid.

69. Centers for Disease Control. 1996. CDC National AIDS Hotline Bulletin no. 168, February 2.

70. Elmer DeWitt. "Turning the Tide." *Time*, pp. 54–55.

71. David Gilden. 1998. "Moods Brighten as Statistics Lighten." *GMHC Treatment Issues* 12, no., 3, March: 1.

72. Ibid., p. 2.

73. John G. Bartlett. 1997. "Why Some Patients 'Fail' Triple-Drug Therapy." *Baltimore Alternative*, November: 26.

74. Associated Press. 1997. "Doctors: New AIDS Drugs Failing." September 29.

75. Ibid.

76. Ibid.

77. Stephen Gendin. "Living on the Edge." *Poz*, November: 81.

78. Lauran Neergard. 1997. "Money an Issue for AIDS Patients: AIDS Patients Living Longer, Money Problem Grows." Associated Press, July 15.

79. Catherine Hanssens (panel discussion moderator). 1998. "Who's Responsible for New Infections/Criminalization Says It's the PWA. Prevention Says Both Partners. Right Now, Criminalization's Winning." *Poz*, May, p. 62.

80. Awo Fa'lokun Fatunmbi. 1994. *Ìbà'Ṣẹ Òrìṣà*. (Bronx, N.Y.: Original Publications), p. 34.

Chronology 2

This chapter contains a chronology of selected events in the development of the Human Immunodeficiency Virus/Acquired Immune Deficiency Syndrome (HIV/AIDS) crisis in the United States. Events in the early 1980s, the first decade of the U.S. HIV/AIDS epidemic, reflect the scientific groundwork necessary to allow researchers to understand the challenges ahead when they first saw cases of mysterious diseases. Later events demonstrate the significant social, economic, scientific, and political impact of the epidemic. Events were chosen because of their historical significance or their representative qualities. For instance, the court cases cited are representative of a number of similar cases.

1959   According to the Associated Press and a report published in the February 1998 edition of *Nature*, scientists have identified what they believe is the earliest case of AIDS in a Bantu man from the Congo who died in 1959. According to *Time* magazine's 1997 Man of the Year, David Ho, who coauthored

1959   the *Nature* article, "This is the oldest known HIV case."
cont.   HIV was found in a preserved blood sample.

1970   Temin and S. Mitzutani, as well as D. Baltimore, dis-
cover reverse transcriptase. This enzyme is produced
by retroviruses, a group of viruses containing the genetic material ribonucleic acid (RNA) and having the
ability to copy RNA into deoxyribonucleic acid (DNA)
inside an infected cell. The DNA that results from this
process is then included in the genetic structure of the
cell and passed to each infected cell's offspring cells.

1976   The T cell growth factor, also called interleukin-2, is discovered by D. A. Morgan, F. W. Ruscetti, and Robert
Gallo. T cells are white blood cells used by the immune
system to fight infection. Interleukin-2 is a substance
important to immune response and results in expanded
T cell function.

1980   The first human retrovirus is discovered by Robert
Gallo, B. J. Poiesz, and others. It is called human T cell
leukemia virus type I (HTLV-I).

By the end of 1980, the unknown virus is established in
Africa, Europe, and North America. It is later shown
that by the end of 1980, 80 young men have been diagnosed with at least one of the opportunistic infections
that are the hallmarks of HIV.

1981   In February, Dr. C. Everett Koop, a prominent Philadelphia pediatric surgeon, is named assistant secretary of
the U.S. Department of Health and Human Services; he
is later named U.S. surgeon general after a yearlong
confirmation battle. Koop's highly publicized antiabortion position led both supporters and critics of his nomination to conclude that they could predict his actions
once in office. He surprises observers by approaching
critical issues as public health problems rather than ideological campaigns. His vigorous work to educate
Americans about HIV/AIDS and his advocacy of the
need for sex education in the public schools eventually
establish his reputation as an effective surgeon general.

On June 5, the Centers for Disease Control (CDC) publishes the *Morbidity and Mortality Weekly Report,* its first report on the HIV/AIDS epidemic. The report is based on five Los Angeles cases of *Pneumocystis carinii* pneumonia (PCP) diagnosed among homosexual men in recent months.

On July 4, the CDC releases its first official report on Kaposi's sarcoma (KS) in the *Morbidity and Mortality Weekly Report.* Cases of KS and PCP among homosexual men in New York City are reported.

On November 30, George Kenneth Horne Jr., the first KS case reported to the CDC, dies in San Francisco.

In December, a CDC report describes the case of an infant who had received blood transfusions and developed the same immune deficiency disease previously reported in homosexual men.

The number of U.S. AIDS cases diagnosed in 1981 is 298.

1982   In January a new organization, the Gay Men's Health Crisis, forms in New York City to provide services to men with the new disease.

As of March 19, the CDC reports 285 cases of the disease in 17 states. Outside the United States, 5 European nations have confirmed the presence of the disease. Even though scientists cannot agree on a name for the illness, the number of cases is increasing. Two weeks after the March report, the CDC affirms cases in 2 additional states and 2 more European countries. U.S. cases now total 300—242 in gay or bisexual men, 30 in heterosexual men, 10 in heterosexual women, and 18 in persons whose sexual preference is unknown.

In June, the CDC reports clusters of KS and PCP cases in both Los Angeles and Orange County, California.

By July, 471 cases of the newly named AIDS disease are reported; of those, 184 patients have died. Reported cases are found in 24 states.

1982
cont.

Also in July, the CDC reports that cases of PCP have been found among hemophiliacs and opportunistic infections are present among Haitian immigrants living in the United States.

In August, the CDC reports that nearly half of the AIDS cases reported to date are in New York City.

In October, under the leadership of Representative William Natcher (D-KY), Congress appropriates $5.6 million for research—the first federal funds set aside to study the epidemic.

In November, guidelines for clinical and laboratory staff who work with blood are released by the CDC to address occupational health concerns. The American Red Cross announces a review of its policies for choosing blood donors after a child who received a blood transfusion develops AIDS. The CDC reports a case of AIDS possibly linked to a blood transfusion.

The number of U.S. AIDS cases diagnosed in 1982 is 1,113. Of the small number of cases identified in 1979, 85 percent of the patients are dead. Of cases in 1981, 60 percent of those diagnosed are dead. The 1982 rate of reported cases is triple that of the previous year.

1983

The January 7 issue of *Morbidity and Mortality Weekly Report* names two cases that identify yet another group to be affected by the epidemic: female sexual partners of males with AIDS. The cases involve a 37-year-old woman with PCP who lived with an intravenous drug user for 5 years and a 23-year-old Hispanic woman with lymphadenopathy who lived with a bisexual with both KS and PCP. The CDC also has reports of 43 other women who have developed the opportunistic infections of AIDS; in most of those cases, the women had previously had sexual relations with IV drug users. These cases give weight to the theory that the men are carrying an agent that can infect their partners while leaving the men themselves asymptomatic. The *Morbidity and Mortality Weekly Report* also addresses the growing number of AIDS cases in prisons, mostly among prisoners who have been IV drug users.

The February 2 CDC report indicates that the number of U.S. AIDS cases has surpassed 1,000. Almost half of the 1,025 cases reported are in New York state; at least 394 U.S. residents have died. Almost 25 percent of cases have been reported in the previous two months, during which 100 people have died.

In March, the American Red Cross announces that homosexual males, intravenous drug users, and Haitian immigrants living in the United States—all believed to be at great risk for carrying the virus—are advised not to donate blood.

In April, Health and Human Services (HHS) Secretary Margaret Heckler testifies before the House Appropriations Committee, saying, "I really don't think there is another dollar that would make a difference, because the attempt is all out to find the answer."

In May, more than 6,000 people in San Francisco march to focus attention on the growing wave of illness and death. Marchers with AIDS carry a banner that reflects the outlook of those with the disease: Fighting for Our Lives.

Later in May, conservative political commentator Patrick Buchanan writes, "The poor homosexuals; they have declared war upon nature, and now nature is exacting an awful retribution."

Also in May, the journal *Science* reports that both U.S. and French scientists have detected a retrovirus (referred to as HTLV-III/LAV) among those with AIDS or at risk for AIDS. U.S. scientists subsequently release findings of a direct connection between the leukemia virus and the development of AIDS. Confusion remains about whether differences exist between the French and U.S. findings and about which country's scientists made the breakthrough discovery.

In late May the Conference of State and Territorial Epidemiologists recommends that AIDS be added to the list of notifiable diseases, meaning it should be reported to the CDC through local public health departments.

1983   Also in May, Assistant Secretary of Health and Human
cont.   Services Edward Brandt announces that the Public
        Health Service has made HIV/AIDS research its top
        priority.

        In June, French researcher Dr. Luc Montagnier of the
        Pasteur Institute announces that French scientists have
        isolated an equine lentivirus (a virus that can remain
        dormant in the cells and then become active) he calls
        Lymphadenopathy-Associated Virus (LAV).

        In September, the CDC issues guidelines for health care
        workers and other health professionals who might be
        exposed to HIV. The government also announces that
        dentists, morticians, and medical examiners should
        take special precautions to avoid infection.

        The number of U.S. AIDS cases diagnosed in 1983 is
        3,001.

1984   In March, research into the virus causing AIDS takes an
        important step forward when the CDC isolates French
        researchers' LAV from the blood of an asymptomatic
        Los Angeles nurse who had become infected from a
        blood transfusion. This finding demonstrates the virus's
        presence before illness begins and shows that LAV in a
        blood donor's system can be transmitted to others.

        In April, Dr. Mervyn Silverman, director of the San
        Francisco Department of Public Health, announces reg-
        ulations to restrict high-risk sexual practices in the city's
        bathhouses. This enormously controversial move, taken
        after months of debate over the public health, political,
        economic, and social ramifications of the popular gay
        men's gathering places, only serves to anger both sides.

        Also in April, HHS Secretary Heckler announces the
        U.S. discovery of HTLV-III, the agent that causes AIDS.
        Heckler only briefly mentions the work of French re-
        searchers in identifying LAV.

        In May, the research group of Dr. Robert C. Gallo an-
        nounces the development of the Western blot technique
        for detecting antibodies to the virus that causes AIDS.

In June and subsequent months, the availability of the HIV antibody test allows medical researchers to learn how the virus is moving through the population. One study of IV drug users in a New York clinic shows an 87 percent rate of infection; studies of hemophiliacs who had used contaminated clotting factor show infection rates from 72 percent to 90 percent. Tests at a San Francisco venereal disease (VD) clinic show a 65 percent infection rate, and an East Coast testing project finds a 35 percent positive result.

In August, Bobbi Campbell dies of cryptosporidiosis in San Francisco. Campbell, diagnosed with KS when it was still regarded as gay cancer, had publicly declared himself the AIDS poster boy two years earlier in an effort to focus attention on and increase funding for those who are ill. He appeared on the cover of *Newsweek* in 1983.

Also in August, scientists find HTLV-III in the semen of both a man with AIDS and an asymptomatic man, which shows conclusively that one can be a carrier of the virus without showing symptoms. The virus is also isolated in the vaginal fluid of a symptomatic woman, thereby establishing the mother-to-infant mode of transmission.

In September, new studies are released showing high rates of infection among severe hemophiliacs who use Factor VIII, a clotting agent.

In October, Dr. Mervyn Silverman of the San Francisco Department of Public Health orders the closing of the city's bathhouses.

Also in October, U.S. House-Senate budget negotiators agree on $93 million in AIDS funding for the fiscal year, a 60 percent increase over Reagan administration requests. Of that amount, $8.35 million is earmarked for expedited development of an HTLV-III antibody test. The Reagan administration announces that it will use less than half a million dollars for this purpose and that the rest of the funds will be returned to the treasury.

1984   In December, University of California researchers an-
cont.   nounce that 10,000 human blood samples will be tested
        in 1985 using a new method to detect HIV in blood.

        The number of U.S. AIDS cases diagnosed in 1984 is
        6,049.

1985   In January, interim Public Health Service guidelines for
        screening blood donations are announced by the CDC;
        blood will be examined for antibodies to HTLV-
        III/LAV.

        Total reported AIDS cases surpass 8,000 during January.

        Also in January, the Reagan administration announces
        its budget proposal for the coming fiscal year, which
        calls for a reduction in AIDS spending from $96 million
        to $85.5 million, with a 20 percent cut at the CDC. Only
        about 5 percent of the budget is designated for preven-
        tion and education.

        In March, blood supply screening begins across the
        United States with an Abbott Laboratories test licensed
        by the federal government. The use of the test is her-
        alded as an opportunity to virtually eliminate the
        chance of contracting HIV from a blood transfusion.
        Gay community leaders, however, are concerned that
        the test could be used to discriminate against gays.

        In April, the CDC deletes the category of recent immi-
        grants from Haiti from the list of those most at risk for
        AIDS.

        Also in April, HHS Secretary Heckler tells the first In-
        ternational Conference on Acquired Immune Defi-
        ciency Syndrome in Atlanta, Georgia, that AIDS will
        remain the top U.S. public health priority until it has
        been conquered.

        In May, the *New England Journal of Medicine* reports that
        persons infected with HIV could be asymptomatic for
        four years or longer. Also, Martin Delaney starts Pro-
        ject Inform in San Francisco to bring together informa-

tion on AIDS therapies and to improve access to those therapies.

In June, Drs. Robert C. Gallo, Mikulas Popovic, and M. G. Sarngadharan patent an antibody test for HTLV-III for the Department of Health and Human Services.

In July, pharmaceutical manufacturer Burroughs Wellcome begins testing the drug azidothymidine, or AZT, on more than 30 patients with HIV illness. In an important scientific report, federal researchers announce their discovery that the virus attacks the T4 helper cells, a set of important blood cells that identify agents such as viruses and prompt the immune system to attack those agents.

On July 25, it is officially confirmed that actor Rock Hudson is dying of AIDS in a Paris hospital.

In August, Ryan White, a 13-year-old hemophiliac infected with HIV through a blood transfusion, is barred from public school in Kokomo, Indiana, because authorities fear he might infect other students. CDC guidelines issued the same month state that the privacy of students with the virus should be protected by school administrators and that they should be allowed to attend school. Preschool students and handicapped children, however, are to be kept out of school under the guidelines, pending more information on how the virus is transmitted. The CDC also recommends that the HIV antibody test be administered to children in adoption or foster care settings if their natural parents are in high-risk groups for the virus or if their natural parents' personal histories are unknown.

Also in August, the Pentagon announces that all potential military recruits will be screened for HIV.

Two polls by the Gallup Organization, released by the CDC in August, show that 95 percent of U.S. residents have heard of AIDS.

In September, $1.3 million for HIV/AIDS research is raised by the gala Hollywood Night of 1,000 Stars. The newly formed National AIDS Research Foundation names actress Elizabeth Taylor its national chairperson.

According to a *New York Times*/CBS News poll released in September, about half of Americans believe HIV can possibly be transmitted by casual contact despite strong medical evidence to the contrary.

Also in September, the Food and Drug Administration (FDA) redefines the gay high-risk group for HIV/AIDS to include any male who has had sex with another male since 1977.The FDA also approves for U.S. use the experimental drug HPA-23, which might inhibit the reproduction of HIV although it does not eliminate the resultant immune system suppression.

Federal officials tell a U.S. House subcommittee in September that $70 million more is needed for HIV/AIDS research and treatment, an amount twice as high as the Reagan administration has requested.

In October, the Public Health Service announces its long-range plan for halting the spread of HIV. The plan focuses on curbing steady increases in the growth of the virus by 1990 and eliminating its spread by 2000. The CDC announces that the risk of transmission through daily contact in ordinary household situations is nonexistent and that voluntary behavioral changes are being undertaken by gay and bisexual men in San Francisco, one of the epicenters of the disease. The CDC also announces that Miami, Newark, and Houston have joined New York, San Francisco, and Los Angeles as cities with large numbers of AIDS cases. At the same time, the Harvard School of Public Health announces that sexual transmission is responsible for the spread of the virus into the heterosexual population.

Actor Rock Hudson dies of AIDS in October. His death is widely viewed as a turning point in the public perception of the epidemic. In response to the renowned actor's death, President Ronald Reagan makes his first public comment on AIDS.

Also in October, the Pentagon announces plans to increase its screening to include all 2.1 million military personnel, promising treatment, counseling, and honorable medical discharges for those who develop the disease. One rationale for this move is that the military acts as its own blood bank in times of need.

The National Education Association (NEA) suggests in October that school officials should decide on a case-by-case basis whether children with HIV will be permitted in the classroom. The NEA also endorses testing for students and teachers if there is reason to think they have contracted the virus.

In November, school officials grant Ryan White leave to attend classes. The Public Health Service announces that no special restrictions should be placed on food handlers and health care workers with HIV, as there is no medical evidence that casual contact transmits the virus. Prostitutes, targeted as a primary transmission source of heterosexual infection, are not found to present any particular risk for their customers according to scientists, who state that female-to-male sexual transmission has been extremely rare.

The number of U.S. AIDS cases diagnosed in 1985 is 11,359.

1986   In April, John James publishes the first issue of *AIDS Treatment News,* which soon becomes the underground medical movement's chief source of information and communication on HIV/AIDS issues. The first issue discusses AL 721, the egg lipid solution popular in the gay community and tested in Israel and France.

In June, the 85 top government HIV/AIDS experts meet in Coolfont, West Virginia, to review Public Health Service plans regarding the epidemic. The group projects 270,000 cases of AIDS and 179,000 deaths in the United States by 1991.

In October, the Institute of Medicine releases a massive report calling the federal response to the AIDS crisis

1986
cont.
woefully inadequate. U.S. Surgeon General C. Everett Koop releases the *Surgeon General's Report on the Acquired Immune Deficiency Syndrome*. The frank nature of the report and its emphasis on the epidemic as a public health problem rather than a political issue surprise both conservatives and liberals. The report advises starting sex education for children at the earliest grade possible, using condoms, and abandoning as useless the quarantine or identification of HIV-infected people. Tens of thousands of copies of the report are distributed.

In November, the New York state health commissioner announces that he will consider a small demonstration project to provide needle exchange services for IV drug users with the goal of reducing the spread of HIV by cutting down on needle sharing within that group.

The number of U.S. AIDS cases diagnosed in 1986 is 18,494.

1987
In January, the FDA's Anti-Infective Drugs Advisory Committee votes to release AZT as the only drug approved for use against HIV infection. The annual cost per person is estimated at $10,000.

In March, gay activist and writer Larry Kramer, speaking to a New York City audience, calls for the angry advocacy that leads to the creation of the AIDS Coalition to Unleash Power (ACT UP). Days later, on March 24, hundreds of demonstrators block traffic on Wall Street to protest the cost of AZT; seventeen people are arrested. Shortly after the demonstration, the FDA announces it will shorten its drug-approval process by two years.

In May, the Third International Conference on Acquired Immune Deficiency Syndrome convenes in Washington, D.C. At an awards dinner held in conjunction with the conference, President Reagan gives his first speech on HIV/AIDS, focusing on testing people for the virus. The next morning, Vice President George Bush gives the conference's opening address, defending the administration's testing proposals. More than 60 activists are arrested at the White House that day for protesting federal policy. Washington police don rubber gloves to make the arrests.

On June 4, when Northwest Orient Airlines refuses passage to people with AIDS (PWAs), ACT UP erupts in protest at the airline's New York offices. Two lawsuits are brought against Northwest. The policy is reversed.

On September 9, the Presidential Advisory Council on AIDS meets for the first time in Washington, D.C. ACT UP protests the inadequacies of the newly formed commission.

In October, a U.S. scientist begins the first tests of an experimental AIDS vaccine on HIV-negative human subjects.

Also in October, the NAMES Project AIDS Memorial Quilt is displayed on the Mall in Washington, D.C. Every panel of the huge quilt has been made by a friend or relative to commemorate a person who has died of HIV/AIDS.

The number of U.S. AIDS cases diagnosed in 1987 is 27,558.

1988   In January, New York state health officials announce that they have approved a plan to distribute clean syringes to IV drug users in an effort to curb the spread of HIV.

On January 15, ACT UP New York's Women's Caucus organizes the group's first action focused on women and HIV. Five hundred people protest an article in *Cosmopolitan* telling heterosexual women that having unprotected vaginal intercourse with an HIV-positive man is safe.

In March, young hemophiliac Ryan White testifies before the Watkins, or Presidential, Commission on AIDS, which subsequently releases a report identifying complacency as a major obstacle to ending the epidemic.

1988
cont.

During the period May 1–9, ACT UP branches around the United States mount protests focusing on specific, unattended aspects of the AIDS epidemic such as IV drug use, homophobia, people of color, women, testing programs, prison programs, and children with AIDS. More than 50 cities participate.

In August, New York City officials announce they will adopt the proposed needle exchange plan over the strenuous objections of law enforcement officials.

On October 11, the ACT UP coalition closes down the FDA outside Washington, D.C., when 1,000 activists stage a series of demonstrations; almost 180 are arrested. The event receives international press coverage.

In November, New York City Mayor Edward Koch announces that he has ruled out a needle exchange program at one city site because it is located too close to a school. Another site is also found unacceptable. The city then begins a needle distribution program from an office in the Health Department in downtown Manhattan.

The number of U.S. AIDS cases diagnosed in 1988 is 33,590.

1989

In January, New York City officials admit that their needle exchange program has attracted few participants. Critics charge that the program's location in a city office building in downtown Manhattan does not encourage participation. Health officials say they will focus their efforts on drug treatment.

On March 28, ACT UP's second anniversary protest draws 3,000 people to New York's City Hall, making "Target City Hall" the largest AIDS activist demonstration to date. The group protests New York's AIDS policy under Mayor Edward Koch; about 200 are arrested.

In April, the independent and star-studded American Foundation for AIDS Research (AmFAR) announces an award of $1.4 million to 16 community-based research centers for further work on AIDS drug therapies.

On April 21, ACT UP New York joins ACT UP Atlanta to protest a South Carolina provision that would allow PWAs to be quarantined. That same day, four ACT UP members barricade themselves in a Burroughs Wellcome office in North Carolina demanding a cut in the price of AZT, still the most expensive medicine in history at $8,000 for a year's dosage.

On May 2, the FDA Advisory Committee finally approves aerosolized Pentamidine, a major advance in prophylaxis against PCP, the leading killer of people with AIDS.

In June, ACT UP members take over the stage at the Fifth International Conference on AIDS in Montreal to read 12 principles on drugs and drug testing aimed at the FDA.

On September 14, ACT UP stages demonstrations at the Stock Exchanges in New York, San Francisco, and London to protest Burroughs Wellcome's pricing of AZT. Four days later, Burroughs Wellcome lowers the price of AZT by 20 percent, to $6,400 per year.

In December, ACT UP brings 5,000 demonstrators to New York City's St. Patrick's Cathedral to protest the Roman Catholic Church's positions on homosexuality, safe sex, birth control, and abortion; 111 are arrested. Six people arrested for interrupting a church service become known as the St. Patrick's Six.

Also in December, the National Commission on AIDS (NCOA), formed earlier in the year by the U.S. Congress, issues its first report, *Failure of the U.S. Health Care System to Deal with the HIV Epidemic.* The report finds dangerous levels of complacency regarding an epidemic the public wants to believe is over and laments the lack of a national plan to address that epidemic.

A major article by Gina Koalata appears in the *New York Times* in December that reports critical information from ACT UP about the effectiveness of lower doses of AZT. Within weeks, the FDA cuts the standard dosage of AZT in half.

1989
cont.

The first Day without Art is held in December, in which gallery owners across the United States are asked to close their galleries to acknowledge the losses to the art world as a result of AIDS.

The number of U.S. AIDS cases diagnosed in 1989 is 38,154.

1990

In February, New York City Mayor David Dinkins, who had previously stated he fears needle exchange will encourage drug use, announces he will drop the needle distribution program.

In March, President George Bush responds to the call by NCOA and issues a statement on the AIDS epidemic to a national meeting of business leaders.

On March 6, ACT UP forms its Needle Exchange Committee, dedicated to decriminalizing needle possession, offering education on safer injection, and providing drug treatment on demand. Activists exchange clean needles for used ones and distribute information on safe drug injection, condoms, and safe sex/AIDS prevention to intravenous drug users (IVDUs) on a Lower East Side street corner. Six are arrested.

In April, NCOA issues its second report, *Leadership, Legislation, and Regulation.* The report finds that a clear national plan with well-defined goals and responsibilities is essential to battling the AIDS epidemic.

Also in April, one of the earliest and most highly publicized cases involving HIV transmission to a health care worker through an accidental needle stick that occurred in 1983 is settled in New York City. Dr. Veronica Prego, who had sued the city's Health and Hospitals Corporation and two other physicians for $175 million, accepts a settlement of $1.4 million. Prego had sued her supervising intern for leaving a needle in a patient's bed and the other physician for revealing her HIV status to hospital personnel.

In June, the National Institutes of Health (NIH) begins an investigation into the procedures involved in Dr.

Robert C. Gallo's discovery of the virus that causes AIDS. Allegations persist that in the highly competitive world of research, Gallo's virus might, in fact, have been the French virus that was discovered before his.

In July, the first book to document the history of HIV disease in women, *Women, AIDS, and Activism*, is published. The book was originally developed by ACT UP New York's Women's Caucus in 1989.

In November, the CDC announces that HIV is more prevalent in those over age 50 than among children under age 13. Statistics show that whereas the majority of those affected are homosexual or bisexual, around 17 percent of those who are HIV positive acquired the virus from blood products used in surgery, a phenomenon that occurs more frequently among older people.

December 1 is the World Health Organization's third annual AIDS Awareness Day and also marks the second annual Day without Art, observed by 3,000 organizations across the United States to highlight the toll the epidemic has taken on the arts community and the artistic contributions that have been lost because of artists' deaths. In museums, paintings are covered or removed for the day. The lights of the Manhattan skyline—including the Empire State Building, Rockefeller Center, the World Trade Center, and the Chrysler Building—are dimmed for 15 minutes to commemorate those who have died from AIDS. Cable television stations are black, and Broadway theaters dim their lights.

Later in December, ACT UP conducts a demonstration at New York City's St. Patrick's Cathedral to protest the role of the Roman Catholic Church in influencing public policy on abortion, safe sex, birth control, and homosexuality, much like the demonstration in December 1989. The organization also announces a lawsuit brought by advocates over the church's refusal to provide safe sex, birth control, and abortion information to HIV-positive clients in publicly financed, church-operated health care facilities. New York state officials

1990
cont.

waived requirements for those services to ensure church participation in providing health facilities.

The number of U.S. AIDS cases diagnosed in 1990 is 38,280.

1991

On January 23, ACT UP stages a "Day of Desperation" in New York City, targeting "every aspect of City life" and demanding that "everyone realize that every day is a day of desperation for those in the AIDS community." Activities include invasions of PBS and CBS Evening News broadcasts the previous night; a demonstration on Wall Street with more than 2,000 protesters marching with coffins they deliver to city, state, and federal officials; a demonstration at the state office building in Harlem to demand an end to the city's homeless shelter system and to protest the lack of housing and services for people with HIV/AIDS; and a Latino/a Caucus invasion of the Bronx Borough president's office. At 5:07 P.M., Grand Central Station is taken over by thousands of activists, and a banner announcing "One AIDS Death Every Eight Minutes" is hung over the arrivals board. Later, 263 people are arrested as the group attempts to march to the United Nations.

Also in January, the American Dental Association (ADA), acting in response to the apparent infection of five patients by a Florida dentist, issues an interim policy urging dentists either to refrain from invasive procedures or disclose their seropositive status. The ADA pledges to assist and support infected dentists who stop practicing, states that all HIV-infected patients should disclose their status to their dentists, and urges dentists to develop confidentiality protocols.

In late January, the St. Patrick Six are sentenced to six months of community service by a Manhattan Criminal Court judge who compares them to Ghandi and Martin Luther King.

In February, the New York City Board of Education narrowly votes to proceed with Chancellor Joseph Fernandez's plan to provide condoms in the city's high schools. Under the plan, students will be the first high school students in the nation to have unrestricted access to condoms with no fees, parental consent, or counseling requirements. The plan is vigorously opposed by religious groups and others, but a Gallup poll finds 54 percent of parents of public school students support it. Also in New York City, 10 activists charged with possession of needles with the intent to distribute them to IV drug users on the Lower East Side are acquitted by a judge who agrees that the "necessity defense" applies because the activists are trying to save the lives of those vulnerable to HIV infection.

On March 31, 6,436 health care workers in the United States are known to be HIV positive, including 703 physicians, 47 surgeons, 1,358 nurses, and 171 dentists and dental hygienists. The nation's largest organization of bone and joint surgeons calls for HIV-infected surgeons to inform their patients and stop performing all procedures except for emergency surgery, although no federal law to this effect has been enacted.

In April, a San Francisco jury deadlocks when trying to reach a verdict in the case of two people arrested for distributing new syringes to drug addicts on the street. Jury foreperson Spero Saridakis, swayed by the testimony, subsequently joins the Prevention Point program and begins distributing syringes himself.

Also in April, a federal judge awards $3.8 million to a 42-year-old Marine, Martin Gaffney, whose wife and one child have died from AIDS. Gaffney's wife received a tainted blood transfusion at a Navy hospital in 1981 while giving birth. A subsequent child died of AIDS, and Gaffney also tests positive for the virus. At the time of the court ruling, Gaffney is asymptomatic. (He dies in November 1991, leaving one daughter who is seronegative. He receives his settlement just ten days before his death after a four-year court battle.)

In May, NIH scientist Robert C. Gallo drops his claim of having codiscovered HIV, ending a seven-year dispute with French scientist Dr. Luc Montagnier.

1991
cont.

Also in May, NIH director Dr. Bernadine Healy says she thinks the National Cancer Institute (NCI) should be named coinventor of the drug AZT. Such a move would end the often criticized monopoly of pharmaceutical manufacturer Burroughs Wellcome.

Later in May, tobacco company Philip Morris announces it will increase its charitable contributions to AIDS research. ACT UP had called for a boycott of the company in 1990 because of its support of conservative Republican Senator Jesse Helms of North Carolina.

Three people die of AIDS in May after receiving organ transplants from a man who died in 1985; two others who received transplants test positive for HIV. Although 58 of the 61 organs and tissues donated when the man died were used, some were processed in ways that would have killed the virus, whereas others were not.

In June, the Seventh International Conference on AIDS convenes in Florence, Italy. Demonstrators protest continuing U.S. immigration policy banning HIV-positive persons from entering the country. The policy poses a threat to the Eighth International Conference, planned originally for Boston in 1992 but held instead in Amsterdam.

Also in June, the American Medical Association votes in favor of voluntary testing of health care workers, and the American Nurses Association votes 577 to 13 to oppose compulsory HIV testing for its members and patients.

Also in June, the CDC announces that 1 million Americans are infected with HIV and proposes to change the 1987 case definition of AIDS to take effect in April 1992. Proposed definition changes, focusing on T4 cell counts, could raise the 193,000 reported AIDS cases by 160,000 cases.

In July, the U.S. Senate votes 81 to 18 in favor of a proposal by Senator Jesse Helms (R-NC) to set a prison term of at least 10 years and a fine of $10,000 for any

HIV-infected medical professional who performs an invasive procedure without disclosing his or her serostatus. Helms says, "I don't think 10 years is severe when you consider what these people are willing to do to innocent patients." The provision is dropped in September during House-Senate budget negotiations.

The CDC recommends in July that HIV-infected physicians and dentists stop performing certain procedures that involve a greater-than-normal chance of patients being exposed to the worker's blood during an accident and that anyone performing such procedures be tested for the virus.

Also in July, the FDA recommends that a new drug (didanosine, or dideoxyinoisine [ddI]) be approved for marketing even though the drug has not been thoroughly tested in clinical trials. The drug would be used for those in advanced stages of AIDS who cannot tolerate the more common AZT because of side effects or who are no longer responding to AZT.

In August, the ADA amends its January 1991 interim policy on HIV to include a recommendation that dentists who believe they are at risk for HIV infection should seek testing.

Also in August, former U.S. surgeon general C. Everett Koop appeals for caution in public and legislative responses to the possible HIV infection of patients by health care providers. "Let me assure the American public that the chances of getting AIDS from a health care worker are essentially nil," Koop states. He condemns mandatory testing proposals for health care workers, as well as state and federal efforts to regulate HIV-infected practitioners.

On August 28, just before school opens, Massachusetts state officials announce their recommendation that high schools make condoms available to students. Although some local schools already distribute condoms, this is the first announced statewide policy in the nation.

That same day, the statute of limitations expires on possible prosecution for arson in the torching of the Ray family home in Arcadia, Florida, in 1987. Florida authorities never learned who started the fire, which destroyed the home of three hemophiliac brothers, Ricky (15), Robert (13), and Randy (12), after officials learned the boys had acquired HIV from contaminated blood products. The family subsequently moved to Sarasota, Florida.

On September 1, 2,500 AIDS activists march on President Bush's vacation home in Kennebunkport, Maine, to demand leadership on the AIDS crisis and to declare that the crisis can be ended. The next day the president says he was moved more deeply by a demonstration by the unemployed the week before. "That one hit home," he says, "because when a family is out of work, that's one that I care very much about."

Later in September, 12,000 people—up from 3,000 the previous year—take part in the fifth annual AIDSWALK in Washington, D.C., to raise funds for local AIDS-related services; the walkers raise $450,000.

Also in September, the CDC issues draft guidelines proposing that hospitals routinely offer and encourage HIV testing for patients, especially in areas with high rates of infection. The CDC estimates that only 12 percent of those infected are aware of their serostatus. The proposed guidelines represent the CDC's first update of its advice to hospitals since 1987.

In October, Congress passes legislation requiring that states adopt guidelines for physicians, dentists, and others who perform invasive surgery within a year or risk losing federal public health funding. This move is made in the wake of publicity from an alleged case of dentist-to-patient transmission of HIV in Florida, although the CDC has found this case to be the only instance of such transmission in the 11 years of the epidemic.

The World Health Organization estimates in October

that approximately 10 million people are infected with HIV worldwide.

In November, Earvin "Magic" Johnson, well-known National Basketball Association star of the Los Angeles Lakers, announces his immediate retirement after learning he is HIV positive during a routine insurance physical. Johnson, who has recently married and whose wife is pregnant, says his wife has tested HIV negative. He states that he acquired the virus through heterosexual activity with another woman. Johnson, a role model for many young people, says he will devote his time to AIDS education, especially regarding the importance of safe sexual practices. President Bush subsequently announces that Johnson will replace Belinda Mason, recently deceased, on the National Commission on AIDS.

Also in November, the CDC publishes a draft of proposed revisions to the HIV/AIDS surveillance case definition; the new definition is to take effect in April 1992. The CDC also reports that in some areas up to 20 percent of homeless people are HIV positive and that infection rates among homeless teens are alarmingly high.

In December, Kimberly Bergalis, the Florida college student believed to have been one of five patients of an HIV-infected dentist to acquire the virus through doctor-patient transmission, dies.

The number of U.S. AIDS cases diagnosed in 1991 is 101,000. The number of U.S. AIDS deaths for that year is 36,600.

1992   In March, researchers announce they are making progress in finding ways to block the transmission of HIV from a mother to her unborn child, which occurs in about 30 percent of cases.

In April, the CDC fails to implement the proposed new case surveillance definition as scheduled and makes no announcement of its intention to do so.

Also in April, New York state announces it will make Medicaid payments to those who watch tuberculosis

1992
cont.

(TB) patients swallow their prescription medicine, which is called directly observed therapy. The $5.8 million program will involve up to 1,000 TB patients identified by physicians as recalcitrant about taking their medications. Workers will be paid $32.82 per patient per week in a hospital or shelter and $95.90 if they visit a patient at home.

That same month, a New York state judge upholds the New York City public high school system's access to condoms program, ruling that the program does not violate parents' religious freedom or require their consent. The ruling follows the first legal challenge to the program and others like it in San Francisco, Philadelphia, Chicago, Seattle, and Los Angeles.

Also in April, scientific experts announce that the accelerated approval of ddI in July 1991 seems justified. The drug had not been fully tested when it was released for limited use against HIV by those who cannot take or have stopped responding to AZT.

Conditional FDA approval is given in April to a new drug, dideoxycytidine (ddC), to be used in combination with AZT. The drug will be available under an expanded access program in which patients who cannot tolerate other treatments receive the drug free of charge.

Also in April, tennis player Arthur Ashe announces he has AIDS.

In May, New York City Mayor Dinkins announces he will drop his long-standing opposition to a needle exchange program for drug users and commence an ambitious effort to exchange 2.53 million syringes.

Also in May, Washington, D.C., Mayor Sharon Pratt Kelly calls for condom distribution programs to be instituted in public high schools and prisons and for a needle exchange effort. Robert Martinez, director of the federal Office of Drug Control Policy, denounces the programs as wrong on moral grounds.

A federal judge rules in May that the so-called Helms rule is unconstitutional. The 1987 CDC rule, adopted at the urging of Senator Jesse Helms (R-NC), decrees that HIV/AIDS education materials cannot contain any material that could be deemed offensive to the target audience or to anyone else. Critics argued that this restriction cripples their efforts to distribute materials that were sexually explicit and geared toward specific audiences.

The May issue of the *New England Journal of Medicine* reports that a study of AZT shows that the drug prolongs the lives of patients with HIV. This result seems to contradict the earlier findings of a Veterans Administration study that showed AZT did not affect survival.

In June, scientists at the University of Washington and Northwestern University announce a breakthrough in HIV vaccine research with the discovery that an Asian monkey, the pigtail macaque, becomes ill with HIV when infected by direct injection or exposure to infected blood. Previously, scientists had been unable to identify an animal whose immune system responds to the virus the same way as a human's, a factor they consider necessary for possible vaccine testing.

Also in June, it is revealed that federal officials have shelved plans to loosen proposed restrictions on HIV-infected physicians, dentists, and others who perform invasive procedures. This action leaves the states free to issue their own prohibitions and could mean that if such persons continue to practice, they could be required to disclose their seropositive status to their patients.

In July, the Eighth International Conference on AIDS convenes in Amsterdam. The conference was originally scheduled for Boston but was moved when the United States refused to lift travel restrictions on HIV-positive people.

In September, Earvin Magic Johnson resigns from the National Commission on AIDS because of official inaction on HIV/AIDS policy. Johnson announces that he will return to professional basketball next season.

1992
cont.

In December, in a continuing struggle to win the release of HIV-positive Haitian refugees from a detainment camp in Guantanamo, Cuba, a coalition including ACT UP, Housing Works, and the Coalition for the Homeless begins providing an "underground railroad" of housing and services for the refugees.

On December 21, ACT UP and Haitian activists demand the release of Siliese Success, an HIV-positive Haitian woman jailed after the death of her baby. They threaten to hold a Christmas Eve vigil at the Immigration and Naturalization Services detention center. Following the threat, Success is released.

The number of people living with AIDS in the United States is 136,600. The number of U.S. AIDS deaths is 41,100.

1993

The CDC revises its definition of AIDS to include new opportunistic infections, including some most common to women, and to include individuals whose T cells measure less than 200.

The so-called female condom is approved. In the United States, the FDA refuses to allow testing for anal sex because sodomy is illegal in many states.

In March, actress Susan Sarandon protests the detention of HIV-positive Haitians at Guantanamo during the Academy Awards presentation before an international television audience of billions of viewers.

In April, researchers in Europe release the Concorde Study, which shows that taking AZT early in the progression of HIV/AIDS has no benefits.

On April 4 and 8, ACT UP members bring the first 36 Haitian refugees with T cell counts under 200 to New York from the Guantanamo detention center. In the first week alone, they house 22 Haitian PWAs.

On April 23, Donna Shalala, the new secretary of Health and Human Services, meets with 15 lesbians with AIDS. Several hundred protesters gather, gaining coverage in *Newsweek*.

On April 24 and 25, the largest group of gay men and lesbians in U.S. history gathers in Washington, D.C. Organizers estimate participation at 1 million, although the federal government halves that figure. Many AIDS activists, including Larry Kramer, address the attendees.

In May, a British study confirms suspicions that smokers infected with HIV develop full-blown AIDS twice as quickly as nonsmokers who have the virus. Also, the Social Security Administration changes disability regulations for people with HIV, adding a wide range of female-specific opportunistic infections.

In June, the Guantanamo Bay detention camp is closed. ACT UP New York members bring 78 Haitian refugees to New York. By September, all of the refugees are living in permanent, medically appropriate housing.

The number of people living with AIDS in the United States is 173,100. The number of U.S. AIDS deaths is 44,600.

1994 A Benetton advertisement appears in numerous publications depicting former President Ronald Reagan with KS lesions.

In February, the first HIV detection saliva test, Orasure, developed by Epitope, is approved by the FDA.

In March, a Maryland court rules that an HIV-positive surgeon has a legal obligation to identify his HIV status to patients before he performs invasive surgery (*Faya v. Almaraz*, 620 A.2d 327). Also, in the case of *Aetna Casualty and Surety Co. v. Sheft* (989 F.2d 1105 [9th Cir.]), a former lover wins a tort suit against his dead lover's estate for intentional concealment of AIDS and recovers damages from an insurance company.

In May, bowing to pressure from activists, New York Mayor Rudolph Giuliani releases his proposed city budget, which leaves intact the threatened Division of AIDS Services. Also, in the case of *Anderson v. Boston Store of Texas* (No. 330931430 [EEOC, Houston Dist.

1994
cont.

Off.]), the court rules that a store violated ADA regulations by not allowing an HIV-infected employee to participate in its group health plan.

In July, the courts reject challenges to Burrough Wellcome's exclusive patent on AZT in *Burroughs Wellcome Co. v. Barr Laboratories, Inc.* (828 F. Supp. 1208).

In August, two medical supply companies—Baxter International of Deerfield, Illinois, and Rhone Poulenc Rorer of Collegeville, Pennsylvania—agree to pay $160 million to HIV-positive hemophiliacs and their survivors to settle allegations that they sold HIV-tainted blood-clotting products.

In October, a West Virginia court rules that a plaintiff in an HIV transmission case can be given the name of a deceased donor to secure medical records (*Doe v. American Nat. Red Cross*, 151 F.R.D. 71 [S.D.W.Va.]). Also, in the case of *Alt v. Parker* (435 S.E.2d 773), assault with a deadly weapon charges are dismissed against an HIV-positive man who spat at police officers.

3TC (Zerit®)—Bristol-Myers Squibb—a nucleoside reverse transcriptase inhibitor, is approved by the FDA for use in the United States.

In December, Dr. Peter Palo, chief of the UN AIDS program, announces testing of two AIDS vaccines among heterosexual male drug users in Thailand and homosexual men in Brazil.

Also in December, Barbara Webb, the fourth of six people infected with HIV by Florida dentist Dr. Acer (the group includes Kimberly Bergalis), dies at age 68 on her 45th wedding anniversary.

News reports in December indicate that Sarah Ferguson, the Duchess of York, has tested twice for HIV.

A Philadelphia church marks the Christmas holiday season by posting placards on its door, including a large one that reads "All Are Welcome" and a smaller one that reads "Only those who have tested negative for the AIDS virus."

The FDA announces in December that 18 pints of blood that lacked complete medical histories were distributed by a Florida blood bank.

Also in December, in Auckland, New Zealand, an HIV-positive Kenyan man, Peter Mwai, age 29, is found guilty of having unprotected sex with five women and is convicted of causing grievous bodily harm to one woman.

The number of people living with AIDS in the United States is 196,200. The number of U.S. AIDS deaths is 49,400.

1995   In January, a milestone is marked as AIDS surpasses accidents as the leading cause of death in the United States for adults ages 25 to 44. Also, Dr. David Ho and (independently) Dr. George Shaw of the University of Alabama, Birmingham, announce that HIV infection has no dormancy period, as once believed, and studies reveal a protein in human saliva that blocks HIV infection.

Also in February, Olympic gold medalist Greg Louganis announces he has full-blown AIDS during a televised interview with Barbara Walters.

That same month, Nike begins featuring HIV-positive Latino athlete Rick Muñoz in a new television promotion for its "Just Do It" campaign.

In March, the CDC reports that two of three Americans who are tested voluntarily for HIV go to private physicians rather than public clinics.

The *Chicago Tribune* reports in March that the Abundant Life Clinic in Chicago, which is affiliated with the Nation of Islam and has received nearly $600,000 in federal funds, is dispensing Kemron, an unlicensed "miracle cure" for AIDS.

1995
cont.

Also in March, a five-year-old Los Angeles boy infected with HIV at birth is reported to be free of the virus.

In April, the *Annals of Internal Medicine* reports that viral load assays are more effective than CD4 counts in measuring how quickly an HIV-positive patient will progress to AIDS.

Also in April, Russian President Boris Yeltsin signs into law a bill that mandates that foreigners must test negative for HIV if they want to stay in Russia for more than three months.

Later in April, Jacksonville, Florida, teenager Tammy Lynn Esckilsen, who called former hospital patients and told them they had tested positive for HIV, is sentenced to probation and therapy following a guilty plea.

That same month, a CDC study finds no evidence to support the risk of transmission of HIV from health care workers to patients.

In May, the Associated Press reports that the FBI is spying on AIDS activists and gay rights groups, allegedly out of fear they might resort to violence or throw infected blood during demonstrations.

A government survey released in May reveals that nearly one-third of U.S. adults are interested in using soon-to-be-approved home AIDS tests to find out whether they are infected.

Also in May, an Indiana woman, LaDonna Cleve, who sold her blood despite knowing she is HIV positive, is sentenced to four years in prison. In a related story, witnesses tell a Canadian government panel that blood products from Arkansas prison inmates, some of whom later tested positive for HIV, were used by Canadian hemophiliacs during the 1980s.

That same month, in a surprise move the federal government ends anonymous testing of newborns for

AIDS just as a member of Congress is pushing legislation to allow the mothers to learn the test results.

Lured in part by $12 million in incentives, AIDS scientist Robert C. Gallo announces in May that he will establish the Center for Human Virology in Baltimore, Maryland.

A study released in May reveals that hospitals can lose up to $260,000 a year caring for AIDS-infected patients, the vast majority of whom depend on Medicaid or charity for life-prolonging treatment.

In June, the CDC advises those who are HIV positive and, in fact, anyone with a weakened immune system to boil their drinking water to avoid contracting cryptosporidium, a dangerous illness caused by waterborne parasites that has caused numerous deaths among people with AIDS in the Midwest.

The World Health Organization announces in June that AIDS and tuberculosis are creating a deadly partnership as both diseases spiral out of control.

Also in June, Hoffman-LaRoche announces it will offer Invirase®, one of the first protease inhibitors, without charge to 2,000 AIDS patients through a government-administered lottery.

In Phoenix, Arizona, 44-year-old Michael Kent Bilbrey receives a five-year prison sentence in June for selling an AIDS cure made from cranberry juice, a salt solution, and household bleach.

In July, the CDC recommends that all expectant mothers voluntarily be tested for HIV.

Senator Jesse Helms is quoted in the *New York Times* in July as saying that the government should spend less money on people with AIDS because they became ill as a result of "deliberate, disgusting, revolting conduct."

A government report released in July says a failure of leadership, coupled with uncertainty over the threat

1995
cont.

posed by AIDS, allowed the U.S. blood supply to become contaminated with HIV in the early 1980s.

Also in July, a U.S. House grievance board finds Representative Barbara-Rose Collins (D-Michigan) guilty of firing a former aide, Bruce Taylor, who is gay, because she was afraid he might be HIV positive.

That same month, the Presidential Advisory Council on AIDS urges President Clinton to show more leadership on AIDS and to convene a presidential summit on the issue.

In August, a study published in the *Journal of Acquired Immune Deficiency Syndromes* reports that needle sharing among drug users dropped 40 percent in Connecticut after the state passed a law permitting sales of syringes without prescriptions.

Also in August, David Geffen, a millionaire record producer and cofounder of Dreamworks SKG Studio, donates $4 million to two AIDS organizations. The Gay Men's Health Crisis receives $2.5 million to build a testing and counseling center, and God's Love We Deliver, which provides meals for home-bound AIDS patients in New York City, receives $1.5 million.

That same month, the Fort Myers, Florida, school district drops voluntary HIV testing of high school students after receiving complaints that the program is inappropriate for schools.

The August issue of the British journal *Lancet* reports that improved treatment of sexually transmitted diseases such as gonorrhea and syphilis has helped to reduce the spread of HIV in Tanzania.

Also in August, it is announced by the Celgene Corporation that Thalidomide, the tranquilizer that caused birth defects throughout Europe in the 1950s, will be offered on an experimental basis to U.S. AIDS patients suffering wasting syndrome and who have failed other treatments or are near death.

In September, the state of Missouri cancels its program that assists nearly 1,400 AIDS patients with rent, food, and health care needs.

In September, the *New York Times* reports that the American Red Cross, at the behest of its president, Elizabeth Dole, is seeking to remove explicit content from its AIDS-prevention program that describes safe sex and sterile syringes for drug users as prevention methods for HIV.

In September, the CDC reports that more than 8 million needles were exchanged in 1994 under programs that allow drug addicts to trade dirty syringes for sterile ones.

A September report by the World Health Organization states that Indian health authorities are investigating reports that a U.S. foundation, the Bhattacharya, illegally tested a new HIV vaccine on residents of Bombay and Calcutta.

In October, New York state announces that the results of HIV tests administered to newborns will be made available to their mothers.

On October 6, the government of Taiwan denies Magic Johnson entry into the country because of his HIV-positive status even though the Taiwanese president had invited him to visit.

In November, the FDA announces that 3TC used in combination with AZT is the preferred first line of treatment in primary HIV care.

Also in November, it is revealed that six Australians remain healthy more that 10 years after having been infected with HIV, spurring hopes that they may hold the secret to an effective anti-HIV vaccine.

The United Nations announces in November that the spread of HIV may have peaked in northern Europe, where the number of new infections appears to have leveled off.

1995
cont.
In December, Invirase®, developed by Roche, is approved for use in the United States—the first anti-HIV drug in the protease inhibitor class to receive such approval. Approval of Ritonavir (Norvir®), developed by Abbott, and Indinavir (Crixivan®), developed by Merck, follows shortly.

Also in December, AIDS patient Jeff Getty receives a bone marrow transplant from a baboon. He is still alive in March 1998, although his condition has worsened in recent months.

That same month, Medicaid announces a project to be run in four states that will encourage voluntary testing to minimize the risk of vertical transmission from mother to child.

Later in December, President Clinton convenes the first White House Conference on AIDS with the goal of finding "a cure and a vaccine."

Also in December, Australia bars HIV-positive people from joining the military.

That same month, Abbott Labs offers its protease inhibitor Ritonavir to 2,000 people in the late stages of AIDS.

In December, the *New England Journal of Medicine* publishes a study by the CDC revealing that only about 24 of the 12 million pints of blood used in transfusions each year are infected with HIV.

Also in December, in an effort to stem the country's growing HIV/AIDS epidemic, Ukraine health inspectors shut down hair salons in Odessa after scissors and razors are found to be improperly sanitized.

The number of people living with AIDS in the United States is 215,600. The number of U.S. AIDS deaths is 50,700.

1996
In January, scientists infect a chimpanzee with AIDS,

suggesting a possible substitute for humans in testing anti-HIV treatments.

In February, the CDC announces that AIDS causes one-third of all deaths of black men ages 25 to 44.

Also in February, heavyweight boxer Tommy Morrison announces he is HIV positive after being tested by the Nevada Boxing Commission prior to a scheduled bout in Las Vegas. He is forced to withdraw from the fight and is effectively barred from the ring everywhere. He later creates a great deal of controversy by advocating his practice of having unprotected sexual relations with his wife in an interview in *Poz*.

An HIV-positive New York man is sentenced to 90 years in jail in February for assault with the intent to murder in the sexual assault of his step-grandson.

In March, scientists announce that a herpes-related virus is the cause of Kaposi's sarcoma, one of the leading killers of people with AIDS, a discovery they hope will lead to the development of a vaccination.

Also in March, a therapeutic HIV vaccine (one designed to treat those already HIV positive) developed by the late Jonas Salk, who also developed the polio vaccine, enters human trials.

In April, four members of ACT UP New York are arrested after plastering Stadtlanders Pharmacy's showcase store with signs decrying "PRICE GOUGING" and "AIDS profiteering." Stadtlanders is charging a 37 percent markup on the protease inhibitor Crixivan® and at the time is the sole distributor of the drug. The next day, Stadtlanders's Mail Order Pharmacy announces a 19.5 percent cash discount on the retail price of Crixivan®.

In May, President Clinton signs legislation extending the Ryan White Care Act for another five years; the appropriation is $738 million, compared with $632 million in 1995. The bill has been stalled for over nine months because of a debate over mandatory testing of

1996
cont.

newborns. A compromise is developed wherein testing of newborns will be implemented only if the number of expectant mothers being tested is unexpectedly low.

Health and Human Services Secretary Shalala announces in May that over the next four years $100 million will be spent on research to develop an effective microbicide against HIV.

Also in May, the FDA approves the first home HIV testing kit.

In June, the FDA approves Nevirapine (Viramune®), developed by Roxane Laboratories, the first in a new class of AIDS medicines called nonnucleoside reverse transcriptase inhibitors.

In July, at the Eleventh International Conference in Vancouver, groundbreaking announcements are made regarding the use of triple combination therapy in reducing HIV/AIDS patients' viral loads to undetectable levels, which is heralded as the greatest medical advance to date in the fight against HIV and AIDS because it represents the first hope that HIV might be effectively managed. In response to the good news, one major viatical company announces it will no longer buy insurance policies from PWAs. A study unveiled at the conference reveals that the cases of vertical transmission of HIV from mother to infant have been cut in half in the United States as a result of AZT monotherapy. In a speech at the conference, Elizabeth Taylor harshly criticizes the Clinton administration's inaction on the issue of needle exchange.

Also in July, a Los Angeles County woman is diagnosed with a strain of HIV not previously found in the United States.

In Louisiana in July, Dr. Richard J. Schmidt is charged with trying to murder his girlfriend by injecting her with blood from an HIV-infected patient.

In August, a study by the Aaron Diamond AIDS Research Center in New York City reveals that 1 percent of Caucasians carry a gene that provides protection against HIV infection.

Also in August, a San Francisco sheriff refuses to enforce a court order to close down a buyer's club that provides marijuana for medical use by those suffering from AIDS and other terminally ill patients.

In September, a study by the National Institute of Health and Human Development finds that the hormones used in implanted contraceptives may make women more susceptible to HIV infection.

Also in September, Louis Rochon begins a 5,200-mile walk across the United States to raise money for AIDS.

In October, San Francisco erects a public monument to those who have died of AIDS. The largest AIDS Quilt to date is displayed on the Mall in Washington, D.C.

Also in October, four network-affiliated television stations begin to air advertisements for condoms.

In November, by a 55.7 percent to 44.3 percent margin, California voters pass Proposition 215 to allow the medicinal use of marijuana. Arizona voters pass Proposition 200, which also allows the medicinal use of marijuana, by a much larger margin—65.3 percent to 34.7 percent. Neither law goes into effect because of opposition from the Clinton administration.

Russian officials announce in November that the number of HIV infections has quadrupled in the past year.

In December, *Time* magazine names David Ho, research director at the Aaron Diamond AIDS Research Center, its 1997 Man of the Year because of his work in the development of triple combination therapies.

1996
cont.

Also in December, the United States grants political asylum to an HIV-positive man, José Cruz, on the grounds that he faces undue persecution in his home country, El Salvador, because of his HIV status. This precedent-setting decision is the first of many successful asylum petitions, even though the United State still denies entry to HIV-positive foreigners.

In what has been described as a precedent-setting settlement, in December the owners of a seniors-only housing development, Shorecliffs Mobile Home Park in Huntington Beach, California, agree not to evict Shirley Lewis for allowing her son, who has AIDS, to live with her. Lewis had brought suit under the Americans with Disabilities Act and the Fair Housing Act.

Playboy centerfold Rebekka Armstrong announces she is HIV positive and embarks on a career as an advocate for the rights of people with HIV/AIDS.

The number of people living with AIDS in the United States is 239,600. The number of U.S. AIDS deaths is 38,200.

1997

In January, officials in New York City—the U.S. city with the highest number of HIV/AIDS cases—report that AIDS deaths dropped by 30 percent in 1996.

A study by the National Cancer Institute reported in January reveals that high doses of AZT can cause cancer in the pups of pregnant mice.

In February, the virus responsible for Kaposi's sarcoma is identified in a blood sample from a healthy man.

In March, the FDA approves the first two protease inhibitors for use by children.

Also in March, ACT UP New York marks its tenth anniversary.

The Drug Enforcement Administration raids a San Francisco buyer's club that sells marijuana for medicinal use to people with AIDS and other terminal conditions.

In April, a study released by Family Health International reveals that condoms used with spermicides provide no more protection against HIV and other sexually transmitted diseases than those used without spermicides.

In May, Crixivan®, the protease inhibitor prescribed most often to patients with HIV, becomes available throughout the United States. Previously, it had been available only through Stadtlanders.

Also in May, four companies that may have distributed HIV-tainted blood reimburse the federal government for nearly $12.2 million in payments for that blood.

President Clinton announces a national goal of developing an AIDS vaccine within 10 years in a speech given in May in Baltimore, Maryland.

A study led by Dr. Jeffrey M. Jacobson of the Bronx Veterans Affairs Medical Center in New York City and published in the *New England Journal of Medicine* reveals that Thalidomide, a sedative banned since the 1960s for causing birth defects, is determined to be the only effective treatment for AIDS-related mouth ulcers.

In June, figures show that condom use among U.S. women has more than doubled since 1982.

The United Nations announces in June that worldwide, more than 1,000 children are infected with HIV each day. In July, the CDC believes it has identified the first case of HIV transmission through kissing when a woman apparently became infected after receiving a "deep kiss" from an HIV-positive man who had bleeding gums.

Also in July, the CDC announces that the number of AIDS deaths fell nearly 20 percent during the first nine months of 1996 compared to 1995.

In July, a study released by the Dana Farber Cancer Institute proves that HIV produces a protein called TAT that enhances its own reproduction.

1997
cont.

In August, New Jersey residents Diane McCague and Thomas Scozzre, who started a needle exchange program, are found guilty under a state law that prohibits the commercial sale and distribution of syringes. Municipal Court Judge Terrill Brenner is not swayed by arguments about the proven reduction in HIV transmissions when such programs are operated.

Also in August, Johnson and Johnson announces it is shutting down its toll-free number through which consumers obtain the results of their home HIV tests.

On August 31, Diana, Princess of Wales, is killed in a car accident in Paris. She was one of the first public figures to play an active role in increasing public sensitivity toward people with AIDS and in raising money for AIDS charities.

In September, the CDC announces that the number of HIV infections in the United States fell by 6 percent in 1996, the first drop it has reported since the beginning of the epidemic. Two-thirds of Americans who are infected are now aware of their status.

The September issue of the *New England Journal of Medicine* contains an article urging mandatory reporting of HIV infection to state health departments.

Also in September, 50 volunteers who want to help advance the search for an AIDS vaccine by being injected with a live, weakened strain of HIV are identified at a Washington, D.C., meeting of the International Association of Physicians in AIDS Care. The vaccine was developed by Ronald Desrosiers of Harvard University.

Data released in September by the University of California at San Francisco's large public AIDS clinic at San Francisco General Hospital show that resistance to HIV eventually develops in 53 percent of patients treated with triple combination therapy.

In October, David Ho and Catherine M. Wilfert resign from the editorial board of the *New England Journal of*

Medicine because of an article in the journal that criticizes the ethics of a clinical trial to explore the effectiveness of vitamin therapy compared with AZT monotherapy in pregnant women in Africa.

Also in October, light heavyweight David Lawhorn is allowed to fight in a professional bout even though he is HIV positive.

In November, the Pharmaceutical Research and Manufacturers of America announces that 124 new HIV medicines and vaccines are undergoing clinical trials, the greatest number since the AIDS epidemic began.

Also in November, the FDA approves a more powerful version of the protease inhibitor Saquinavir.

A study released by the U.S. Centers for Disease Control and Prevention in November reveals that AZT monotherapy dramatically reduces the risk of infection from accidental job-related exposure to HIV through needle sticks and similar incidents.

Also in November, the United Nations announces that it has underestimated the number of people in the world who are HIV positive. Its revised estimate is that 30 million people are living with HIV and that around 16,000 new victims are infected every day.

In December, the Presidential Advisory Council on AIDS issues a report on the Clinton administration that is critical of the lack of initiative during the president's second term and of the lack of federal support for needle exchange programs. The administration rejects as too expensive a proposal to extend Medicaid coverage to people with HIV to give them access to the latest anti-HIV therapies. A few days later, Vice President Al Gore expresses disappointment that the Department of Health and Human Services has been unable to extend Medicaid coverage to people with HIV.

Also in December, a California Appeals Court rules that buyer's clubs cannot sell marijuana for medicinal use in spite of the state's medical marijuana initiative.

1997
cont.

A report released in December reveals that fever, joint pain, and night sweats can indicate HIV infection before it shows up in standard blood tests, which may have practical implications for people in parts of the world where access to HIV tests is limited.

Also in December, a study by the University of California published in the *New England Journal of Medicine* reports that germs spread by cats and lice can threaten the health of those whose immune systems are weakened by HIV.

Researchers from Melbourne, Australia's MacFarlane Burnet Center for Medical Research announce in December that they will use a grant from the International AIDS Vaccine Initiative of New York to study a crippled strain of HIV in hopes of developing a vaccine for the illness.

Biographical Sketches 3

It would be impossible in a few pages to mention everyone who has played a significant role in the AIDS epidemic. The challenge of the epidemic has brought out the best and the worst in people. Since the epidemic began in the early 1980s, some people have been captured by the media in indelible images: Rock Hudson, an epitome of virility, appearing as a withered old man on the front pages of the tabloids; Diana, Princess of Wales, holding hands with an AIDS patient at a time when many believed AIDS could be transmitted through casual contact; David Ho on the cover of *Time* magazine with the magnified image of an HIV-infected T cell mirrored in his glasses; President Ronald Reagan's face digitally altered to be covered with Kaposi's sarcoma lesions in a Benetton ad; a fragile Kimberly Bergalis being escorted into Congress in a wheelchair; and countless demonstrators across the world conducting protests. These are some of the first people who come to mind when we think about AIDS.

There have been many, however, who have spent tireless hours involved in medical research, advocacy, and education. Rather than try to list them all here, the biographical sketches in this chapter aim to depict those whose work and contributions are representative of many. No one is included here simply because he or she died of AIDS. For the decadent yet wistful performance artist Klaus Nomi who died early in the epidemic, the provocative photographer Robert Mapplethorpe, the brilliant Cuban writer Reinaldo Arenas, the popular television actress Amanda Blake, tennis great Arthur Ashe, and far too many others, it is more respectful to remember them for the brilliance they achieved in their lives rather than for the pain and desolation their sensationalized deaths brought them. Therefore, the people included here are among those who shaped the course of the AIDS epidemic through a conscious commitment to make AIDS part of their business. Some of those included here are famous, and some have worked in relative obscurity. But they all have responded to an appalling epidemic and, through their contributions, have made it a little more bearable for those who have suffered from its affliction or have helped the rest of us to better understand the scourge that is AIDS.

John G. Bartlett, M.D.

Dr. John G. Bartlett is a national authority on the medical treatment of HIV infection and is among a relative handful of physicians directly involved in nearly every aspect of AIDS medical care. Dr. Bartlett has authored at least five major books on the clinical care of AIDS patients and is widely regarded by peers, patients, and AIDS activists as one of the finest AIDS doctors in the world. He is a fellow of the American College of Physicians, an active member of numerous clinical and laboratory standards committees, and an editor and reviewer for several major professional medical publications. Dr. Bartlett is a member of the Executive Committee of the National Institutes of Health/National Institute of Allergies and Infectious Diseases AIDS Clinical Trials Group and serves as principal investigator of the Johns Hopkins AIDS Clinical Trials Unit. He is also cochair of an ongoing National Institutes of Health (NIH) panel to establish the first universally accepted standard of care for HIV, an important and historic effort.

Kimberly Bergalis

Kimberly Bergalis, who died at age 23, became the most visible of the five patients believed to have been infected with HIV by

Stuart, Florida, dentist Dr. David Acer. Bergalis developed symptoms in early 1989 while she was in college. In 1991, she wrote a blunt letter to Florida officials who were considering legislation to regulate the testing of health care workers, stating, "I blame Dr. Acer and every single one of you bastards. Anyone who knew Dr. Acer was infected and had full-blown AIDS and stood by not doing a damn thing about it. You are all just as guilty as he was. You've ruined my life and my family's."

Bergalis traveled to Washington, D.C., in the final stages of her illness to testify before Congress for a few seconds on a mandatory HIV testing measure for health care workers. Her presentation of herself as an innocent victim did not endear her to many other AIDS sufferers, although a blond, blue-eyed girl who was a victim did underscore to the American public that HIV was a virus and nothing more. Bergalis claimed she was a virgin at the time of her infection, although her medical records revealed she had been treated for at least one sexually transmitted disease prior to her AIDS diagnosis. Later, the CDC reported that the strain of HIV she carried likely came from Dr. Acer and that the mode of transmission may have been improperly cleaned dental equipment he might have used on himself. She died in December 1991.

Michael Callen

Michael Callen survived for a long time with HIV; he was first diagnosed with AIDS in 1982 and died in 1994. He was a singer who continued to perform with his group, the Flirtations, until his death. Callen cofounded the People with AIDS Coalition in New York City and the Community Research Initiative. He wrote several books: *Surviving AIDS; Surviving and Thriving with AIDS:* Volume I, *Hints for the Newly Diagnosed* and Volume II, *Collected Wisdom.* He became a national spokesperson, appearing frequently on talk shows and always eager to talk about his strategy for survival.

Controversy surrounded Callen because of his position that HIV may not be the cause of AIDS. He never took AZT or any other antiretroviral treatment. Of long-term survivors he said in a 1992 Amsterdam, Netherlands, speech:

> "The first thing I want to say about long-term survivors is that there definitely is a survivor personality. But for every pattern I found, I found exceptions. And

that actually made me very happy, because it says to me that there is no single way, there is no recipe, no magic way to become a long-term survivor. I personally believe that each person's AIDS is unique, is different. They probably arrived in it in a slightly different way. We are each biochemically, biologically, genetically unique. And so I never expected that any one approach would work for everybody with AIDS. But I did find patterns that I found fascinating and I will provide them to you. If I had to summarize in one word the common characteristic among survivors, it would be 'grit': people are incredibly feisty, incredibly knowledgeable, not at all passive, very aggressively involved in the struggle to survive."

Robert C. Gallo

Dr. Robert C. Gallo is a leading retrovirologist with the National Cancer Institute who isolated the first retroviruses in humans and garnered international fame in 1984 when he codiscovered the virus that causes AIDS and developed a test for its presence. The discovery was surrounded by controversy because of allegations that Gallo had, in fact, discovered the same virus found earlier by codiscoverer Dr. Luc Montagnier of Paris's Pasteur Institute. (In 1983, Dr. Montagnier was chief of the research team that first isolated the virus that causes AIDS, which he referred to as Lymphadenopathy-Associated Virus). Montagnier became embroiled in a dispute with Gallo over the original discovery of the virus since the actual virus studied by Gallo proved genetically identical to a sample he had "borrowed" from the Pasteur Institute. In 1991, Gallo and Montagnier agreed to be considered codiscoverers.

This incident showed the competitive nature of the research environment. Although all evidence strongly suggested that Gallo's team had appropriated the virus and grown it from the Pasteur sample, Gallo was eventually cleared of scientific misconduct. Regardless of whether he actually discovered HIV, he did grow the virus in a lab and thus helped to prove that HIV is the causative factor in AIDS. He also developed an HIV antibody test and has identified people who may be naturally resistant to the virus. Gallo established the Institute for Human Virology in Baltimore, Maryland.

Stephen Gendin

Stephen Gendin was diagnosed HIV positive in 1986. He was an original member of ACT UP New York who founded the group's *Treatment and Data Digest* and served on the Executive Committee of the 1987 March on Washington for Lesbian and Gay Rights. In 1991, along with Sean Strub, who also had AIDS and was the founder of *Poz*, Gendin cofounded the Community Prescription Service designed to cater to the needs of HIV-positive clientele. In 1994, Gendin formed the AIDS Prevention Action League to address the increasing HIV transmission rates among gay men. He is a member of the Treatment Action Group—the only community-based organization in the United States dedicated solely to AIDS research and treatment advocacy—and the Institutional Review Board of the Clinical Director Network, a trial network for new HIV drugs. He is a frequent contributor to *Poz*. He wrote in the May 1998 issue: "For 12 years, I've had HIV, more or less without symptoms. So I've long thought of it as an emotional burden, never a physical threat. Now, suddenly at a gut level, I understand that it can kill me." Gendin has been arrested almost a dozen times during protests and acts of civil disobedience.

Judy Greenspan

Judy Greenspan is widely recognized as the nation's leading authority on the incidence of HIV in prisons. She is director of the HIV/AIDS in Prison Project of Catholic Charities of the East Bay. She frequently testifies on HIV/AIDS issues and correctional policy before state, national, and international scientific and government bodies. A founder of the California Coalition for Women Prisoners, she was the AIDS information coordinator for the American Civil Liberties Union's National Prison Project. She has conducted lifesaving advocacy for thousands of persons with HIV and AIDS through her work with the Prison Issues Committee of ACT UP San Francisco, which fought for the groundbreaking investigation by the Assembly Public Safety Committee of the California legislature that exposed the appalling quality of medical care at the California Medical Facility at Vacaville. That institution is now a model for the treatment of HIV/AIDS in prisons.

Imani Harrington

Imani Harrington was diagnosed HIV positive in 1987. Her background in counseling and substance abuse led her to become a visible spokesperson and advocate for women and AIDS. Harrington was a member of the San Francisco Mayor's Joint Task Force on AIDS in 1994 and wrote articles for the Seventh and Eighth International Conferences on AIDS. Her talent as a playwright and creative writer has earned national acclaim. Two of her plays have been produced: *Love and Danger,* which deals with women and AIDS, and *Do You Have Time to Die.* Two more plays—*In Seven Moon* and *Ashes to Dust*—are in progress. Harrington was quoted in Bill Jacobson's article "Healing Prescription" in the March 28, 1998, issue of *A&U: America's AIDS Magazine* about the impact of HIV on women: "We get lost in labeling. We get lost in the language, and the important issue is the disease. To this day no one will talk about how my friend [who died of AIDS] died. How women struggle with this disease is often ignored, and it relegates us to an unstable existence. . . . We are living with HIV. Are people recognizing that women are greatly impacted by this disease? That is something that resonates in my art."

David Ho

David Ho is a doctor at the Aaron Diamond AIDS Research Center who received national recognition when he was named *Time* magazine's Man of the Year in 1997. Ho has been credited with developing a medical strategy to rid a patient of HIV by using protease inhibitors in combination with nucleoside analogs to suppress HIV to undetectable levels long enough for it to die off. Although the strategy is not feasible for everyone, it has produced dramatic results for many living with HIV disease. Earlier, Ho observed that HIV rises to dramatic levels in an infected person's bloodstream shortly after the initial infection, then lowers, then again reaches high levels as the patient advances toward full-blown AIDS. He and coauthor George Shaw published this finding in the *New England Journal of Medicine* in 1991.

Earvin "Magic" Johnson

Earvin "Magic" Johnson, a famous National Basketball Association star who played for the Los Angeles Lakers, announced in

November 1991 that he was infected with HIV and was immediately retiring from basketball. Johnson, who had appeared in many television commercials and endorsements and was a role model for many young people, said he would devote himself to AIDS education. Shortly after his public admission, calls to local AIDS hot lines in California increased by as much as 600 percent. President George Bush named Johnson in 1991 to the National Commission on AIDS, from which he resigned in protest over the Bush administration's inaction on AIDS. He returned to basketball, playing on both the U.S. Olympic gold medal team in 1992 and again professionally for the Los Angeles Lakers. Johnson remains a popular public figure and is seen in commercials for a wide variety of goods and services, including the American Express Card.

C. Everett Koop

Dr. C. Everett Koop was one of the nation's leading pediatric surgeons when he was nominated by President Ronald Reagan as the U.S. surgeon general. Koop's highly publicized antiabortion position led both supporters and critics of his nomination to conclude they could predict his actions when he took office. He surprised both groups, however, by approaching critical issues as public health problems rather than ideological campaigns. Koop issued blunt statements on the rights of handicapped children and the dangers of passive cigarette smoke, but it was his vigorous work to educate U.S. citizens about HIV/AIDS and the need for sex education in the schools that gave him the reputation as an effective surgeon general.

In his 1986 *Surgeon General's Report on AIDS*, Koop stated: "At the beginning of the AIDS epidemic, many Americans had little sympathy for people with AIDS. The feeling was that somehow people from certain groups deserved their illness. Let us put those feelings behind us. We are fighting a disease, not people. Those who are already afflicted are sick people and need our care, as do all sick patients. The country must face this epidemic as a unified society. We must prevent the spread of AIDS while at the same time preserving our humanity and intimacy." Koop was stripped of many accolades he had received from antiabortion groups when he assumed a leadership role in educating the public on AIDS.

Larry Kramer

Larry Kramer is a New York City novelist, playwright, colum-
nist, and film producer who helped to found the Gay Men's
Health Crisis in early 1982. Kramer became a controversial figure
in the gay community for advising men to stop having sex to halt
the epidemic. In March 1983, he wrote in the *New York Native*,
later cited in *And the Band Played On*:

> There have been so many AIDS victims that the CDC
> is no longer able to get to them fast enough. . . . This is
> a woeful waste with as terrifying implications for us
> as the alarming rise in case numbers and doctors fi-
> nally admitting they don't know what's going on. As
> each man dies, as one or both sets of men who inter-
> acted with each other come down with AIDS, yet
> more information that might reveal patterns of trans-
> missibility is not being monitored and collected and
> studied. . . . How is AIDS transmitted? Through which
> bodily fluids, by which sexual behaviors, in what so-
> cial environments? For months the CDC has been
> asked to begin such preparations for continued sur-
> veillance. The CDC is stretched to its limits and is
> dreadfully underfunded for what it's being asked, in
> all areas, to do.

Some of Kramer's sharpest barbs were reserved for his fellow gay men. "I am sick of guys who moan that giving up care-
less sex until this thing blows over is worse than death. . . . How
can they value life so little and cocks and asses so much?" In
1987, Kramer called for the angry advocacy that gave birth to
ACT UP. A prolific and often controversial writer, Kramer has authored works of fiction—*Faggots*—nonfiction—*Reports from the
Holocaust: The Making of an AIDS Activist*—drama—*The Normal
Heart*—and the screenplay for *Women in Love* based on D. H.
Lawrence's book. Diagnosed seropositive in 1986, Kramer continues to thrive, write, and provoke controversy.

Mathilde Krim

Dr. Mathilde Krim worked on biomedical research projects at the
Weizmann Institute of Science (Israel) from 1953 through 1959
and at Cornell Medical College in New York City from 1959 to

1962. She joined the staff of New York's Sloan-Kettering Medical Institute and later headed its interferon laboratory. She also worked in pediatrics at St. Luke's Roosevelt Hospital Center and Columbia University from 1986 to 1990. In 1990, she became an adjunct professor of public health and management at Columbia University.

In addition to being a distinguished scientist, Krim established a significant presence as a glamorous socialite as the wife of Arthur B. Krim, lawyer and Hollywood executive. Her social connections helped her to finance a crusade against AIDS, first through establishing the AIDS Medical Foundation in 1983, which eventually became the American Foundation for AIDS Research (AmFAR)—the nation's largest privately funded nonprofit organization devoted to ending the AIDS epidemic through education, clinical research, and public policy. By 1990, Krim had used her social connections to raise around $40 million for AmFAR. In spite of her image as an elegant, highly educated woman, Krim— who had smuggled guns for the Zionist underground in Europe during World War II—showed great grit by joining the fight against AIDS at the very beginning of the epidemic.

Belinda Mason

Belinda Mason was the only original member of the National Commission on AIDS to have HIV/AIDS, from which she died in September 1991 at age 33. A Kentucky journalist, Mason received a contaminated blood transfusion while giving birth to her second child in 1987. Mason served as president of the People with AIDS Coalition and founded the Kentucky branch of that coalition. She attributed her appointment to the commission to the fact that "I was Southern, I was white, I was articulate, and I got AIDS in a nice way." In 1990, she wrote a highly publicized letter to President Bush, urging him to reject federal policies that would further stigmatize persons with AIDS by prohibiting the immigration of infected individuals and promoting mandatory screening of health care workers: "After more than ten years of the AIDS crisis, it is disheartening to realize that some people are still pointing fingers and looking for a place to lay blame. Only our effort as a united people has any hope of slowing the epidemic and avoiding the further human tragedy that statistics tell us we will all surely face one day. Mr. President, those who come after me are counting on you."

Jonas Salk

Jonas Salk was credited as being a codiscoverer of the polio vaccine in the 1950s. In 1963, he established the Institute for Biological Studies (the Salk Institute) in La Jolla, California, for the study of infectious diseases and served as its director until his death in 1995. Salk acted as a scientific diplomat to negotiate an end to the dispute between Gallo and Montagnier over who had discovered the virus that causes AIDS. This allowed the release of an HIV antibody test that had been held up because of the Pasteur Institute's pending court case against Gallo.

Salk eventually applied a principle similar to the one he had used for his polio vaccine to develop a therapeutic vaccine for HIV, although he died before wide-scale studies of the vaccine could be conducted. In light of recent breakthroughs in HIV treatment, the true value of this scientific pioneer's work may never be realized, although leading researchers have commented that a therapeutic vaccine could be the key to treating AIDS in much of the world. In 1993, Salk spoke to young people on the role of an AIDS vaccine: "[Regarding the goal of developing an HIV vaccine], it is a matter of those of us who are working toward that objective to do so as expeditiously as possible. Until that time, we know how AIDS can be acquired. . . . We must focus their attention on what one can do to protect one's own individual self. It is a matter, it seems to me, of understanding that one factor—the mode of transmission. And to focus the attention on the individual and what they can do to protect themselves until such time as a vaccine becomes available, then they are free to do as they please."

Randy Shilts

Randy Shilts was the first major chronicler of the AIDS epidemic. As a reporter for the *San Francisco Chronicle,* he began reporting on the epidemic from its onset in 1982. His 1987 book *And the Band Played On* is an essential historical document for understanding the AIDS epidemic and the United States in the early 1980s. The book documents the heroic efforts of people like Don Francis to spearhead an effective public health response to HIV/AIDS and, through their silence, the complicity of the U.S. government and the blood-products industry in spreading HIV/AIDS. The proposal for the book was rejected by nearly a dozen publishers and was turned down twice by St. Martin's Press, which eventually published it.

Shilts also wrote *The Mayor of Castro Street: The Life and Times of Harvey Milk* and *Conduct Unbecoming*—a history of gays in the military—on which he was working when he succumbed to AIDS in 1993 after a lengthy hospital stay. Shilts struggled to keep his illness a secret from the public, explaining to friends that he wanted to keep the public focused on what he was writing rather than on the sensational impact of his death from AIDS.

Sister Mary Elizabeth

Sister Mary Elizabeth of the Sisters of St. Elizabeth of Hungary is nearly blind, yet she is the guiding force behind the AIDS Education Global Information System (AEGIS) website—the largest available on-line database of AIDS information, containing around 50,000 documents. Her odyssey into the world of AIDS began in 1990, when she founded the "HIV/AIDS Info BBS," a computer bulletin board for AIDS information. She had met several AIDS patients while staying in a small Midwestern farming community. Recognizing that they "were profoundly isolated by illness, small town fears, and geography," she saw a computer bulletin board as a way she could use her computer genius to satisfy her spiritual aspirations by providing useful information and telecommunications services on-line to all those affected by the AIDS epidemic.

In 1991, Sister Mary Elizabeth met Jamie Jemison who had created an on-line bulletin board system devoted to HIV/AIDS, called ÆEGIS, in the 1980s. She suggested joining forces, but he had gone on to other pursuits and ceded the use of the name ÆEGIS to her. From September 1990 through April 1995, the on-line information service operated out of the Sisters of St. Elizabeth of Hungary, a small religious community founded in 1988. AEGIS was reorganized as a charitable educational corporation in April 1995 and was recognized as a nonprofit organization by the Internal Revenue Service in 1996. The AEGIS mission statement reads as follows: "The 'magic bullet' to cure or prevent HIV infection has not been found, and too many people with or affected by HIV/AIDS are isolated by cultural, geographic, and economic barriers. In these times, how must we fight AIDS and relieve the human suffering it causes? We believe the answer will be found in the transformation of information into knowledge. For that to happen, information must be easily accessible and widely disseminated. It must be used."

Ryan White

Ryan White, a hemophiliac from Kokomo, Indiana, was 13 when he was diagnosed with HIV, which he received from a contaminated transfusion of Factor VIII (a clotting agent). He was subsequently denied the right to return to his school; he and his mother fought a lengthy public legal battle over that right. Although he won in the courts, Ryan's family was the target of enormous hostility and ignorance in Kokomo; when a bullet was fired into their home, they moved to Cicero, Indiana. There, Ryan met a welcoming community and found his battle had attracted the attention of numerous celebrities such as Michael Jackson and Elton John.

Ryan was memorialized on the NAMES Project AIDS Memorial Quilt as "Educator for Life" because of his efforts to speak out about HIV/AIDS and his numerous public appearances at fundraisers, before the Presidential Commission on AIDS, and in schools. Ryan White died on April 8, 1990, at age 18; his grave has been repeatedly vandalized. His name has become synonymous with the Ryan White CARE Act and is used popularly by AIDS service providers to represent federal monies.

Maxine Wolfe

Maxine Wolfe has been a member of ACT UP New York since 1987 and has organized many ACT UP actions and campaigns. She cofounded the Women's Caucus, the ACT UP National Women's Committee, and the Lesbian Avengers and is the coordinator of the Lesbian Herstory Archives. She has lectured widely about AIDS and AIDS activism, and her work has been published in *Women, AIDS and Activism* and *AIDS Prevention and Services: Community Based Research.*

Wolfe is a formidable and articulate champion of the rights of women with HIV (and of the HIV-infected population as a whole). An example of her incisive analysis follows:

> This is the fourth year of the women's epidemiology study. They are not giving the participants any information from their tests, and they wonder why so many women have dropped out. I doubt that they will ever have decent data. They continually present papers at conferences, papers that simply describe their sample demographics. Their resumés are grow-

ing, their universities get money, but the women are getting nothing. When Mary Lucey put a questionnaire about protease inhibitor use in the *Women Alive* newsletter, several of these researchers wanted to get their hands on the data, analyze it, and present it "along with" Mary.

Facts and Statistics

4

Centers for Disease Control Surveillance Case Definition

The surveillance case definition is the official Centers for Disease Control (CDC) definition of AIDS; many aspects of an individual's treatment and access to benefits revolve around whether a clinical diagnosis of "CDC AIDS" is present. The definition adopted in 1987 was criticized for shortcomings that included its rigidity and the omission of many manifestations seen in women with HIV.

In January 1993, the CDC adopted a revised classification system for HIV infection and an expanded AIDS surveillance case definition for adolescents and adults. The key points of this revision are summarized in the December 18, 1992 CDC *Morbidity and Mortality Weekly Report:*

> CDC has revised the classification system for HIV infection to emphasize the clinical importance of the CD4+ T-lymphocyte count in the categorization of HIV-related clinical conditions. This classification system replaces the system published by CDC in 1986 and is primarily intended for use in

public health practice. Consistent with the 1993 revised classification system, CDC has also expanded the AIDS surveillance case definition to include all HIV-infected persons who have less than 200 CD4+ T-lymphocytes/µ L, or a CD4+ T-lymphocyte percentage of total lymphocytes of less than 14. This expansion includes the addition of three clinical conditions—pulmonary tuberculosis, recurrent pneumonia, and invasive cervical cancer—and retains the 23 clinical conditions in the AIDS surveillance case definition published in 1987; it is to be used by all states for AIDS case reporting effective January 1, 1993.

The key indicator is an absolute CD4 count of 200, which indicates that an individual has AIDS whether or not other indicator conditions are present. The diseases listed below also qualify an individual for an AIDS diagnosis in the presence of a documented HIV infection regardless of CD4 count:

- Candidiasis of bronchi, trachea, or lungs
- Candidiasis, esophageal
- Coccidioidomycosis, disseminated or extrapulmonary
- Cryptococcosis, extrapulmonary
- Cryptosporidiosis, chronic intestinal (greater than one month's duration)
- Cytomegalovirus disease (other than liver, spleen, or nodes)
- Cytomegalovirus retinitis (with loss of vision)
- Encephalopathy
- HIV-related herpes simplex: chronic ulcer(s) (greater than one month's duration); or bronchitis, pneumonitis, or esophagitis
- Histoplasmosis, disseminated or extrapulmonary
- Isosporiasis, chronic intestinal (greater than one month's duration)
- Kaposi's sarcoma
- Lymphoma, Burkitt's (or equivalent term)
- Lymphoma, immunoblastic (or equivalent term)
- Lymphoma, primary, of brain
- Mycobacterium avium complex or M. kansasii, disseminated or extrapulmonary
- Mycobacterium tuberculosis, any site (extrapulmonary)

- Mycobacterium, other species or unidentified species, disseminated or extrapulmonary
- Pneumocystis carinii pneumonia
- Progressive multifocal leukoencephalopathy
- Salmonella septicemia, recurrent
- Toxoplasmosis of brain
- Wasting syndrome due to HIV

The change of definition resulted in increased numbers of reported AIDS cases as well as changes to AIDS mortality statistics for the previous years.

Opportunistic Infections

If untreated, HIV infection almost inevitably leads to AIDS. The mechanisms for illness and death are opportunistic infections that take advantage of the host's compromised immune system. Descriptions follow of the infections that appear most frequently in AIDS sufferers in the United States. The descriptions are taken from the second edition of the AIDS Research Information Center's *Encyclopedic AIDS Medical Glossary*.

Pneumocystis carinii **pneumonia (PCP):** PCP is caused by a protozoan (one-celled) parasite common in the environment that infects more than half of the world's adult population. As is the case with many other opportunistic diseases, the organism lives quietly within the body, causing little or no damage and no outward sign of disease. The parasite causes serious illness only in those whose immune systems are suppressed or who are weakened by another disease.

In spite of major progress in the treatment and prevention of this disease, it can still cause death in people with HIV/AIDS. PCP is especially troublesome in children with HIV, who may develop the disease even at very high T4 cell levels. In adults, it rarely becomes a problem until the T4 cell count falls below 200, at which point antibiotic drugs are given to either prevent or treat the infection. Additional complementary therapy may be necessary, especially with the drug *leucovorin*, which replaces folic acid, a vital substance lost during the metabolism of these drugs.

Symptoms of an active PCP infection are shortness of breath and a persistent but unproductive cough (no phlegm or sputum is coughed up), low-grade fever, pain when breathing deeply, and other common signs of respiratory trouble. Diagnosis is usually made through a chest X-ray and a careful examination of lung function, combined with a microscopic exam of respiratory secretions (mucous from the throat and lungs) seeking evidence of the parasite. Such samples can be difficult to obtain, since little phlegm is produced with PCP infection. It is often necessary to do a bronchoscopy (an examination of the inner breathing tubes of the chest, the bronchi, usually done with a thin, fiber-optic viewing device, a bronchoscope). If the organism is not found through this procedure, a bronchial-alveolar lavage or even a lung biopsy may be required to obtain the samples.

Although these procedures are difficult for the patient, the tests are essential so proper treatment can be prescribed. Since PCP is an AIDS-defining illness, a firm diagnosis may help the patient gain disability status and its accompanying medical and financial benefits. PCP infection usually responds to treatment, but the disease has nearly a 70 percent recurrence rate.

Cytomegalovirus (CMV): One of the family of herpes viruses, CMV is common within the population but normally causes only minor illness in healthy people. In immune-suppressed persons, however, CMV can cause serious illness. Disease is usually localized in a single organ system but in some cases can spread throughout the body.

CMV can be the root cause of many different chronic diseases, including varieties of pneumonia, sinusitis, diseases of the liver and bone marrow, destruction of the intestinal cell lining leading to malnutrition, inflammation of the spleen and pancreas, heart valve infections, kidney disease, and an eye infection—CMV retinitis—that can lead to blindness. CMV most often appears in HIV-positive persons as CMV retinitis and as an infection of the digestive tract called CMV colitis.

Symptoms of CMV retinitis (an inflammation of the retina, the nerve lining at the back of the eye) include an increase in the number of "floaters" or spots in the field of vision, slow loss of peripheral vision, and—without treatment—the eventual dimming or complete loss of vision. Diagnosis is made through a careful examination of the eye by a specialist, who in those infected will see white patches on and around the retina and indications of damage to the tiny blood vessels around the optic nerve, as well as to tissues of the retina. A limited self-diagnosis can be done with a simple eye-chart test called the Amsler Grid, which quickly reveals some distortions in vision common in early CMV retinitis.

Toxoplasmosis/Toxoplasmic Encephalitis (TE): TE involves an infection of the brain and central nervous system, rarely of the eye, with the microscopic protozoan parasite *Toxoplasma gondii*, carried by cats and excreted in their stool and also found in raw meats. About 30 percent of adults in the United States are infected with Toxoplasma, but in healthy people the immune system keeps the organisms suppressed so they do not cause disease. In immune-compromised persons, however, the dormant infection rises and causes serious disease. Symptoms include memory loss, motor control problems, mood swings, and, eventually, seizures, convulsions, and coma. Diagnosis is made through CAT, MRI, or SPECT scans, EEG, all of which make images of the brain using magnetic resonance, or brain biopsy.

The disease mimics many other neurological problems (progressive multifocal leukoencephalopathy, meningitis, dementia, and the like) and thus is difficult to diagnose. TE progresses quickly, so it is important to begin treatment immediately; thus, proper and accurate diagnosis is essential. If symptoms are present and progressing but the diagnosis is uncertain, it is sometimes necessary to treat presumptively.

Progressive Multifocal Leukoencephalopathy (PML): PML is a viral infection of the brain with type a papovavirus, which causes memory loss, motor control problems, loss of strength and coordination, and, eventually, seizures, coma, and death. The virus is present in the majority of individuals and is harbored in the kidneys, causing no problems until immune suppression becomes severe. It then rises, possibly using macrophages as a carrier, and infects the brain, usually fatally. The average time from the appearance of symptoms to death is four to six months.

PML has only recently (with the advent of the AIDS epidemic and the development of organ transplants) been seen in a large number of patients. Previously, it was so rare and so devastating when it did occur that doctors did not usually attempt to treat it. Some medical professionals now believe a treatment for the disease may be found. Happily, it is fairly uncommon in HIV-positive persons, occurring in only about 2 percent of cases.

Cryptococcal meningitis (CM): CM is a disease caused by infection with the fungus *Cryptococcus neoformans*, transmitted by tiny egglike spores that are breathed in with dust particles. *Cryptococcus* can cause a mild form of disease even in healthy people, but in those with suppressed immune systems, especially those who are HIV positive, it easily infects and can completely destroy the fatty myelin covering of the peripheral nerves (the nerves in arms and legs), leading to nerve damage and loss of muscle control. But the most serious disease caused by *Cryptococcus* is a type of meningitis, an infection of the meninges, the membrane that protects the brain.

Symptoms of CM include headaches, fever, vision problems, and seizures or convulsions, usually followed by coma and death in those left untreated. Diagnosis is made by examining the cerebrospinal fluid, the liquid that surrounds and cushions the brain and spinal cord. A sample of the fluid is obtained through a lumbar puncture (spinal tap) and is examined by microscope. Immediate treatment and accurate diagnosis are vital for survival. Happily, CM can be successfully treated, although "maintenance" therapy with treatment drugs must be continued for the rest of a patient's life to prevent a return of the disease.

Mycobacterium avium complex (MAC): MAC is a mycobacterial infection similar to—and, in fact, related to—tuberculosis that infects cells of the liver, spleen, lymph nodes, bone marrow, and other vital organs and tissues important to the immune system. These tissues are called reticuloendothelial.

MAI is an intracellular parasite, or a parasite that hides inside cells and remains dormant. This condition is very difficult to treat because the cell must practically be destroyed to reach the germ. Further, the immune system does not recognize the germ when it is lying dormant inside a cell. The mycobacteria are "visible" to the immune system only when MAI is actively reproducing. Since mycobacteria grow very slowly and reproduce infrequently, the immune system rarely has a chance to fight these germs. Unfortunately, treatment drugs for MAC infections have the same limitation: They can kill MAI germs only when they are actively reproducing.

The use of combinations of drugs for a very long time is the only effective treatment for MAC. Treatment must be continued long enough to kill a majority of the germs, which can take a long time. People with HIV/AIDS must often be treated for life once they are infected with MAC. Recent studies have proven that MAI/MAC is prevalent in the environment and that the vast majority of PWAs are infected with MAI. Autopsy results have revealed that the disease is present in about 75 percent of PWAs who survive more than four years after an AIDS diagnosis. In those persons organ damage is almost always widespread and severe, although the damage usually goes unnoticed.

Cryptosporidiosis: This disease occurs when the intestines are infected with the microparasite *Cryptosporidium* (or a similar parasite, *Microsporidium*, and others), causing severe, chronic diarrhea. Patients are in danger of severe dehydration and malnutrition, which weakens them and exposes them to further infections. Diagnosis is made by examining stool to find the parasites.

Kaposi's sarcoma (KS): KS is a neoplasia, a type of precancer, the cause of which remains unknown. KS may occur from an interaction between HIV and an as yet unidentified organism, possibly a common bacterium or virus that is activated by immune suppression. The characteristic pink, red, or purple lesions are composed mainly of blood vessels, which grow in unusually large concentrations at the lesion sites through a little understood process called angiogenesis in which growth factors are somehow made to stimulate the endothelial tissues that line all blood vessels and to cause them to grow. The endothelial cells are normal, but they grow very quickly under the influence of the growth factors (as they do in normal healing). But in this case, growth concentrates the blood vessels in one place, expressly to nourish the abnormal tissues of the tumors, which enlarge and can block circulation or other vital functions. Tumors appear on the skin but can also grow within the body, in or on organs and other vital tissues.

A number of other opportunistic infections occur with HIV/AIDS, but they are less common than those listed previously. They include lymphoma; AIDS dementia complex; cachexia, or Wasting Syndrome; tuberculosis; the fungal infections histoplasmosis and coccidiomycosis; herpes simplex and herpes zoster infections; and invasive cervical cancer in women with HIV. Of these, only candidiasis, recurrent herpes infections, and certain lymphomas are currently considered AIDS-defining diagnoses, but the guidelines for diagnosis are not fully accurate.

Candidiasis, especially oral thrush and vaginal thrush, and other so-called minor fungal infections are very common in AIDS. They are caused by a yeast, *Candida albicans,* that is present almost everywhere in the environment but causes little or no disease in normal people. Immune-suppressed persons, however, can become heavily infected in any mucous membrane, including the mouth, nose, eyes, anus, vagina, ears, and the digestive tract. Normal, beneficial, harmless bacteria always compete with yeasts in these membranes, but immune suppression allows the yeast to outgrow and overcome the other organisms. When that happens, the yeast becomes firmly established and can be very difficult to eliminate.

Candida normally grows in a small, round shape that is unattached, but when it becomes established the yeast changes into another form, shaped more like a plant, that has "roots" (mycelia) that reach into and destroy tissues. At that point, infection is said to be severe. In this form, candida can invade organs of the body and cause death if not treated. Such infection is often seen in HIV-positive persons with T4 counts below 50.

Herpes infections are caused by herpes viruses such as simplex or zoster. Herpes simplex is a common sexually transmitted disease and thus is seen in many AIDS patients, especially in the anogenital area (between the legs), sometimes as large lesions, especially when T4 counts are very low. It can also occur in the eyes, mouth, and elsewhere.

Herpes zoster is the later stage of infection with the virus that causes chicken pox in almost every child. When a person is immune suppressed, that virus can rise again from dormant life in the base of the spinal nerves and cause large, painful lesions on the trunk of the body (chest, back).

Lymphoma involves any tumor that arises in lymphatic tissues—such as lymph nodes, bone marrow, the thymus gland, and the spleen—or in lymphatic cells (lymphocytes) such as B cells. When a cancer develops in lymphatic tissues, it is classed by the type of cells it affects and changes.

Two basic forms of lymphoma occur with AIDS: Hodgkin's disease and non-Hodgkin's B cell lymphomas. Most lymphomas arise on the cellular level, in B cells, as a non-Hodgkins lymphoma. This form of cancer can directly affect the number of antibodies present in the blood and how well they work, which often means immune suppression becomes even more severe in those with both HIV and non-Hodgkins lymphoma. Less common in HIV-positive persons is Hodgkin's disease, which produces painless swellings of the lymph nodes, liver, and spleen. This lymphoma often affects children, and the current rise in HIV infection rates among teenagers may mean the disease will become more common. Early symptoms include sweating, fever, weight loss, and weakness. Diagnosis is made through a biopsy of lymphatic tissues, blood samples, and direct examination.

Vaginal thrush (candidiasis infection of the vagina), tuberculosis, and invasive cervical cancer were recently added to the list of AIDS-defining diagnoses after much pressure from AIDS activist groups, who claimed thousands of HIV-positive women were improperly diagnosed (and thus were not receiving the medical and welfare benefits to which they were entitled) because their disease did not follow the original male-oriented list of AIDS-defining diagnoses. Anyone with a T4 cell count below 200 is also now considered to have AIDS.[1]

HIV Testing

Approximately one-third of American adults have been tested for HIV, according to the Center for AIDS Prevention Studies (CAPS) at the University of California, San Francisco.[2] The CDC estimates that 60 percent of HIV-positive individuals know their status.[3] There is great concern, particularly among those whose behavior puts them at risk for contracting HIV/AIDS—such as injection drug users and men who have sex with other men—about the confidentiality of test results. Injection drug use is illegal, as is sodomy in many states.

Public health officials perceive two advantages to testing. Advances in the medical treatment of HIV disease indicate that the onset of full-blown AIDS may be slowed substantially and even prevented with early treatment. The risk of further spreading of the disease can be minimized by behavior modification.[4] For more information on testing and counseling, call the CDC National AIDS Hot Line: 1-800-342-AIDS; Spanish: 1-800-344-SIDA; hearing impaired: 1-800-243-7889 (TTY).

Three kinds of tests are widely available. The Enzyme-Linked-Immuno-Sorbent Assay (ELISA) test is the most common. ELISA is a simple blood test that recognizes the presence of HIV antibodies. If an ELISA test comes back positive, it is confirmed with a second test known as a Western Blot, which is more sensitive in identifying the presence of HIV. Third, oral tests are drawn from swabs taken from inside a patient's cheek and gum. They do not require that blood be drawn, but they are less sensitive than ELISA and the Western Blot.

Outside of a clinical setting, home HIV tests are now available that use a fingertip blood sample individuals can draw themselves. Anonymity is ensured since the sample is mailed to a laboratory and the result is matched only to a personal identification number. Results can be obtained by telephone within three to seven days.

A positive test result means antibodies to HIV have been found. A diagnosis of HIV positive, or seropositive, means the test subject may develop AIDS. If a test result is negative and there has been a risk of exposure, the test should be repeated in six months because it can take that long for the body to make enough HIV antibodies to be detected.

A viral load test, administered to those infected with HIV, measures the amount of HIV in the blood.

Privacy and Testing

It is important to distinguish between confidential and anonymous testing. Confidential testing uses an individual's name, and the records can be released to medical personnel and the State Health Department. Anonymous testing, which is not available in every state, does not record the test subject's name; therefore, the individual decides whether to inform a health professional and can shield the information from his or her insurance company.

Testing Centers

Testing is available through private physicians, publicly funded HIV testing centers, municipal health departments, sexually transmitted disease clinics, and similar organizations. Many publicly funded facilities charge no fee or a minimal fee, but the CDC reports that two-thirds of those tested see a private physician.[5]

Development of an AIDS Vaccine

The National AIDS Strategy, 1997, considers the development of a preventive vaccine for HIV to be one of six major goals in a plan to end the HIV/AIDS epidemic. Two approaches are recognized:

> The Federal government, through the NIH and the Department of Defense, continues to support two approaches to vaccine development. The first approach is based on the belief that gathering basic science information offers the best hope in steering vaccine development. The second approach is guided by the belief that data gathered from clinical efficacy trials of vaccine candidates in humans can lead to the development of a successful candidate and that if a safe candidate vaccine is available, it is not necessary to resolve all scientific questions before proceeding with human trials.[6]

Much federally funded research is conducted through the National Institute of Allergies and Infectious Diseases (NIAID), which conducts clinical trials of candidate vaccines to protect people from becoming infected with HIV. In August 1987, the first clinical trial of an experimental HIV vaccine was begun at the

NIH Clinical Center in Bethesda, Maryland. It was a safety trial that enrolled 138 seronegative volunteers. The candidate vaccine tested caused no serious adverse effects. Since then, more than 40 preventive HIV vaccine trials have been initiated worldwide.

In the United States, vaccine research goes through a process similar to that of other experimental medications. That is, it must go through Phase I trials, which test for safety in human subjects, and Phase II trials to provide further safety data and preliminary information on the drug's ability to stimulate immune responses. The most promising candidate vaccines move into Phase III, or efficacy, trials, which enroll large numbers of seronegative people at high risk for exposure to HIV and are designed to ensure the collection of enough data on safety and effectiveness to support a license application, if warranted.

According to a NIAID fact sheet, the NIAID AIDS Vaccine Evaluation Group (AVEG) is the largest U.S. cooperative HIV vaccine clinical trials group. The AVEG, which began enrolling volunteers in February 1988, includes several facilities:

- The AIDS Vaccine Evaluation Units (AVEUs), located at six U.S. research centers, conduct Phase I and II clinical trials of candidate HIV vaccines in low-risk and high-risk HIV-seronegative volunteers.
- The Central Immunology Laboratory provides state-of-the-art evaluation of humoral and cellular immune responses of vaccines in AVEG trials. The evaluations use standardized tests, permitting comparison of responses in different individuals and between different candidate vaccines.
- The Data Coordinating and Analysis Center provides a central facility for collecting and analyzing data from the trials conducted by the AVEUs.
- The Immunology Laboratory Support for Assessment of Mucosal Immune Responses Induced by AIDS Vaccines evaluates human mucosal immune responses to candidate vaccines in standardized tests, permitting a comparison of responses of volunteers at different AVEUs and of those who receive different candidate vaccines.
- The Specimen Repository collects and maintains blood samples and other specimens from volunteers in AVEG trials for use in current and future studies.
- A Data and Safety Monitoring Board periodically reviews data from AVEG studies.

As of January 1997, more than 2,000 people had participated in preventive HIV vaccine trials conducted at six AVEU sites in Baltimore, Nashville, Seattle, St. Louis, Birmingham, and Rochester, New York.[7]

The wide number of vaccines in development might suggest optimism within the AIDS research community that an effective preventive vaccine may soon be developed. That is not the case. According to a November 1997 Reuters Wire Service report, Dr. David Baltimore, chair of the AIDS Vaccine Research Committee of the U.S. Office of AIDS Research, stated he believes it is "extremely unlikely" that an effective, preventive HIV vaccine will ever be developed. This view is consistent with that of Dr. Luc Montagnier, who stated at the Second Experimental Conference on AIDS Research that it will be extraordinarily difficult to develop a fully protective vaccine. Both men stated that they feel an effective therapeutic vaccine (one that treats those already infected by suppressing HIV) could be developed much sooner than a preventive one. Baltimore said: "A good vaccine needn't actually prevent infection; it can prevent disease and that's critically important."[8]

Some promising results have been produced in clinical trials of therapeutic vaccines. The Salk Immunogen vaccine, developed by Jonas Salk who developed the first polio vaccine in the 1950s, is designed to help those already infected with HIV form a long-term effective immune response to the virus. This unique approach, which started clinical trials in 1987, has been met with derision from the scientific community. The vaccine, however, has shown some positive results in the trials. Extensive further research on the effectiveness of the Salk Immunogen has been compromised by a lack of federal support and by economic troubles at Immune Response, the vaccine's manufacturer.[9]

The World Situation

According to UNAIDS,

- As of December 1997, 30.6 million people were infected with HIV worldwide
- People with HIV infection account for 1 percent of the world's population ages 15 to 49
- Nearly 16,000 new HIV infections occur every day
- Nearly 90 percent of those who are infected do not know they are

- Worldwide, nearly 2.3 million people died of AIDS in 1997
- Of that group, 46.0 percent of those who died were women and 3.5 percent were children[10]

In late 1996, *Time* magazine analyzed the exposure factors for adult HIV/AIDS cases worldwide, finding that heterosexual transmission accounted for 70 to 75 percent of infections, 5 to 10 percent resulted from intravenous drug use, 5 to 10 percent were caused by male-to-male sexual transmission, and 3 to 5 percent resulted from blood transfusions.[11]

The situation for those affected by HIV/AIDS differs greatly in different geographic areas. Responses to this contemporary plague are shaped by regional economic and social factors. For instance, in Western Europe, the circumstances for people with HIV/AIDS are little different from those in the United States. The disease manifests primarily in men who have sex with other men and in injection drug users. Access to cutting-edge medical treatments such as triple combination therapy and the newer experimental drugs is possible for many infected people.

In sub-Saharan Africa, where two-thirds of HIV-infected people in the world live,[12] in contrast, the disease is spread primarily through heterosexual contact, and the opportunity to benefit from recent medical advances is virtually nonexistent.[13] HIV/AIDS public health directives in Africa focus on prevention because treatment is not economically feasible.[14]

Table 4.1 reveals the number of HIV/AIDS cases worldwide and the primary exposure factors by region.

TABLE 4.1
Regional HIV/AIDS Statistics and Features, December 1997

Region	Epidemic started	People living with HIV/AIDS	Adult prevalence rate	Cumulative number of orphans	Percent women	Main mode(s) of transmission
Sub-Saharan Africa	late 1970s–early 1980s	20.8 million	7.4 percent	7.8 million	50 percent	heterosexual
North Africa/ Middle East	late 1980s	210,000	0.13 percent	14,200	20 percent	IDU, heterosexual
South/ Southeast Asia	late 1980s	6.0 million	0.6 percent	220,000	25 percent	heterosexual
East Asia/ Pacific	late 1980s	440,000	0.05 percent	1,900	11 percent	IDU, hetero-sexual, MSM
Latin America	late 1970s–early 1980s	1.3 million	0.5 percent	91,000	19 percent	MSM, IDU, heterosexual

TABLE 4.1 *(continued)*
Regional HIV/AIDS Statistics and Features, December 1997

Region	Epidemic started	People living with HIV/AIDS	Adult prevalence rate	Cumulative number of orphans	Percent women	Main mode(s) of transmission
Caribbean	late 1970s– early 1980s	310,000	1.9 percent	48,000	33 percent	heterosexual, MSM
Eastern Europe/ Central Asia	early 1990s	150,000	0.07 percent	30	25 percent	IDU, MSM
Western Europe	late 1970s– early 1980s	530,000	0.3 percent	8,700	20 percent	IDU, MSM
North America	late 1970s– early 1980s	860,000	0.6 percent	70,000	20 percent	MSM, IDU, heterosexual
Australia/ New Zealand	late 1970s– early 1980s	12,000	0.1 percent	300	5 percent	MSM, IDU
TOTAL	n/a	30.6 million	1.0 percent	8.2 million	41 percent	n/a

Sub-Saharan Africa

AIDS has exacted a heavier toll in sub-Saharan Africa than anywhere else in the world. Over 20.8 million sub-Saharan Africans
are living with HIV infection, and 7.4 percent of the overall population ages 15 to 45 is infected.[15] Women represent half of those
infected; as mentioned previously, the main mode of infection is
heterosexual contact.[16]

Africa is the only continent that has seen a decrease in
gross national product (GNP) per resident since the mid-
1980s,[17] and AIDS has been a significant factor in the economic
catastrophe. To fully understand the effect of the epidemic on
Africa, one must look at HIV/AIDS as one significant component of a system of health care delivery that is in crisis. According to Dr. François Chieze, director of the Pan-African AIDS
Organization, health care in Africa is marred by the growth in
virulence of major endemics, the foremost being malaria; a high
prevalence of diseases for which much of the world has effective vaccines (measles, whooping cough, tetanus); worsening
malnutrition, particularly among children; and the revival of
traditional medicine and the prosperity of churches and sects as
a result of inaccessible care and the temporary failure of scientific medicine. This degradation of the public health system has
resulted in fewer hospital visits by citizens. Moreover, the AIDS
epidemic has aggravated African doctors' frustration. Faced

with the impossibility of giving their patients the treatment they need, doctors are reluctant to tell their patients they are infected with HIV, which, in turn, causes patients to be unaware of the seriousness of their condition and to be unlikely to take preventive steps.[18]

The quality of care for AIDS sufferers "lucky" enough to be in hospitals is poor. American photographer Anne P. Meredith recently described visiting a woman whose family's savings had been spent to gain her admission to a special AIDS hospital.

> They saved all their money together to send her to the hospital. I could have broken a truck in half after visiting that so-called hospital, I was so enraged. No doctors. No nurses. One woman on the entire ward sitting behind the desk, and she didn't even know [the patient] was there. [She] was on the "diarrhea and vomiting" ward, and she has full-blown AIDS. She's very advanced. The linens were filthy. There were urine and feces everywhere. IVs dripping onto the floor. There was no care there.[19]

The human toll of AIDS in sub-Saharan Africa is inextricable from the economic chaos the epidemic has created. Chieze has analyzed direct and indirect costs. The former include those linked to information, prevention, research, screening, and the treatment of HIV carriers and AIDS sufferers—all of which are much too high for African economies. And antiretroviral treatments are completely out of reach. The risk exists that expenses will be redistributed while other diseases continue to rage (malaria, measles, and tuberculosis) and that public expenditures will be refocused on hospital centers at the expense of primary health care and treatment at home.[20]

In examining indirect costs, Chieze points that the AIDS epidemic has particularly affected the most vital and productive age groups; thus, there are many repercussions. They include:

- An aggravated reduction of agricultural production (the dominant sector of African economies)
- A reduced productivity yield in the industrial sector (because of the loss of qualified personnel)
- A negative effect on the military sector (in Tanzania, for example, over 35 percent of members of the armed forces are HIV positive)

- A disruption of the tertiary sector
- A questioning of the educational system, which has been weakened because so many teachers have died from AIDS
- A reduction of family expenditures for schooling, which has provoked a worrying decrease in the amount of schooling children receive
- The deaths of individuals who had achieved elite status, which puts families' investments into forming the elite into question[21]

Additionally, the loss of people during the prime of life makes their children orphans. To date, 7.8 million orphans have resulted from the AIDS epidemic in sub-Saharan Africa.[22]

To prevent more deaths in this region where treatment is not an option, prevention through safe sex education is the most viable option currently available to health officials. Indeed, there has been some documented success in this area. In Uganda, which began an aggressive public anti-AIDS campaign through the use of billboards and government warnings in the late 1980s, the number of HIV infections among young women decreased by 35 percent between 1990 and 1995.[23]

Other countries in the region have not followed Uganda's lead, however. Sub-Saharan Africa has unique cultural barriers to condom use. Chieze lists three of these. First, Africa has no preventive tradition that follows the model of industrialized countries. Second, condoms were rarely used in Africa before the onset of AIDS, either to prevent sexually transmitted diseases or to promote family planning campaigns based on contraceptive methods. Third, the concept of fertility is an important value in African societies; it is the means by which women establish their status in society. Further, in rural areas, a large workforce still represents the main productive capital.[24]

One other significant obstacle to condom use noted by Meredith involves the subservient role women play in some African cultures. Meredith noted that in those circumstances women are often denied the right to negotiate the terms of sexual engagement. She gives a dramatic illustration:

> And you have this other cultural way of living, where there's polygamy. The men get infected and then infect all their wives. For example the Massai, especially the Red Warriors, they come and they can have sex

with whomever they want, no matter how young the girl is. They come in front of the tent, they throw their spear down, and everyone else has to stay away.[25]

Given the overwhelming scope of the epidemic, compounded by a host of economic and sociological challenges to treatment and prevention, many feel sub-Saharan Africa's (and, indeed, the Third World's in general) best hope to combat AIDS lies in the development of a preventive vaccine.[26]

Asia

UNAIDS estimates that 6.4 million people are living with HIV infection throughout Asia.[27] The disease has a much shorter history there than it does in Africa, and there is more variance in routes of transmission across the continent. Recent advances in genetic typing indicate that multiple epidemics can exist in a given community with little overlap among them, such as the concurrent epidemics among injection drug users and sex workers in Thailand.[28] Because of the relatively recent appearance of HIV and AIDS in Asia, however, few, if any, sophisticated mechanisms exist by which to track the actual numbers of infected people, so estimates may be highly inaccurate. For instance, in late 1996 the Chinese government estimated that up to 200,000 citizens were infected with HIV;[29] the previous December it had estimated that 5,157 people were infected.[30] UNAIDS fears that number may have exceeded 400,000 by the end of 1997.[31] It is widely believed that the number of people in Asia with HIV infection will reach around 17 million by the year 2000.[32]

The number of those infected with HIV/AIDS varies from country to country. UNAIDS gives examples for Southeast Asia. Indonesia, Malaysia, the Philippines, and Singapore have infection rates of under 1 percent. In Cambodia, seropositivity rates are 1 of 20 pregnant women, 1 of 16 soldiers, and half of sex workers. In Myanamar, seropositivity rates among sex workers rose from 4 percent in 1992 to 20 percent in 1996; around 66 percent of injection drug users and 2 percent of pregnant women are HIV positive.[33]

In Asia, the HIV epidemic has been documented the best in Thailand, where 2.3 percent of the adult population is infected.[34] Because of an aggressive education campaign by the Thai government, the number of new HIV infections has dropped dramatically, as evidenced by a fivefold decrease in new HIV cases and a tenfold drop in new cases of other sexually transmitted diseases among young army draftees in northern Thailand.[35] According to UNAIDS, the campaign focused on four issues: increasing condom use among heterosexuals, boosting respect for women, discouraging men from visiting prostitutes, and offering women educational and economic alternatives to becoming prostitutes.[36] The success of these initiatives has not spread to injection drug users, whose numbers still indicate a 40 percent infection rate, or to men who have sex with other men.[37]

A prevention model such as the one used in Thailand may not be successful throughout Asia. A three-year study of social attitudes toward AIDS in Asia appeared recently in the scientific journal *Lancet*. The study revealed that most Asian societies have strict taboos about discussing sex openly and that the media in Asia frequently disseminates misinformation about how HIV is spread, indicating that HIV can be transmitted only through contaminated blood and that in general only injection drug users are infected with the virus.[38]

These findings are contrary to UNAIDS results that most HIV infections in Asia occur through heterosexual contact, even though injection drug use figures prominently in some locales.[39] If, as the *Lancet* report states, Asian societies in general eschew open dialogue about sex and the media inaccurately portrays the risk of infection through heterosexual contact, it will be difficult to apply prevention campaigns that emphasize condom use.

In Asia, the potential exists for a plague that will exceed that seen in Africa in terms of the sheer numbers of afflicted. UNAIDS analyzed the following data for India.

- Even though less than 1 percent of the adult population is infected, India has the largest number of HIV infections in the world—with 3 to 5 million people infected with the virus
- Among truck drivers in Madras (in southern India), the HIV infection rate quadrupled from 1.5 percent to 6.2 percent between 1995 and 1996
- In Manipur (in northeast India) in 1996, some drug clinics showed HIV rates as high as 73 percent among male injection drug users[40]

Given India's vast size and numbers of indigent, it is difficult to imagine that we have seen the real numbers there or to estimate what they will be in the near future.

Latin America

UNAIDS estimates that 1.3 million people in Latin America are living with HIV infection.[41] The pattern of the epidemic there is similar to that in the United States at the start of the epidemic, with the majority of infections occurring among men who have sex with other men and among injection drug users. Only 19 percent of infections have been reported in women.[42] UNAIDS has noted deficiencies in reporting systems throughout Latin America, similar to those in the Third World.

A 1997 Associated Press report analyzed the situation in Mexico created by HIV/AIDS. The report concluded that:

- Whereas Mexico's lagging treatment of AIDS can be attributed largely to economic drawbacks, patients and caretakers must also battle an entrenched "machismo" culture that associates AIDS with homosexuality and responds with derision or denial.
- The Mexican government collects no statistics on the number of HIV/AIDS cases. Most anti-HIV drugs that are distributed come from organizations in the United States that gather unused prescription medicines from those who have died of AIDS. The costs of protease inhibitors and AZT are beyond the means of virtually all Mexican HIV sufferers.
- There is little recognition of the epidemic by the medical establishment. For instance, in Tijuana, which has a population of 1.7 million, there is not a single AIDS ward in the city's hospitals.
- Virtually all funerals for AIDS victims are conducted with closed caskets because morticians will not handle the corpses. According to Skip Rosenthal of the U.S.-Mexico Border Health Association in El Paso, Texas, "The taboo against even talking about [AIDS] is unbelievable. In Mexico, especially on the border, if you're HIV positive the only treatment accessible, maybe, is vitamins."[43]

UNAIDS cites that among Mexican men who have sex with other men, the HIV infection rate is 30 percent. The infection rate among injection drug users is 5 to 10 percent.[44]

Further south in Latin America, Brazil is experiencing its own epidemic. UNAIDS reveals the following:

- The male-to-female ratio of AIDS cases changed from 16:1 in 1986 to 3:1 in 1997
- By 1992, AIDS had become the leading cause of death for 20- to 34-year-old women in São Paulo
- In Porto Allegre, 3 percent of pregnant women are HIV positive
- Nationwide, 60 percent of HIV infections occur in those who completed only primary school or less
- Half of injection drug users are HIV positive
- The number of AIDS deaths in São Paulo has decreased as a result of the newest treatment advances[45]

The Brazil Ministry of Health estimates that as many as 7.5 million Brazilians could be infected with HIV by the beginning of the twenty-first century.[46]

Yet, the December 1997 UNAIDS report stated: "This region of the world still has an important window of opportunity: it is not too late to stop HIV from spreading to the population at large. This will require a much greater focus on meeting the special prevention needs of marginalized and impoverished populations."[47]

The Caribbean

The Caribbean is second only to sub-Saharan Africa in the percentage of the adult population living with HIV infection—1.9 percent. At least a third of those infected are women, and routes of infection include heterosexual and homosexual exposure and injection drug use.[48]

The situation in Haiti, the home of many of the first reported HIV victims in the United States, was examined in a recent Associated Press report. The report found that:

- Haiti's National Strategic Plan reported 101,400 new AIDS cases in 1996, for a total of nearly 324,700 cases.
- Because of poverty, treatment with antiretroviral therapy is not an option for the infected.
- Many HIV/AIDS patients believe they may be the victims of black magic.
- About half of the 8,000 children living on the streets of Port au Prince are believed to be HIV positive.[49]

UNAIDS found that in 1993, 8 percent of pregnant women in Haiti were HIV positive.[50] A later report from the American

Association for World Health indicated that 10 percent of the adult population of urban Haiti is HIV positive.[51]

Eastern Europe and Central Asia (Russia)

UNAIDS estimated in 1997 that 150,000 HIV-positive people are living in Eastern Europe. The primary mode of infection is from injection drug use, a rapidly rising epidemic in areas once under the dominion of the Soviet Union; male-to-male sexual transmission is also a factor.[52] The rate of HIV infection among injection drug users in Nikolayev, Ukraine, is estimated to have grown from 1.7 percent to 56.6 percent during 1995 alone.[53] Around 25,000 infections were reported in the Ukraine in 1997.[54]

Given the economic uncertainty and more open access to the West as a result of the fall of communism, the former Soviet bloc is another region that is poised for an HIV epidemic. One sign is a huge rise in the number of syphilis cases in Russia, Belarus, and Moldova, which increased from virtually none in the late 1980s to over 2 cases per 1,000 residents in 1996.[55] Since HIV infects people in a similar manner and infection with an STD may heighten the transmissibility of HIV, a rise in the number of STDs is a cause for concern and also indicates that heterosexual transmission will be a factor in the spread of HIV. Currently, 25 percent of those infected with HIV are women.[56]

Western Europe, Australia, and New Zealand

UNAIDS indicates that the number of new AIDS cases in Western Europe declined by 30 percent between 1995 and 1997.[57] The decrease can be traced to two significant factors: a delay in the onset of AIDS-defining symptoms among the infected because of advances in antiretroviral therapy and a drop in infection rates among men who have sex with other men as a result of successful safer sex initiatives implemented in the early 1990s.[58]

UNAIDS estimates that in 1997, 530,000 Western Europeans were infected with HIV.[59] In 1996, 21,000 people in the region died from AIDS.[60] That same year, in Australia and New Zealand, 12,000 people were infected with HIV and 1,000 people died from AIDS.[61] In the early stages, the epidemic has followed a pattern similar to that in the United States, with the greatest number of infections among both men who have sex with men and injection drug users. Current trends in treatment delivery, which include national health care throughout the industrialized world outside of the United States, point to a far more optimistic prognosis for an infected person in an industrialized country than for one in an impoverished area.

AIDS in the United States

Through June 1997, 612,078 AIDS cases had been reported in the United States. Table 4.2 examines the composition of those AIDS patients.

U.S. Government Funding for AIDS Research and Treatment

In October 1982, the U.S. Congress made its first appropriation—$5.6 million—for AIDS research. In FY1990, federal spending for AIDS reached $1.6 billion, and by FY 1996 it was $3.8 billion.

Table 4.3 compares federal government spending in key areas related to AIDS for fiscal years 1996, 1997, and 1998.

The Rise and Decline of AIDS Mortality during the Epidemic

At the Fifth Conference on Retroviruses and Opportunistic Infections in February 1998, the CDC announced that the number of AIDS deaths during the first half of 1997—12,040—fell by 45 percent compared with the same time period in 1996, when 21,460 people died from AIDS.[62] According to the CDC's Dr. Patricia Fleming, "Treatment is having a marked, dramatic impact on AIDS mortality."[63]

Data from New York City, home to 16 percent of all those living with AIDS in the United States,[64] released at the conference were even more optimistic. The New York City Health Department indicated that deaths from AIDS in the city dropped 29 percent from 1995 to 1996 and 33 percent in the first half of 1997. In 1995, 19 people died from AIDS each day compared with 7 a day in 1997. Overall, between 1995 and 1997, AIDS deaths in New York City declined 71 percent among men, 63 percent among women, 73 percent among whites, 66 percent among Hispanics, and 59 percent among blacks.[65]

TABLE 4.2
AIDS Cases by Age Group, Exposure Category, and Sex, Reported July 1995 through June 1996, July 1996 through June 1997; and Cumulative Totals, by Age Group and Exposure Category, through June 1997, United States

Adult/adolescent exposure category	Males				Females				Totals					
	July 1995–June 1996		July 1996–June 1997		July 1995–June 1996		July 1996–June 1997		July 1995–June 1996		July 1996–June 1997		Cumulative total[1]	
	No.	(%)	No.	(%)	No.	(%)	No.	(%)	No.	(%)	No.	(%)	No.	(%)
Men who have sex with men	29,773	(52)	24,146	(48)	—	—	—	—	29,773	(42)	24,146	(38)	298,699	(49)
Injecting drug use	13,701	(24)	11,576	(23)	5,219	(37)	4,574	(33)	18,920	(27)	16,150	(25)	154,664	(26)
Men who have sex with men and inject drugs	3,528	(6)	2,684	(5)	—	—	—	—	3,528	(5)	2,684	(4)	38,923	(6)
Hemophilia/coagulation disorder	366	(1)	250	(0)	27	(0)	15	(0)	393	(1)	265	(0)	4,567	(1)
Heterosexual contact:	3,249	(6)	3,357	(7)	5,940	(43)	5,459	(40)	9,189	(13)	8,816	(14)	54,571	(9)
Sex with injecting drug user	969		794		2,078		1,666		3,047		2,460		22,890	
Sex with bisexual male	—		—		400		298		400		298		2,768	
Sex with person with hemophilia	11		5		37		36		48		41		390	
Sex with transfusion recipient with HIV infection	37		33		69		40		106		73		867	
Sex with HIV-infected person, risk not specified	2,232		2,525		3,356		3,419		5,588		5,944		27,656	
Receipt of blood transfusion, blood components, or tissue[2]	323	(1)	245	(0)	274	(2)	244	(2)	597	(1)	489	(1)	8,075	(1)
Other/risk not reported or identified[3]	6,497	(11)	8,385	(17)	2,479	(18)	3,422	(25)	8,976	(13)	11,807	(18)	44,677	(7)
Adult/adolescent subtotal	57,437	(100)	50,643	(100)	13,939	(100)	13,714	(100)	71,376	(100)	64,357	(100)	604,176	(100)

TABLE 4.2 *(continued)*

AIDS Cases by Age Group, Exposure Category, and Sex, Reported July 1995 through June 1996, July 1996 through June 1997; and Cumulative Totals, by Age Group and Exposure Category, through June 1997, United States

Pediatric (<13 years old) exposure category	Males				Females				Totals					
	July 1995–June 1996		July 1996–June 1997		July 1995–June 1996		July 1996–June 1997		July 1995–June 1996		July 1996–June 1997		Cumulative total[1]	
	No.	(%)	No.	(%)	No.	(%)	No.	(%)	No.	(%)	No.	(%)	No.	(%)
Hemophilia/coagulation disorder	2	(1)	3	(1)	–	–	1	(0)	2	(0)	4	(1)	232	(3)
Mother with/at-risk for HIV infection[3]	331	(93)	291	(91)	335	(95)	261	(90)	666	(94)	552	(91)	7,157	(91)
Injecting drug use	96		79		92		61		188		140		2,878	
Sex with an injecting drug user	55		36		44		36		99		72		1,304	
Sex with a bisexual male	4		7		7		4		11		11		161	
Sex with person with hemophilia	–		2		1		–		1		2		27	
Sex with transfusion recipient with HIV infection											–		26	
Sex with HIV-infected person, risk not specified	60		59		62		58		122		117		982	
Receipt of blood transfusion, blood components, or tissue	2		5		1		5		3		10		150	
Has HIV infection, risk not specified	114		103		128		97		242		200		1,629	
Receipt of blood transfusion, blood components, or tissue[2]	10	(3)	2	(1)	2	(1)	3	(1)	12	(2)	5	(1)	375	(5)
Risk not reported or identified[3]	13	(4)	24	(8)	16	(5)	24	(8)	29	(4)	48	(8)	138	(2)
Pediatric subtotal	356	(100)	320	(100)	353	(100)	289	(100)	709	(100)	609	(100)	7,902	(100)
Total	57,793		50,963		14,292		14,003		72,085		64,966		612,078	

[1] Includes 11 persons known to be infected with human immunodeficiency virus type 2 (HIV-2). See MMWR 1995;44:603-06.

[2] Thirty-seven adults/adolescents and 3 children developed AIDS after receiving blood screened negative for HIV antibody. Twelve additional adults developed AIDS after receiving tissue, organs, or artificial insemination from HIV-infected donors. Four of the 12 received tissue, organs, or artificial insemination from a donor who was negative for HIV antibody at the time of donation. See *N Engl J Med* 1992;326:726-32.

[3] "Other" also includes 63 persons who acquired HIV infection perinatally but were diagnosed with AIDS after age 13. These 63 persons are tabulated under the adult/adolescent, not pediatric, exposure category.

Source: Vol. 9, No. 1 HIV/AIDS Surveillance Report 9.

TABLE 4.3
U.S. Government AIDS Expenditures, Fiscal Years 1996–1998

Federal AIDS Program	FY 96 ($millions)	FY97 ($millions)	FY98 ($millions)
CDC Prevention	$584.1	$617	$634.3
Ryan White CARE Act (Total)	$757.3	$996.3	$1,150.2
RW CARE Act (Title I—Care)	$391.7	$449.9	$464.8
RW CARE Act (Title II—Care)	$208.8	$250	$257.5
RW CARE Act (Title II—ADAP)	$52	$167	$285.5
RW CARE Act (Title IIIb)	$56.9	$69.6	$76.3
RW CARE Act (Title IV)	$29	$36	$41
RW CARE Act (Title V—AETC's)	$12	$16.3	$17.3
RW CARE Act (Title V—Dental)	$6.9	$7.5	$7.8
NIH Research	$1,407.8	$1,501.7	$1,608
HUD-HOPWA	$171	$196	$204

The decline in the number of deaths in New York City and nationwide was attributed primarily to the use of triple combination therapy. Because fewer people are dying, the number of Americans living with AIDS increased in the first half of 1997 by 13 percent, to 259,000 people, even though the number of new AIDS cases reported during the period fell by 12 percent.[66]

Table 4.4 shows the number of AIDS cases, mortality rates, and the number of deaths occurring each year from the beginning of the epidemic in 1981 through the first half of 1997.

AIDS in Individual States

Some states and territories have been disproportionately affected by HIV/AIDS. As of June 1997, the CDC reported that in terms of the number of AIDS cases, the states with the highest totals are New York, with 113,549 cases; California, with 101,569; Florida, with 62,200; Texas, with 42,185; and New Jersey, with 34,871.[67]

Perhaps a better indicator of the impact of AIDS on a state or territory is the rate of cases per 100,000 people. The CDC reports that between July 1996 and June 1997, the highest rates among states and territories were seen in the District of Columbia, with 220.2 cases per 100,000 residents; New York, with 69.9 cases per 100,000; Puerto Rico, 58.4 cases per 100,000; the Virgin Islands, 53.4 cases per 100,000; and New Jersey, 47.3 cases per 100,000.[68]

A breakdown of the numbers of cases and the rates of cases per 100,000 people by U.S. state and territory from July 1995 through June 1997 appears in Table 4.5.

States vary in their reporting of HIV infections; as of June 1997, the CDC indicated that only 29 states were recording the

TABLE 4.4
AIDS Cases, Case-Fatality Rates, and Deaths, by Half-Year and Age Group,
through June 1997, United States[1]

	Adults/adolescents			Children <13 years old		
	Cases diagnosed during interval	Case-fatality rate	Deaths occurring during interval	Cases diagnosed during interval	Case-fatality rate	Deaths occurring during interval
Before 1981	85	91.8	29	8	75.0	1
1981 Jan.–June	107	88.8	37	10	80.0	2
July–Dec.	206	93.7	83	6	100.0	6
1982 Jan.–June	437	92.9	151	14	92.9	10
July–Dec.	727	92.3	296	17	82.4	4
1983 Jan.–June	1,352	94.3	527	33	100.0	14
July–Dec.	1,717	94.2	949	44	93.2	16
1984 Jan.–June	2,691	93.8	1,428	53	86.8	27
July–Dec.	3,513	94.2	2,026	66	86.4	24
1985 Jan.–June	5,175	92.9	2,875	113	82.3	47
July–Dec.	6,552	93.4	3,979	140	87.1	72
1986 Jan.–June	8,702	92.4	5,203	144	85.4	70
July–Dec.	10,254	92.9	6,729	199	80.9	98
1987 Jan.–June	13,556	91.8	7,813	229	80.3	121
July–Dec.	14,908	90.6	8,285	269	77.3	173
1988 Jan.–June	17,419	88.8	9,716	265	69.8	140
July–Dec.	17,887	88.9	11,070	347	70.0	179
1989 Jan.–June	21,039	86.2	12,755	367	69.5	175
July–Dec.	21,341	85.5	14,653	348	71.3	192
1990 Jan.–June	24,372	83.4	15,068	392	65.3	196
July–Dec.	23,749	82.2	16,052	408	60.0	199
1991 Jan.–June	28,462	79.6	17,129	409	60.6	174
July–Dec.	30,575	77.5	19,046	394	56.6	220
1992 Jan.–June	37,250	72.3	19,681	488	54.7	194
July–Dec.	40,169	69.0	20,906	448	57.1	226
1993 Jan.–June	42,367	59.8	21,309	439	51.9	254
July–Dec.	35,204	55.1	22,460	442	51.6	268
1994 Jan.–June	36,660	47.5	23,388	418	47.4	295
July–Dec.	32,786	40.4	24,275	351	44.4	253
1995 Jan.–June	34,505	31.5	23,806	303	32.7	263
July–Dec.	29,292	24.0	23,474	291	26.8	236
1996 Jan.–June	28,453	16.9	19,658	232	20.7	214
July–Dec.	21,341	12.1	13,852	150	12.7	159
1997 Jan.–June	11,323	6.4	5,551	65	10.8	71
Total[2]	604,176	62.0	374,656	7,902	58.2	4,602

[1]Persons whose vital status is unknown are included in counts of diagnosed cases, but excluded from counts of deaths. Case-fatality rates are calculated for each half-year by date of diagnosis. Each 6-month case-fatality rate is the number of deaths ever reported among cases diagnosed in that period (regardless of the year of death), divided by the number of total cases diagnosed in that period, multiplied by 100. For example, during the interval January through June 1982, AIDS was diagnosed in 437 adults/adolescents. Through June 1997, 406 of these 437 were reported as dead. Therefore, the case fatality rate is 92.9 (406 divided by 437, multiplied by 100). The case-fatality rates shown here may be underestimates because of incomplete reporting of deaths. Reported deaths are not necessarily caused by HIV-related disease.
[2]Death totals include 397 adults/adolescents and 9 children known to have died, but whose dates of death are unknown.
Source: Vol. 9, No. 1 HIV/AIDS Surveillance Report 15.

TABLE 4.5
AIDS Cases and Annual Rates per 100,000 Population, by State, Reported July 1995
through June 1996, July 1996 through June 1997; and Cumulative Totals, by State
and Age group, through June 1997, United States

State of residence	July 1995–June 1996		July 1996–June 1997		Cumulative totals		
	No.	Rate	No.	Rate	Adults/adolescents	Children < 13 years old	Total
Alabama	664	15.6	521	12.2	4,441	63	4,504
Alaska	37	6.1	44	7.2	380	5	385
Arizona	656	15.2	532	12.0	5,237	21	5,258
Arkansas	285	11.5	243	9.7	2,238	32	2,270
California	10,540	33.4	8,177	25.7	101,020	549	101,569
Colorado	597	15.9	432	11.3	5,935	27	5,962
Connecticut	1,518	46.4	1,198	36.6	9,002	172	9,174
Delaware	319	44.5	264	36.4	1,908	14	1,922
District of Columbia	1,049	189.2	1,196	220.2	9,799	147	9,946
Florida	7,686	54.2	6,725	46.7	60,930	1,270	62,200
Georgia	2,495	34.6	2,108	28.7	17,808	177	17,985
Hawaii	207	17.6	144	12.2	2,014	14	2,028
Idaho	45	3.9	44	3.7	392	2	394
Illinois	2,148	18.2	1,753	14.8	19,095	224	19,319
Indiana	653	11.3	564	9.7	4,746	33	4,779
Iowa	129	4.5	105	3.7	1,020	8	1,028
Kansas	256	10.0	189	7.3	1,909	10	1,919
Kentucky	314	8.1	405	10.4	2,380	21	2,401
Louisiana	1,361	31.4	1,232	28.3	9,548	112	9,660
Maine	80	6.5	55	4.4	774	9	783
Maryland	2,287	45.4	2,175	42.9	15,955	268	16,223
Massachusetts	1,294	21.3	1,126	18.5	12,331	192	12,523
Michigan	1,032	10.8	949	9.9	8,681	89	8,770
Minnesota	322	7.0	248	5.3	3,075	20	3,095
Mississippi	414	15.4	448	16.5	3,006	44	3,050
Missouri	845	15.9	691	12.9	7,437	50	7,487
Montana	30	3.4	42	4.8	246	3	249
Nebraska	98	6.0	99	6.0	834	9	843
Nevada	457	29.8	466	29.1	3,275	25	3,300
New Hampshire	99	8.6	68	5.8	721	8	729
New Jersey	3,981	50.1	3,777	47.3	34,178	693	34,871
New Mexico	113	6.7	229	13.4	1,517	5	1,522
New York	13,242	72.8	12,525	68.9	111,541	2,008	113,549
North Carolina	977	13.6	859	11.7	7,637	105	7,742
North Dakota	10	1.6	10	1.6	85	–	85
Ohio	1,107	9.9	930	8.3	9,001	108	9,109
Oklahoma	279	8.5	288	8.7	2,861	25	2,886
Oregon	500	15.9	357	11.1	4,007	14	4,021
Pennsylvania	2,266	18.8	2,127	17.6	18,136	252	18,388
Rhode Island	181	18.3	162	16.4	1,652	16	1,668
South Carolina	967	26.4	815	22.0	6,592	69	6,661
South Dakota	17	2.3	10	1.4	118	4	122
Tennessee	901	17.2	796	15.0	5,901	46	5,947
Texas	4,375	23.3	4,928	25.8	41,863	322	42,185
Utah	197	10.1	159	7.9	1,429	20	1,449
Vermont	40	6.8	32	5.4	313	3	316

TABLE 4.5 (continued)
AIDS Cases and Annual Rates per 100,000 Population, by State, Reported July 1995
through June 1996, July 1996 through June 1997; and Cumulative Totals, by State
and Age group, through June 1997, United States

| State of residence | July 1995– June 1996 | | July 1996– June 1997 | | Cumulative totals | | |
	No.	Rate	No.	Rate	Adults/ adolescents	Children < 13 years old	Total
Virginia	1,506	22.8	1,255	18.8	9,548	151	9,699
Washington	773	14.2	764	13.8	7,898	32	7,930
West Virginia	147	8.1	113	6.2	793	8	801
Wisconsin	326	6.4	253	4.9	2,892	24	2,916
Wyoming	14	2.9	17	3.5	151	2	153
Subtotal	69,836	26.6	62,649	23.6	584,250	7,525	591,775
U.S. dependencies, possessions, and associated nations							
Guam	4	2.8	2	1.4	19	–	19
Pacific Islands, U.S.	–	–	2	0.7	4	–	4
Puerto Rico	2,135	56.9	2,210	58.4	19,220	363	19,583
Virgin Islands, U.S.	32	30.6	56	53.4	317	13	330
Total[1]	72,085	27.0	64,966	24.1	604,176	7,902	612,078

[1]U.S. totals presented in this report include data from the United States (50 states and the District of Columbia), and from U.S. dependencies, possessions, and independent nations in free association with the United States. Totals include 367 persons whose state of residence is unknown.
Source: HIV/AIDS Surveillance Report 6 Vol. 9, No. 1

infections.[69] That group did not include the three states—New York, California, and Florida—with the greatest numbers of AIDS cases. This lack of reporting makes an accurate representation of the number of HIV infections in the United States difficult to determine. Recent statistics on the number of new HIV infections compared with new AIDS cases by U.S. state and territory are given in Table 4.6.

TABLE 4.6
Persons Reported To Be Living with HIV Infection[1] and with AIDS,
by State and Age Group, Reported through June 1997[2]

| U.S. state of residence (Date HIV reporting initiated) | Living with HIV infection[3] | | | Living with AIDS[4] | | | Cumulative totals | | |
	Adults/ adolescents	Children <13 years old	Total	Adults/ adolescents	Children <13 years old	Total	Adults/ adolescents	Children <13 years old	Total
Alabama (Jan. 1988)	4,144	35	4,179	1,956	21	1,977	6,100	56	6,156
Alaska	–	–	–	182	2	184	182	2	184
Arizona (Jan. 1987)	3,168	34	3,202	1,806	6	1,812	4,974	40	5,014
Arkansas (July 1989)	1,511	19	1,530	1,077	17	1,094	2,588	36	2,624

TABLE 4.6 *(continued)*
Persons Reported To Be Living with HIV Infection[1] and with AIDS,
by State and Age Group, Reported through June 1997[2]

U.S. state of residence (Date HIV reporting initiated)	Living with HIV infection[3]			Living with AIDS[4]			Cumulative totals		
	Adults/ adolescents	Children <13 years old	Total	Adults/ adolescents	Children <13 years old	Total	Adults/ adolescents	Children <13 years old	Total
California	—	—	—	34,627	205	34,832	34,627	205	34,832
Colorado (Nov. 1985)	4,976	28	5,004	2,352	7	2,359	7,328	35	7,363
Connecticut (July 1992)[5]	—	87	87	4,344	80	4,424	4,344	167	4,511
Delaware	—	—	—	850	7	857	850	7	857
District of Columbia	—	—	—	4,112	81	4,193	4,112	81	4,193
Florida	—	—	—	25,326	574	25,900	25,326	574	25,900
Georgia	—	—	—	7,662	77	7,739	7,662	77	7,739
Hawaii	—	—	—	682	4	686	682	4	686
Idaho (June 1986)	230	2	232	160	—	160	390	2	392
Illinois	—	—	—	6,493	104	6,597	6,493	104	6,597
Indiana (July 1988)	2,798	22	2,820	2,031	14	2,045	4,829	36	4,865
Iowa	—	—	—	435	4	439	435	4	439
Kansas	—	—	—	712	3	715	712	3	715
Kentucky	—	—	—	963	12	975	963	12	975
Louisiana (Feb. 1993)	4,947	86	5,033	3,983	57	4,040	8,930	143	9,073
Maine	—	—	—	337	8	345	337	8	345
Maryland	—	—	—	6,656	147	6,803	6,656	147	6,803
Massachusetts	—	—	—	4,126	76	4,202	4,126	76	4,202
Michigan (April 1992)	3,188	81	3,269	3,459	28	3,487	6,647	109	6,756
Minnesota (Oct. 1985)	2,061	23	2,084	1,207	10	1,217	3,268	33	3,301
Mississippi (Aug. 1988)	3,372	40	3,412	1,232	21	1,253	4,604	61	4,665
Missouri (Oct. 1987)	3,507	41	3,548	3,211	16	3,227	6,718	57	6,775
Montana	—	—	—	115	1	116	115	1	116
Nebraska (Sept. 1995)	301	5	306	327	4	331	628	9	637
Nevada (Feb. 1992)	2,198	19	2,217	1,512	13	1,525	3,710	32	3,742
New Hampshire	—	—	—	379	3	382	379	3	382
New Jersey (Jan. 1992)	10,615	318	10,933	11,906	259	12,165	22,521	577	23,098
New Mexico	—	—	—	598	3	601	598	3	601
New York	—	—	—	36,362	729	37,091	36,362	729	37,091
North Carolina (Feb. 1990)	6,773	89	6,862	2,797	50	2,847	9,570	139	9,709
North Dakota (Jan. 1988)	55	—	55	33	—	33	88	—	88

TABLE 4.6 *(continued)*
Persons Reported To Be Living with HIV Infection[1] and with AIDS,
by State and Age Group, Reported through June 1997[2]

U.S. state of residence (Date HIV reporting initiated)	Living with HIV infection[3]			Living with AIDS[4]			Cumulative totals		
	Adults/ adolescents	Children <13 years old	Total	Adults/ adolescents	Children <13 years old	Total	Adults/ adolescents	Children <13 years old	Total
Ohio (June 1990)	3,224	53	3,277	3,055	36	3,091	6,279	89	6,368
Oklahoma (June 1988)	1,734	11	1,745	1,200	9	1,209	2,934	20	2,954
Oregon (Sept. 1988)[5]	–	3	3	1,552	5	1,557	1,552	8	1,560
Pennsylvania	–	–	–	7,160	127	7,287	7,160	127	7,287
Rhode Island	–	–	–	686	3	689	686	3	689
South Carolina (Feb. 1986)	5,707	106	5,813	2,960	25	2,985	8,667	131	8,798
South Dakota (Jan. 1988)	152	5	157	44	1	45	196	6	202
Tennessee (Jan. 1992)	4,056	43	4,099	2,722	18	2,740	6,778	61	6,839
Texas (Feb. 1994)[5]	–	211	211	17,006	127	17,133	17,006	338	17,344
Utah (April 1989)	773	4	777	599	6	605	1,372	10	1,382
Vermont	–	–	–	137	1	138	137	1	138
Virginia (July 1989)	6,177	67	6,244	3,732	81	3,813	9,909	148	10,057
Washington	–	–	–	3,115	14	3,129	3,115	14	3,129
West Virginia (Jan. 1989)	396	1	397	330	3	333	726	4	730
Wisconsin (Nov. 1985)	1,932	29	1,961	1,228	9	1,237	3,160	38	3,198
Wyoming (June 1989)	55	–	55	58	2	60	113	2	115
Subtotal	78,050	1,462	79,512	219,594	3,110	222,704	297,644	4,572	302,216
U.S. dependencies, possessions, and associated nations									
Guam	–	–	–	7	–	7	7	–	7
Pacific Islands, U.S.	–	–	–	2	–	2	2	–	2
Puerto Rico	–	–	–	6,746	166	6,912	6,746	166	6,912
Virgin Islands, U.S.	–	–	–	166	8	174	166	8	174
Total	78,050	1,462	79,512	226,726	3,285	230,011	304,776	4,747	309,523

[1]Includes only persons reported with HIV infection who have not developed AIDS.
[2]Persons reported with vital status "alive" as of the last update. Excludes persons whose vital status is unknown.
[3]Includes only persons reported from states with confidential HIV reporting. Excludes 1,789 adults/adolescents and 42 children reported from states with confidential HIV infection reporting whose state of residence is unknown or are residents of other states.
[4]Includes 211 adults/adolescents and 1 child whose state of residence is unknown.
[5]Connecticut and Texas have confidential HIV infection reporting for pediatric cases only; Oregon has confidential infection reporting for children less than 6 years old.
Source: Vol. 9, No. 1 33 HIV/AIDS Surveillance Report

Another variation among states involves the types of public assistance a person living with HIV/AIDS can expect to receive. A useful indicator of help available is the AIDS Drug Assistance Program (ADAP), which is administered through the states and funded through Title II of the Ryan White CARE Act. ADAP funding for FY1998 is a record $285.4 million, an increase of 71 percent over FY1997.[70] The funds are distributed to the states to help uninsured and underinsured people living with HIV infection purchase essential medicines. Table 4.7 indicates the amount of funding each state received from ADAP in FY1997 and the amount each state contributed to the program.

TABLE 4.7
Fiscal Year ADAP Funding by State and Source: Federal and State Funds

State	Federal/State Total FY 1997 ADAP Funds	Title II Base Funds	ADAP Supp. Funds	State Funds	Title I EMA Contribution	Other Federal/State Funds
Alabama	$ 3,150,604	$ 1,670,294	$ 1,329,706	$ 150,604		
Alaska	212,320		112,917			99,403
Arizona	3,333,000	849,248	1,450,752	600,000	407,000	26,000
Arkansas	2,050,008	1,395,995	654,013			
California	79,471,892	12,900,000	26,371,892	40,200,000		
Colorado	2,819,681	136,000	1,607,932	301,000	774,749	
Connecticut	4,178,675	352,389	2,790,394	592,000	443,892	
Delaware	934,000	314,314	619,686			
DC	5,416,836	754,876	2,613,341	800,000	1,150,873	97,746
Florida	29,355,935	9,957,303	17,898,632	1,500,000		
Georgia	8,449,959	2,000,000	5,125,509	324,450	1,000,000	
Hawaii	1,102,594	268,691	542,903	291,000		
Idaho	193,000	80,083	112,917			
Illinois	14,466,503	714,281	5,427,222	8,325,000		
Indiana	2,615,048	800,886	1,372,162	442,000		
Iowa	292,680		292,680			
Kansas	957,620	389,424	568,196			
Kentucky	1,147,265	356,275	663,046	127,944		
Louisiana	23,206,330	489,106	2,717,224	20,000,000		
Maine	389,446	100,000	229,446	60,000		
Maryland	5,955,633		5,025,239	600,000	330,394	
Massachusetts	11,288,179		3,310,714	6,800,000	1,177,465	
Michigan	2,862,921	154,636	2,408,285		300,000	
Minnesota	991,003		841,003	150,000		
Mississippi	2,040,326	1,159,577	880,749			
Missouri	5,652,428	2,620,796	1,965,652	600,000		465,980
Montana	201,037	136,900	64,137			
Nebraska	893,499	659,536	233,963			
Nevada	2,834,199	576,666	957,533	1,300,000		
New Hampshire	563,790	93,507	214,993		102,388	152,902
New Jersey	18,280,738	4,556,141	9,448,859	700,000	1,410,738	2,165,000
New Mexico	1,923,568	805,975	377,593	740,000		
New York	71,466,311	9,354,309	29,381,796	9,900,000	16,043,941	6,786,265
North Carolina	3,660,201	660,000	2,250,201	750,000		

TABLE 4.7 (continued)
Fiscal Year ADAP Funding by State and Source: Federal and State Funds

State	Federal/State Total FY 1997 ADAP Funds	Title II Base Funds	ADAP Supp. Funds	State Funds	Title I EMA Contribution	Other Federal/State Funds
North Dakota	124,390	100,000	24,390			
Ohio	6,524,500	822,792	2,577,208	3,124,500		
Oklahoma	2,065,187	606,101	728,086	431,000		300,000
Oregon	1,885,136	200,000	1,148,136		537,000	
Pennsylvania	11,917,646		5,258,299	6,659,347		
Puerto Rico	12,920,475	3,437,230	5,315,209	4,168,036		
Rhode Island	762,972	268,849	494,123			
South Carolina	3,486,578	423,683	2,112,895	500,000		450,000
South Dakota	138,843	100,000	38,843			
Tennessee	2,440,202		1,830,152	610,050		
Texas	19,959,044	3,000,000	11,061,308	2,697,736		3,200,000
Utah	780,946	266,873	399,273	114,800		
Vermont	400,000	157,860	92,140	150,000		
Virginia	6,410,469	2,714,138	2,881,631	667,200		127,500
Washington	6,181,728	276,000	2,067,728	3,263,000	575,000	
West Virginia	815,189	492,843	247,513	74,833		
Wisconsin	1,477,701	280,362	823,839	373,500		
Wyoming	137,940	100,000	37,940			
Total	$390,786,175	$67,553,939	$167,000,000	$118,108,000	$24,253,440	$13,870,796
Percent	100	17.29	42.73	30.22	6.21	3.55

Source: National ADAP Monitoring Project: Interim Technical Report, March 1998, p. 42.

Criteria for receiving ADAP funding are set by each state, and income requirements vary. Table 4.8 presents an estimate of income levels of ADAP clients broken down by state. (Note: The federal poverty level is $7,890 annual income.)

A client's overall health may also be a factor in qualifying for ADAP assistance. Some states limit the availability of drugs based on a client's T4 cell counts and viral loads. For instance, in March 1998 the National ADAP Monitoring Project reported that: "Texas ADAP continues to restrict RTI [Reverse Transcriptase Inhibitor] antiretrovirals to those with less than 500 CD4 cells. For access to protease inhibitors, Texas requires clients to have a viral load of over 10,000 copies but does not specify a CD4 count. Virginia has instituted a medical exception form for clients who do not meet current requirements for access to protease inhibitors: a CD4 count of 500 or less or a viral load of over 10,000 copies."[71]

Even a client who qualifies for ADAP may not receive assistance depending on where he or she lives. The following states have limits on the numbers of clients they accept, have waiting lists, or both.

TABLE 4.8
Estimated State ADAP Client Income Levels Based on Federal Poverty Guidelines[1]

State	ADAP Clients Served July 1997	ADAP Clients <100% FPL	Estimated Number of Clients <100%	ADAP Clients 101%–200%	Estimated Number of Clients 101%–200%	ADAP Clients 201%–300%	Estimated Number of Clients 201%–300%	ADAP Clients 301%–400%
Alabama	486							
Alaska	11	10	1	40	4	50	–	0
Arizona	448	30	134	70	314		6	
Arkansas	426	100	426				–	
California	8,539	47	4,039	36	3,083	10	854	6
Colorado	534				–		–	
Connecticut	519	48	249	38	197	14	73	
Delaware	47		–	80	38	13	6	5
DC	312	40	125	30	94	20	62	5
Florida	4,868	86	4,186	14	682		–	
Georgia	1,041	73	762	24	248	3	26	0
Hawaii	104	2	2	55	57	35	36	8
Idaho	48	20	10	65	31	10	5	5
Illinois	1,319	70	923	22	290	6	79	1
Indiana	280	10	28	30	84	60	168	
Iowa	45		–	100	45		–	
Kansas	110	40	44	44	48	10	11	6
Kentucky	191	73	140	19	36	6	12	2
Louisiana	175	22	38	78	137		–	
Maine	52		–		–	0	–	0

TABLE 4.8 *(continued)*
Estimated State ADAP Client Income Levels Based on Federal Poverty Guidelines[1]

State	ADAP Clients Served July 1997	ADAP Clients <100% FPL	Estimated Number of Clients <100%	ADAP Clients 101%–200%	Estimated Number of Clients 101%–200%	ADAP Clients 201%–300%	Estimated Number of Clients 201%–300%	ADAP Clients 301%–400%
Maryland	493	2	10	49	242	35	173	7
Massachusetts	858	69	592	20	172	8	69	3
Michigan	259	96	249	3	8	1	3	0
Minnesota	201	22	44	54	109	23	46	
Mississippi	188	85	160	15	28		–	0
Missouri	371	11	41	89	330	0	–	
Montana	18	90	16	10	2		–	
Nebraska	85	30	26	70	60		–	
Nevada	336		–		–	100	336	
New Hampshire	57	62	35	29	17	9	5	
New Jersey	1,960	55	1,078	35	686	8	157	2
New Mexico	465	5	23	60	279	30	140	5
New York	7,595	34	2,582	33	2,506	15	1,139	11
North Carolina	470	85	400	15	71		–	
North Dakota	12	57	7	30	4	4	0	
Ohio	596	21	125	68	405	11	66	9
Oklahoma	293	65	190	35	103		–	
Oregon	91	1	1	90	82	9	8	
Pennsylvania	1,268		–	20	254	65	824	15
Puerto Rico	2,320		–		–		–	

Rhode Island	140	43	60	40	56	15	21	2
South Carolina	310	60	186	30	93	10	31	
South Dakota	17	10	2	75	13	15	3	
Tennessee	145	50	73	43	62	7	10	0
Texas	3,215	70	2,251	30	965	–	–	
Utah	95	58	55	26	25	13	12	2
Vermont	41	28	11	42	17	20	8	10
Virginia	1,189	–	–	100	1,189	–	–	
Washington	543	43	233	43	233	12	65	2
West Virginia	43	45	19	20	9	35	15	0
Wisconsin	202	46	93	54	109	0	–	0
Wyoming	63	–	–	–	–			
Total	43,494		19,670		13,512		4,469	
Percent			49.13		33.75		11.16	

[1] National percentages are based on a total of 40,034 clients served by ADAPs in July 1997. Estimated client income levels were not reported by Alabama, Colorado, Maine, Puerto Rico, and Wyoming.
Source: National ADAP Monitoring Project: Interim Technical Report, March 1998, p. 57.

- Ten states—Alabama, Florida, Georgia, Indiana, Mississippi, Montana, Nevada, North Carolina, South Carolina, and South Dakota—have caps on program enrollment
- Nine states—the District of Columbia, Florida, Idaho, Kentucky, Maine, Mississippi, Missouri, Nevada, and Oklahoma—have caps on or restricted access to protease inhibitors
- Nine states—Alabama, Florida, Georgia, Indiana, Mississippi, Montana, Nevada, South Carolina, and South Dakota—have waiting lists for ADAP enrollment
- Seven states—the District of Columbia, Idaho, Kentucky, Maine, Mississippi, Nevada, and Oklahoma—have waiting lists for protease inhibitors[72]

No consistent standard exists for what medications a state will cover. Some states cover only antiretrovirals, whereas others also cover drugs for opportunistic infections and their prophylaxis. At least two states—Arkansas and South Dakota—did not cover even one protease inhibitor as of March 1998, although Arkansas indicated it would do so by April 1, 1998.[73]

Needle Exchange in the States

Needle exchange programs offer injection drug users an opportunity to reduce their chances of acquiring HIV through the use of contaminated syringes by allowing them to exchange used syringes for clean ones. Compelling evidence shows that this practice reduces the rate of new HIV infections. A study conducted in New York City showed that the rate of new HIV infections among participants in a needle exchange program was 2 percent compared with a 4–7 percent infection rate among injection drug users not enrolled in such a program.[74] The June 1997 issue of *Lancet* published an Australian study of needle exchange programs worldwide. It reported that 52 cities without needle exchange programs had experienced a 6 percent increase in HIV infections annually compared with a 6 percent decrease in the number of infections in 29 cities with such programs.[75]

In spite of such evidence, federal funding cannot be used to support needle exchange programs. The Presidential Advisory Council on HIV/AIDS found this restriction to be a significant shortcoming in developing an effective national HIV prevention policy:

Perhaps most disturbing is the continued prohibition on federal funding for needle exchange programs despite clear scientific evidence on the efficacy of such programs in preventing new HIV infections without increasing substance use. At least 50 percent of new HIV infections are traceable to injection drug use. The HHS Secretary [Donna Shalala] has for some time had the legal authority to lift funding restrictions, yet she has failed to do so. The Administration has thus far expended little effort to educate Congress and the American public about the effectiveness of needle exchange programs or to build political support for such programs.[76]

The argument most commonly used to reject needle exchange is that it encourages drug use. Evidence does not support this belief; on the contrary, data show that such programs reduce both drug use and the number of new users. According to a study of a San Francisco needle exchange program conducted from 1987 to 1992, the frequency of drug injection among participants was reduced from 1.9 to 0.7 injections per day, the average age of injection drug users increased from 36 to 42, and the number of new users decreased from 3 percent to 1 percent.[77]

Furthermore, needle exchange is cost-effective in terms of public health dollars. Over a five-year period, needle exchange will cost an estimated $9,400 per HIV infection averted[78] compared with $120,000 per course of treatment for each person infected with HIV.[79]

Without federal funding, most needle exchange programs in the United States are under the auspices of the North American Syringe Exchange Network (NASEN), which as of November 1996 had 101 U.S. member organizations. (The CDC has stated that it believes the vast majority—if not all—of the needle exchange programs in the United States are NASEN members.)[80] In 1996, NASEN and Beth Israel Medical Center in New York City conducted an extensive survey of member exchange programs. There were 87 respondents, from which the following data were derived.

Organizations fit one of three legal categories: (1) 46 (53 percent) operated in states that had no law requiring a prescription to acquire syringes or had state-level exemption to operate, (2) 20 (23 percent) operated in states with a prescription law but had the sanction of a municipal elected body, and (3) 21 (24 percent) operated in a state with a prescription law and had no expressed legal sanction.[81]

The 87 respondents were located in 71 cities, 28 states, and one territory. The breakdown by state was 17 in California; 11 in Washington; 10 in New York; 6 in Connecticut; 3 each in Illinois and Michigan; 2 each in Massachusetts, Puerto Rico, Texas, and Wisconsin; and 1 each in Colorado, Florida, Indiana, Louisiana, Maryland, Minnesota, Missouri, New Hampshire, New Jersey, North Carolina, Ohio, Oregon, Pennsylvania, Rhode Island, and Tennessee. Twenty-four respondents requested that their locations not be disclosed.[82]

All of the respondents give participants information about safer injection techniques, and 97 percent offer instruction in safer sex practices. Nearly half (42 percent) offer on-site HIV testing and counseling, and all but three offer referrals for drug treatment.[83]

HIV/AIDS in Specific U.S. Populations

In this section, all statistics come from the July 1997 Centers for Disease Control HIV/AIDS Surveillance Report unless otherwise noted.

Men Who Have Sex with Other Men

July 1997 CDC statistics revealed that, for the time period of July 1995–June 1997, men who have sex with men had accounted for 49 percent of AIDS cases to that date, or 298,699 cases, plus another 6 percent of cases (33,600) that also involved injection drug use. Thus, this group constituted 55 percent of AIDS cases as of that reporting date.

Racially, the makeup of those with AIDS among men who have sex with other men is 65 percent white, 21 percent black, and 11 percent Hispanic. Among men who have sex with other men and also use injection drugs, the racial makeup is 52 percent white, 31 percent black, and 15 percent Hispanic. Among ethnic groups, AIDS cases among men who have sex with men (including those who also use injection drugs) account for 84 percent of whites, 66 percent of Native Americans/Alaska Natives, 46 percent of blacks, and 51 percent of Hispanics.

Table 4.9 gives a breakdown by exposure factor and race of U.S. male adult and adolescent AIDS cases for the period July 1996–June 1997.

TABLE 4.9

Male Adult/Adolescent AIDS Cases by Exposure Category and Race/Ethnicity, Reported July 1996 through June 1997, and Cumulative Totals, through June 1997, United States

Exposure category	White, not Hispanic				Black, not Hispanic				Hispanic			
	July 1996–June 1997		Cumulative total		July 1996–June 1997		Cumulative total		July 1996–June 1997		Cumulative total	
	No.	(%)	No.	(%)	No.	(%)	No.	(%)	No.	(%)	No.	(%)
Men who have sex with men	13,805	(68)	194,042	(76)	6,251	(32)	61,894	(38)	3,675	(37)	38,765	(44)
Injecting drug use	2,302	(11)	22,962	(9)	5,984	(31)	57,409	(36)	3,198	(32)	32,724	(37)
Men who have sex with men and inject drugs	1,309	(6)	20,385	(8)	951	(5)	12,246	(8)	391	(4)	5,915	(7)
Hemophilia/coagulation disorder	181	(1)	3,442	(1)	36	(0)	466	(0)	26	(0)	376	(0)
Heterosexual contact:	585	(3)	3,881	(2)	1,883	(10)	10,511	(7)	841	(8)	4,263	(5)
Sex with an injecting drug user	151		1,505		451		4,036		182		1,323	
Sex with person with hemophilia	1		3		1	8						
Sex with transfusion recipient with HIV infection	14	24	138	12	14		120		5		75	
Sex with HIV-infected person, risk not specified	419		2,214		1,415		6,343		653		2,857	
Receipt of blood transfusion, blood components, or tissue	119	(1)	3,043	(1)	81	(0)	960	(1)	39	(0)	516	(1)
Risk not reported or identified	2,026	(10)	8,598	(3)	4,425	(23)	17,498	(11)	1,738	(18)	6,197	(7)
Total	20,327	(100)	256,353	(100)	19,611	(100)	160,984	(100)	9,908	(100)	88,756	(100)

Exposure category	Asian/Pacific Islander				American Indian/Alaska Native				Cumulative totals[1]			
	July 1996–June 1997		Cumulative total		July 1996–June 1997		Cumulative total		July 1996–June 1997		Cumulative total	
	No.	(%)	No.	(%)	No.	(%)	No.	(%)	No.	(%)	No.	(%)
Men who have sex with men	267	(60)	2,884	(75)	91	(51)	822	(59)	24,146	(48)	298,699	(58)
Injecting drug use	23	(5)	203	(5)	34	(19)	210	(15)	11,576	(23)	113,635	(22)

TABLE 4.9 (continued)

Male Adult/Adolescent AIDS Cases by Exposure Category and Race/Ethnicity, Reported July 1996 through June 1997, and Cumulative Totals, through June 1997, United States

	Asian/Pacific Islander				American Indian/Alaska Native				Cumulative totals[1]			
	July 1996–June 1997		Cumulative total		July 1996–June 1997		Cumulative total		July 1996–June 1997		Cumulative total	
Exposure category	No.	(%)	No.	(%)	No.	(%)	No.	(%)	No.	(%)	No.	(%)
Men who have sex with men and inject drugs	9	(2)	128	(3)	22	(12)	231	(17)	2,684	(5)	38,923	(8)
Hemophilia/coagulation disorder	4	(1)	61	(2)	2	(1)	27	(2)	250	(0)	4,378	(1)
Heterosexual contact:	32	(7)	111	(3)	8	(4)	28	(2)	3,357	(7)	18,811	(4)
Sex with an injecting drug user	6		27		3		12		794		6,906	
Sex with person with hemophilia	–		–		–		–		5		44	
Sex with transfusion recipient with HIV infection	–		7		–		1		33		342	
Sex with HIV-infected person, risk not specified	26		77		5		15		2,525		11,519	
Receipt of blood transfusion, blood components, or tissue	3	(1)	98	(3)	2	(1)	7	(1)	245	(0)	4,634	(1)
Risk not reported or identified	106	(24)	365	(9)	20	(11)	65	(5)	8,385	(17)	32,854	(6)
Total	444	(100)	3,850	(100)	179	(100)	1,390	(100)	50,643	(100)	511,934	(100)

[1] Includes 601 men whose race/ethnicity is unknown.

Source: HIV/AIDS Surveillance Report 10 Vol. 9, No. 1

Historically, most of the early cases of AIDS in America—particularly those cited by the media—were found within the gay white community. In the intervening years, the way that group has responded to the AIDS epidemic has given social scientists a model for the effective prevention of behavior-based infectious disease. (The gay white community and minority gay communities have responded differently to the epidemic. Gay African Americans, Hispanics, and Native Americans are discussed in the sections on their respective ethnic groups.) The behavior modifications the gay white community has made have had an impact on the number of new AIDS case in the United States (and in the industrial world as a whole). According to UN-AIDS, the United States experienced a 6 percent drop in the number of new AIDS cases from 1995 to 1996, facilitated primarily by an 11 percent decrease in new cases among men who have sex with other men—an extenuation of a 10-year pattern.[84]

In dealing with a disease such as HIV/AIDS that has no vaccine or cure, the only way to minimize the number of those infected is to prevent the transmission of the virus. Since HIV is transmitted through behaviors that involve the exchange of bodily fluids, its spread can be controlled by behavior modification. A detailed study of behavior modification in the white male gay community by John C. Gonsiorek and Michael Shernoff was published in 1991.[85] Much of the following analysis is derived from that source.

The study cites five tenets for a successful health epidemic control behavior modification plan:

1. The goals should be as simple as possible to achieve the desired change. Increasing the complexity of goals reduces the likelihood of success. Goals should be specific and concrete. Goals that are vague or global reduce the likelihood of success.
2. Behavior change should be accomplished in a gradual step-by-step fashion, which allows for the program to be tuned and, more important, for rewards and a sense of accomplishment to be achieved throughout the process.
3. Although mild fear-based messages can motivate target groups to change behaviors, programs themselves should be based on reinforcement rather than on punishment or fear.
4. To be effective in the long term, behavioral intervention should have an ongoing, follow-up component to

address relapse and recurrence of problem behaviors and new contingencies that may arise.

5. Behavioral programs should be carefully planned and individually tailored to the individuals for whom the program is intended. Different populations usually require programmatic changes.[86]

Gonsiorek and Shernoff note: "Studies on gay men reflect the number of partners as a risk factor only as an artifact, since research has repeatedly shown that it is specific behaviors that directly place an individual at risk for HIV infection." They note the failure of prevention programs that advocate celibacy or solitary masturbation as goals, as well as the failure of the federal government to produce HIV prevention materials that explicitly address gay sexuality. As a result, public health authorities as high as the CDC have been "operating more to avoid offending right-wing political constituencies than to control disease."[87]

In spite of this impediment, the white gay community has employed many of the tenets of a successful behavior modification program, according to the authors, and has produced an effective community-based prevention strategy. Explicit posters detailing ways to use a condom and to perform safe sex acts have decorated the walls of bars. Condoms have been freely distributed at community-oriented businesses. Gay papers have scrupulously documented the latest medical advances and prevention information. As a result, the study noted, dramatic changes occurred in the spread of the epidemic among gay men as early as the late 1980s.

> Gay males have changed their behavior on an unprecedented scale. Becker and Joseph, in their review of the literature on AIDS and behavior change, state, "Indeed, in some populations of homosexual/bisexual men, this may be the most rapid and profound response to a health threat which has ever been documented."
>
> Similarly, Stall, Coates, and Hoff . . . described the behavior changes reducing risk for HIV infection among bisexual and gay men as "the most profound modifications of personal health-related behaviors ever recorded."[88]

The Gonsiorek/Shernoff study analyzed the reasons the gay community's response to the AIDS crisis has been so effective:

The decade of the 1980s saw a concentrated effort within gay male communities to develop a variety of education and prevention programs. These programs coming from within the affected community were viewed positively. Despite lack of funding or underfunding, political criticism, governmental interference, bigotry, and scientific scorn, numerous programs were developed within the gay male community.[89]

The authors suggest that similar appropriate response models could be developed by other communities, noting that part of the key to success is that the programs are developed by members of the affected groups.

With any successful change, there is the problem of relapse, which has occurred within the gay community. One manifestation of this problem is seen in the phenomenon of "barebacking," a practice in which an HIV-positive man and his partner deliberately have unprotected sex, particularly anal sex.

A problem facing the gay community that has far greater scope is that of educating its younger members. In 1996, the San Francisco Young Men's Health Study revealed some startling statistics: an HIV seroprevalence rate of nearly 18 percent in young gay men between ages 18 and 29 and a 4.8 percent infection rate in 18- to 23-year-olds and a rate of 28.9 percent in 27- to 29-year-olds.[90]

Unfortunately, a similar study of young gay men in Holland, conducted by John de Wit at the University of Utrecht, produced similar results—results that have been reproduced consistently across the industrial world. De Wit's data revealed that risky sexual behavior was the reason for so many infections among a generation that had always been aware of the threat of HIV/AIDS. He noted that similar behavior has been shown within the same age group in the heterosexual community.[91]

Women

As of July 1997, the CDC reported 92,242 cases of AIDS among women in the United States. The racial breakdown was 23 percent white, 55 percent black, and 20 percent Hispanic. Risk factors for exposure among females were injection drug use, 44 percent of cases; heterosexual contact, 39 percent of cases; and blood-product recipients, 4 percent of cases.

According to NIAID, the percentage of AIDS cases represented by women in the United States rose from 7 percent in 1985 to 20 percent in 1996, making AIDS the third leading cause of death for women ages 25 to 44.[92] For women of color in this age group, AIDS is the leading cause of death.[93] In fact, a black woman is sixteen times as likely to have AIDS as a white woman.[94] Table 4.10 presents an analysis of female AIDS cases broken down by risk factor and ethnicity.

HIV disease exhibits a different character in women than it does in men, both medically and socially. Obviously a woman's anatomy creates a different trajectory for any disease to follow. This, in part, led the CDC to include invasive cervical cancer, a common manifestation of HIV in women, in its revised case definition of AIDS in 1993. The National Institute of Allergies and Infectious Diseases' report on women and HIV analyzes ways HIV/AIDS may manifest differently in women:

> Many manifestations of HIV disease are similar in men and women. Both men and women with HIV may have nonspecific symptoms even early in disease, including low-grade fevers, night sweats, fatigue, and weight loss. In the United States, the most common AIDS-associated condition in both women and men is a lung infection called Pneumocystis carinii pneumonia (PCP). Anti-HIV therapies, as well as treatments for the infections associated with HIV (so-called opportunistic infections), appear to be similarly effective in men and women.
>
> Other conditions occur in different frequencies in men and women. HIV-infected men, for instance, are eight times more likely than HIV-infected women to develop a skin cancer known as Kaposi's sarcoma. In some studies, women have had higher rates of esophageal candidiasis (yeast infections of the windpipe) and herpes simplex infections than men. Data from a study conducted by NIAID's Terry Beirn Community Programs for Clinical Research on AIDS (CPCRA) found that HIV-infected women were more likely than HIV-infected men to develop bacterial pneumonia. This finding may be explained by factors such as a delay in care-seeking among HIV-infected women as compared to men, and/or less access to anti-HIV therapies or preventive therapies for PCP.

TABLE 4.10

Female Adult/Adolescent AIDS Cases by Exposure Category and Race/Ethnicity, Reported July 1996 through June 1997, and Cumulative Totals, through June 1997, United States

Exposure category	White, not Hispanic				Black, not Hispanic				Hispanic			
	July 1996–June 1997		Cumulative total		July 1996–June 1997		Cumulative total		July 1996–June 1997		Cumulative total	
	No.	(%)	No.	(%)	No.	(%)	No.	(%)	No.	(%)	No.	(%)
Injecting drug use	1,039	(38)	9,156	(43)	2,627	(32)	23,646	(46)	866	(33)	7,984	(43)
Hemophilia/coagulation disorder	2	(0)	89	(0)	8	(0)	63	(0)	3	(0)	32	(0)
Heterosexual contact:	1,082	(40)	8,338	(39)	3,080	(36)	18,482	(36)	1,236	(47)	8,596	(46)
Sex with an injecting drug user	375		3,567		880		7,961		399		4,335	
Sex with bisexual male	102		1,224		136		1,043		48		426	
Sex with person with hemophilia	19		240		12		59		4		30	
Sex with transfusion recipient with HIV infection	15		275		17		142		7		91	
Sex with HIV-infected person, risk not specified	571		3,022		2,035		9,277		778		3,714	
Receipt of blood transfusion, blood components, or tissue	73	(3)	1,733	(8)	126	(2)	1,098	(2)	37	(1)	508	(3)
Risk not reported or identified	526	(19)	2,003	(9)	2,321	(28)	8,121	(16)	511	(19)	1,543	(8)
Total	2,722	(100)	21,319	(100)	8,162	(100)	51,410	(100)	2,653	(100)	18,663	(100)

Exposure category	Asian/Pacific Islander				American Indian/Alaska Native				Cumulative totals[1]			
	July 1996–June 1997		Cumulative total		July 1996–June 1997		Cumulative total		July 1996–June 1997		Cumulative total	
	No.	(%)	No.	(%)	No.	(%)	No.	(%)	No.	(%)	No.	(%)
Injecting drug use	9	(11)	80	(17)	18	(45)	124	(48)	4,574	(33)	41,029	(44)
Hemophilia/coagulation disorder	1	(1)	4	(1)	1	(3)	1	(0)	15	(0)	189	(0)

TABLE 4.10 (continued)

Female Adult/Adolescent AIDS Cases by Exposure Category and Race/Ethnicity, Reported July 1996 through June 1997, and Cumulative Totals, through June 1997, United States

Exposure category	Asian/Pacific Islander				American Indian/Alaska Native				Cumulative totals[1]			
	July 1996–June 1997		Cumulative total		July 1996–June 1997		Cumulative total		July 1996–June 1997		Cumulative total	
	No.	(%)	No.	(%)	No.	(%)	No.	(%)	No.	(%)	No.	(%)
Heterosexual contact:	36	(44)	219	(46)	12	(30)	95	(36)	5,459	(40)	35,760	(39)
Sex with injecting drug user	8		63		3		49		1,699		15,984	
Sex with bisexual male	5		54		3		15		298		2,768	
Sex with person with hemophilia	1		5		–		2		36		346	
Sex with transfusion recipient with HIV infection	1		16		–		–		7		91	
Sex with HIV-infected person, risk not specified	21		81		6		29		3,419		16,137	
Receipt of blood transfusion, blood components, or tissue	6	(7)	87	(18)	1	(3)	12	(5)	244	(2)	3,441	(4)
Risk not reported or identified	30	(37)	89	(19)	8	(20)	29	(11)	3,422	(25)	11,823	(13)
Total	82	(100)	479	(100)	40	(100)	261	(100)	13,714	(100)	92,242	(100)

[1]Includes 110 women whose race/ethnicity is unknown.

Woman-Specific Symptoms of HIV Infection

Women also experience HIV-associated gynecologic problems, many of which also occur in uninfected women but with less frequency or severity.

Vaginal yeast infections, common and easily treated in most women, often are particularly persistent and difficult to treat in HIV-infected women. Data from the NIAID-supported Women's Interagency Health Study (WIHS) suggest that these infections are considerably more frequent in HIV-infected women.

A drug called fluconazole is commonly used to treat yeast infections. A CPCRA study demonstrated that weekly doses of fluconazole can also safely prevent vaginal and esophageal candidiasis, without resulting in resistance to the drug.

Other vaginal infections may occur more frequently and with greater severity in HIV-infected women, including bacterial vaginosis and common STDs such as gonorrhea, chlamydia, and trichomoniasis. Severe herpes simplex virus ulcerations, sometimes unresponsive to therapy with the standard drug, acyclovir, can severely compromise a woman's quality of life.

Idiopathic genital ulcers—those with no evidence of an infectious organism or cancerous cells in the lesion—are a unique manifestation of HIV disease. These ulcers, for which there is no proven treatment, are sometimes confused with those caused by herpes simplex virus.

NIAID is currently assessing, in a study known as AIDS Clinical Trials Group (ACTG) 842, the prevalence of idiopathic genital ulcer disease in HIV-infected women and the effect of thalidomide treatment. Thalidomide has previously proven effective in the treatment of oral aphthous ulcers in HIV-infected people.

Human papillomavirus (HPV) infections, which cause genital warts and can lead to cervical cancer, occur with increased frequency in HIV-infected women. A precancerous condition associated with HPV called cervical intraepithelial neoplasia (CIN) also is more common and more severe in HIV-infected women, and more apt to recur after treatment . . .

Pelvic inflammatory disease (PID) appears to be more common and more aggressive in HIV-infected women than in uninfected women. PID may become a chronic and relapsing condition as a woman's immune system deteriorates.

Menstrual irregularities frequently are reported by HIV-infected women and are being actively studied by NIAID-supported scientists. Although menstrual irregularities were equally common in HIV-infected women and at-risk HIV-negative women in a recent WIHS survey, women with CD4+ T cell counts below 50 per cubic millimeter (mm³) of blood were more likely to report amenorrhea (no menses within the last three months) than uninfected women, or HIV-infected women with higher CD4+ T cell counts. Because megace, an FDA-approved drug often prescribed for HIV-associated wasting, can cause significant, irregular vaginal bleeding in HIV-infected women, NIAID is planning a trial to assess an alternate drug, nandrolone, in women with HIV-associated weight loss.

Gynecologic Screening

The Public Health Service currently recommends that HIV-positive women have a complete gynecologic evaluation, including a Pap smear, as part of their initial HIV evaluation, or upon entry to prenatal care, and another Pap smear six months later. If both smears are negative, annual screening is recommended thereafter in asymptomatic women. However, more frequent screening—every six months—is recommended for women with symptomatic HIV infection, prior abnormal Pap smears, or signs of human papillomavirus infection.[95]

A woman's childbearing function has figured significantly in the medical research specific to women and HIV. One of the most important studies done in this area was ACTG 076, which revealed that the use of AZT monotherapy by an expectant mother could reduce the rate of HIV transmission from mother to child from 25 percent to 8 percent.[96]

Until recently, most of the medical research on women and HIV prevention centered on pregnant women and vertical transmission. This narrow focus incurred much anger toward the research establishment among HIV-positive women and their advocates. Change has been slow in coming. A recent edition of the newsletter *Women Alive* explained that:

> Until the early 1990s women were generally not included in early phase clinical trials because of a potential risk of pregnancy and a possible dangerous effect on the fetus. (Exclusion criteria often read: "no pregnant women and no non-pregnant women.")
>
> Because of pressure exerted by activism, the FDA revised its clinical guidelines to allow the enrollment of women into clinical trials. Small numbers of women began to enroll into most HIV clinical trials, adhering to strict regulations of using two methods of birth control. (Less than 6 to 8 percent of the total number of enrollees were women.)
>
> During 1994–1995 women finally were allowed to enroll in phase I clinical trials, in which very little information is known about the drug being studied. To date, women still only account for less than 10 percent of the total enrollment into clinical trials, and very few clinical trials are designed strictly for female enrollment.[97]

Women have been excluded from clinical trials because of liability concerns within the pharmaceutical industry that stem from the use of thalidomide as a sedative by pregnant women in the early 1960s. Use of the drug led to hideous birth defects, including children born with severely deformed or missing appendages, that provoked numerous lawsuits. To avoid such suits, the industry began excluding women from medical research. Ironically, thalidomide has reemerged as an AIDS-related treatment, giving relief of recurrent mouth ulcers suffered by PWAs.

The disparity in representation in clinical trials based on gender is one of the strongest social issues unique to HIV-infected women. Additionally, women find it challenging to access care through existing systems. According to Mary Lucey, a cofounder of *Women Alive,* "We must begin to make sense of confusing advice and missing data surrounding our HIV treatment choices. Women have been ignored as HIV treatment decisionmakers and neglected as AIDS study participants even though we represent the fastest growing population of people in the US and the world. We must turn the tide by arming ourselves with knowledge to live by."[98]

Because HIV disease first manifested itself in the United States mostly among gay men and male injection drug users, many systems of care for HIV/AIDS patients were not constructed with women in mind. Further, the initial epidemic pattern may still affect public opinion about who is at risk. A woman who is not at risk through injection drug behavior may find herself at odds with existing systems of care. NIAID's report on women and AIDS states: "Women with HIV frequently have great difficulty accessing health care and carry a large burden of caring for children and other family members who may also be HIV-infected. They often lack social support and face other challenges that may interfere with their ability to adhere to treatment regimens." The report indicates that women who receive early diagnosis and treatment are much more likely to survive than those who do not receive early care but that, overall, women with HIV tend to be diagnosed much later than men and therefore have higher mortality rates. According to a CPCRA study of more than 4,500 people with HIV, women were a third more likely than men to die within the study period.[99]

Children

According to the CDC, by June 1997, in the United States 7,902 children under age thirteen had been diagnosed with AIDS, which accounted for about 1 percent of reported cases. Of these, at least 92 percent were infected perinatally. Racially, the breakdown was 55 percent black, 23 percent Hispanic, and 18 percent white.

Table 4.11 presents a demographic analysis of AIDS cases among children.

Pediatric AIDS poses unique difficulties in treatment because HIV manifests itself differently in children than in adults. According to Dr. Jack Lambert, one of the nation's leading authorities on HIV in children:

AIDS is caused by HIV in adults who have HIV-1 infections. They have a normal immune system, and, with time, the virus damages the immune system. Thus, you have an acquired immune deficiency. Very often with children, who are infected at birth or in the womb prior to delivery, their immune system is damaged from the very beginning; thus, they have more of a primary immune deficiency than an acquired immune deficiency. These children never have a chance to mature their immune system before it is damaged by the virus that causes AIDS. They never have an opportunity to develop antibodies against common infections before their immune system is damaged by the virus. Thus, they are susceptible to a whole different range of bacteria in addition to the many opportunistic infections that commonly appear in adults with HIV, such as pneumocystis pneumonia, cryptococcal disease, CMV disease, tuberculosis, and other infections. Thus, a major difference is that children have their immune systems damaged from early on; the immune system never gets a chance to develop normally.[100]

Furthermore, a child's immune system differs from that of an adult. Healthy infants have CD4+ lymphocyte counts and percent values significantly higher than those in healthy adults. During the first six years of life, these values slowly decline to adult values.[101] Therefore, the clinical markers used to identify the critical points in the progression from HIV infection to AIDS are different in children than in adults. Lambert gives a practical illustration of this phenomenon. Children with HIV develop other infections at different points than do adults with HIV. Children can develop pneumocystis pneumonia, for example, with T cells as high as 2,000; adults usually develop pneumocystis pneumonia only when their T cells are under 200. Not only are the infections children get different from those that plague adults, but there are differences in the ability of child's immune system to fight infection.[102]

One critical problem in creating a standard of care for children and in care delivery is that the development of effective treatments for children lags significantly behind that for adults. According to the *CDC National Center for HIV, STD, and TB Prevention Daily News*, as of January 1998, only 5 of 14 approved AIDS drugs had been tested in children, and no protease inhibitors had

TABLE 4.11
Pediatric AIDS Cases by Exposure Category and Race/Ethnicity, Reported July 1996 through June 1997, and Cumulative Totals, through June 1997, United States

Exposure category	White, not Hispanic July 1996–June 1997 No.	(%)	White, not Hispanic Cumulative total No.	(%)	Black, not Hispanic July 1996–June 1997 No.	(%)	Black, not Hispanic Cumulative total No.	(%)	Hispanic July 1996–June 1997 No.	(%)	Hispanic Cumulative total No.	(%)
Hemophilia/coagulation disorder	2	(2)	157	(11)	1	(0)	34	(1)	1	(1)	37	(2)
Mother with/at risk for HIV infection:	81	(90)	1,037	(74)	345	(90)	4,374	(95)	121	(93)	1,679	(92)
Injecting drug use	20		433		88		1,740		32		685	
Sex with injecting drug user	10		199		42		648		16		444	
Sex with bisexual male	7		65		3		56		1		38	
Sex with person with hemophilia	1		16		—		5		1		6	
Sex with transfusion recipient with HIV infection	—		11		—		8		—		7	
Sex with HIV-infected person, risk not specified	19		121		69		634		29		214	
Receipt of blood transfusion, blood components, or tissue	4		42		3		76		3		31	
Has HIV infection, risk not specified	20		150		140		1,207		39		254	
Receipt of blood transfusion, blood components, or tissue	1	(1)	183	(13)	3	(1)	90	(2)	1	(1)	92	(5)
Risk not reported or identified	6	(7)	23	(2)	34	(9)	88	(2)	7	(5)	25	(1)
Total	90	(100)	1,400	(100)	383	(100)	4,586	(100)	130	(100)	1,833	(100)

	Asian/Pacific Islander July 1996–June 1997	Asian/Pacific Islander Cumulative total	American Indian/Alaska Native July 1996–June 1997	American Indian/Alaska Native Cumulative total	Cumulative totals[1] July 1996–June 1997	Cumulative totals[1] Cumulative total

Exposure category	No.	(%)	No.	(%)	No.	(%)	No.	(%)	No.	(%)	No.	(%)
Hemophilia/coagulation disorder	—	—	3	(7)	—	—	1	(4)	4	(1)	232	(3)
Mother with/at risk for HIV infection:												
Injecting drug use	—		4		—		11		140		2,878	
Sex with injecting drug user	—		4		4		8		72		1,304	
Sex with bisexual male	—		2		—		—		11		161	
Sex with person with hemophilia	—		—		—		—		2		27	
Sex with transfusion recipient with HIV infection									—		26	
Sex with HIV-infected person, risk not specified			8		—		2		117		982	
Receipt of blood transfusion, blood components, or tissue			1		—		—		10		150	
Has HIV infection, risk not specified	—		8		—		4		200		1,629	
Receipt of blood transfusion, blood components, or tissue	—		10	(24)	—		—		5	(1)	375	(5)
Risk not reported or identified	—		1	(2)	—		—		48	(8)	138	(2)
Total	—	—	41	(100)	4	(100)	26	(100)	609	(100)	7,902	(100)

¹Includes 16 children whose race/ethnicity is unknown.

been approved in children under age two.[103] This fact has been a point of contention among those who advocate for the rights of HIV-positive children. In response to activist pressure, the Clinton administration has proposed the Better Pharmaceuticals for Children Act as part of FDA reform legislation. This act would require that drug companies test more drugs in children and report the data to the FDA in the same time frame it does for adults. Activists have identified many loopholes in the proposal, however, that will allow drug companies to continue with their current practices.

Adolescents

The HIV/AIDS epidemic is growing among U.S. youth. According to the CDC, AIDS is the sixth leading cause of death among those ages 15 to 24. Because of the length of time it takes for HIV infection to manifest clinical symptoms, many people who develop AIDS in their twenties were likely infected when they were teenagers. The 1997 CDC report indicated that 17 percent of male AIDS cases and 22 percent of female cases in the United States have occurred in those ages 20 to 29 and that 22,070 cases of AIDS have been reported in those ages 19 to 24 and 2,953 cases in those ages 13 to 19.

Table 4.12 shows the exposure factors for adolescent and young adult AIDS cases. The figures in the table do not include adolescents who are currently infected with HIV but have not yet developed AIDS.

Data from the 29 states that conduct HIV case surveillance indicate that among adolescents ages 13 through 19, 48 percent were male; 52 percent were female; 29 percent were white, not Hispanic; 65 percent were black, not Hispanic; and 1 percent were Hispanic.

As Table 4.12 indicates, the vast majority of young people are infected with HIV through sexual contact. Nearly two-thirds of the 12 million cases of reported sexually transmitted diseases in the United States occur in those under age 25.[104] This statistic is supported by other findings that show that American youth are sexually active. In 1995, the CDC surveyed American youth about their sexual behavior:

- 9 percent of 9th to 12th graders reported they began having sex before age 13
- 40 percent of 9th graders and 70 percent of 12th graders reported having had sexual intercourse

- Only half reported using a latex condom during their last sexual intercourse
- 20 percent had more than four sexual partners[105]

NIAID analyzed the cause of this behavior and its impact on HIV prevention and treatment in its fact sheet on HIV in adolescents:

> Adolescents tend to think they are invincible and, therefore, to deny any risk. This belief may cause them to engage in risky behavior, to delay HIV-testing, and if they test positive, to delay or refuse treatment. Doctors report that many young people, when they learn they are HIV-positive, take several months to accept their diagnosis and return for treatment. Health care professionals may be able to help these adolescents by explaining the information slowly and carefully, eliciting questions from them, and emphasizing the success of newly available treatments.[106]

The Elderly

According to a January 23, 1998, Associated Press report, the CDC has identified adults 50 and older as the population group in which new AIDS cases are growing the most rapidly. The report cited that in 1996, 6,400 cases of AIDS were identified in this age group, compared with 5,260 in 1991—a 22 percent growth rate, compared with 9 percent among those ages 13 to 49. The report revealed that whereas earlier cases of AIDS among the elderly had resulted mostly from tainted blood transfusions, recent infections are linked to unprotected sex and injection drug use. According to Dr. Kimberly Holding of the CDC, "These are older adults engaging in some risky behaviors because they don't perceive themselves to be at risk."[107]

The report also noted that doctors may not be looking for signs of HIV infection among the elderly and that AIDS-related symptoms may be misdiagnosed. For instance, AIDS-related dementia may be interpreted as Alzheimer's, and dramatic weight loss may be mistaken for age-related depression. As a result, older Americans' HIV infections are more likely to be identified when AIDS is already in its late stages, diminishing their chances for a favorable prognosis. In 1996, 13 percent of those over age 50

TABLE 4.12

AIDS Cases in Adolescents and Adults under Age 25, by Sex and Exposure Category, Reported July 1995 through June 1996, July 1996 through June 1997; and Cumulative Totals through June 1997, United States

Exposure category	13–19 years old						20–24 years old					
	July 1995–June 1996		July 1996–June 1997		Cumulative total		July 1995–June 1996		July 1996–June 1997		Cumulative total	
	No.	(%)	No.	(%)	No.	(%)	No.	(%)	No.	(%)	No.	(%)
Men who have sex with men	68	(34)	85	(39)	629	(34)	874	(59)	750	(57)	10,259	(63)
Injecting drug user	11	(5)	8	(4)	114	(6)	185	(12)	123	(9)	2,038	(12)
Men who have sex with men and inject drugs	6	(3)	5	(2)	83	(4)	100	(7)	67	(5)	1,717	(11)
Hemophilia/coagulation disorder	63	(31)	38	(17)	713	(38)	69	(5)	31	(2)	599	(4)
Heterosexual contact:	11	(5)	15	(7)	62	(3)	95	(6)	99	(8)	655	(4)
Sex with injecting drug user	3		1		17		17		17		230	
Sex with person with hemophilia	–		2		3		–		4			
Sex with transfusion recipient with HIV infection	–		1		1		–		11			
Sex with HIV-infected person, risk not specified	8		13		42		75		82		410	
Receipt of blood transfusion, blood components, or tissue	8	(4)	11	(5)	80	(4)	6	(0)	5	(0)	103	(1)
Risk not reported or identified	35	(17)	56	(26)	171	(9)	159	(11)	234	(18)	979	(6)
Male subtotal	202	(100)	218	(100)	1,852	(100)	1,488	(100)	1,309	(100)	16,350	(100)

Injecting drug user	12 (7)	15 (9)	164 (15)	146 (18)	118 (15)	1,650 (29)
Hemophilia/coagulation disorder	–	–	10 (1)	2 (0)	1 (0)	14 (0)
Heterosexual contact:	100 (56)	71 (41)	590 (54)	445 (56)	439 (56)	3,067 (54)
Sex with injecting drug user	23	16	229	139	101	1,337
Sex with bisexual male	4	6	34	29	22	226
Sex with person with hemophilia	1	–	13	4	3	49
Sex with transfusion recipient with HIV infection	–	1	2	6	2	21
Sex with HIV-infected person, risk 9 not specified	72	48	312	267	311	1,434
Receipt of blood transfusion, blood components, or tissue	7 (4)	10 (6)	76 (7)	9 (1)	7 (1)	112 (2)
Risk not reported or identified	59 (33)	76 (44)	261 (24)	192 (24)	222 (28)	877 (15)
Female subtotal	178 (100)	172 (100)	1,101 (100)	794 (100)	787 (100)	5,720 (100)
Total	380	390	2,953	2,282	2,096	22,070

Source: Vol. 9, No. 1 HIV/AIDS Surveillance Report 13.

with AIDS died within a month of diagnosis, compared with only 6 percent of those ages 13 to 49.[108]

African Americans

HIV/AIDS is increasingly being defined in the United States, as in the rest of the world, as a disease disproportionately affecting people of color. As of June 1997, the CDC reported that 43 percent of adults infected with HIV during the past 12 months were black, compared with 36 percent who were non-Hispanic white. By the year 2000, statistics indicate that blacks will account for more than half of new reported cases.[109]

The American Association for World Health has identified three barriers to HIV/AIDS prevention and education that are unique to African Americans. First, since the Tuskeegee Syphilis Study, the African American community has an underlying distrust of the white public health establishment.[110] Second, African Americans experience persistent inadequacies in social benefits, health care, education, and other opportunities. Third, African American homophobia, coupled with a close attachment to the black community, creates a strong disincentive for gay African American men to respond to AIDS as a gay issue.[111]

The Tuskeegee Syphilis Study has been an underlying factor in the flood of misinformation that has been perpetuated among African Americans. One example that illustrates this point occurred in Miami, Florida, in 1996. The Associated Press reported that a radio talk show host, along with a psychiatrist and a Haitian physician who was unlicensed to practice in the United States, regularly told an estimated audience of 155,000 listeners of Haitian descent that there was no such thing as HIV/AIDS. Listeners were told that people with AIDS should not take medications or use condoms because AIDS had been fabricated by U.S. pharmaceutical companies seeking to increase their business and curtail Haitian population growth. As a result, the number of Haitians keeping appointments at area AIDS clinics declined dramatically. Psychiatrist Laurinus Pierre, head of Miami's Center for Haitian Studies, which works with hundreds of AIDS patients, said: "Everyone has free speech, but this has gone too far. People just refuse to take their medication. This is exactly what we don't need."[112]

Another example was brought to light by the CBS television news program *Sixty Minutes*, which reported on the Nation of Islam's practice of selling the "African Cure for AIDS," a drug called Kemron, to desperate patients at drastically inflated prices. Alpha Oral Interferon supposedly produced dramatic results in a clinical trial conducted in Kenya in the late 1980s by Dr. Davy Koech, who claimed the immune systems of the patients he treated improved dramatically and that some patients even became HIV negative. In more than 20 clinical trials that followed, however, the drug showed no treatment benefit; further, it was not African but was produced by a Japanese company. In 1994, a six-month supply of the drug cost $7,000 if purchased through the Nation of Islam's Abundant Life Clinic; the same amount of the drug cost between $200 and $300 through a buyer's club. The stock of the Japanese company that made the drug increased greatly in value. There were no medically documented cases of any Abundant Life client being cured of AIDS.[113]

In addition to African Americans' innate distrust of the white medical establishment, it is also important to understand the unique dilemma of gay black men. HIV prevention and education messages that have been very effective in helping gay white men have not reached gay black men. In June 1997, the CDC indicated that 38 percent of African American men contracted HIV through sex with another man. In 1996, the number of deaths from AIDS decreased by 13 percent among African Americans compared with a 32 percent decrease among whites.[114]

Although the crisis the AIDS epidemic has created in the African American community continues to fester, some recent evidence indicates a positive direction in public opinion in that community. A 1997 national survey conducted by the Kaiser Foundation revealed these facts:

- 50 percent of African Americans said they are very concerned about becoming infected by HIV, twice the level of concern shown by a national sample of all Americans (24 percent).
- 40 percent of African Americans said their personal concern has heightened from just a few years ago.
- 56 percent said AIDS is a very serious problem for people they know; 49 percent know someone who has HIV or AIDS or who has died from AIDS. By comparison, only a third of a national sample of all Americans said they are or have been as personally affected by the disease.
- 52 percent said the AIDS crisis is the leading health problem facing the nation today; 58 percent said the crisis has become more urgent in recent years.

- 97 percent know how AIDS is transmitted, and 91 percent know a pregnant woman can pass AIDS on to her baby.
- 73 percent know there is no cure for AIDS.
- 56 percent have been tested, including 65 percent of those under age thirty, compared with 38 percent and 51 percent, respectively, of Americans overall.
- 66 percent said the U.S. government does not spend enough on AIDS; 95 percent favored government investment in HIV/AIDS education and prevention activities.
- 95 percent wanted access to more effective new treatments, and 97 percent wanted research on more effective treatments.[115]

These numbers indicate that African Americans are beginning to exhibit more awareness of HIV/AIDS issues. Still, commenting on the study, Professor Henry Louis Gates Jr., director of the W.E.B. Du Bois Institute and chair of the Department of Afro-American Studies at Harvard University, said:

> In my opinion, this survey suggests a disturbing need for more leadership within the African American community—especially from ministers and other church leaders, medical professionals, and educators—about an epidemic that is sixteen times more likely to strike its women and six times more likely to strike its men [compared with members of other races]. Why is it that we are motivated to fight racism in the workplace and the civic square but are not equally motivated to save the lives of our brothers and sisters from this horrible disease?[116]

Hispanics

Hispanics accounted for nearly 20 percent of AIDS cases diagnosed in the United States by June 1997, even though they made up only 11 percent of the U.S. population.[117] According to the CDC, the two largest groups affected are men who have sex with men (who accounted for 44 percent of new HIV infections from July 1996 to June 1997) and injection drug users (37 percent of cases during the same period) plus another 7 percent who fell into both categories. Hispanic women represent the only ethnic group of females in which the percentage for the mode of infection is higher for heterosexual contact (46 percent) than for injection drug use (43 percent). Among the United States and its territories, Puerto Rico—with 59 AIDS cases per 1,000,000 people—ranks third behind the District of Columbia and New York state.[118] According to Antonia Coello de Novello, former U.S. surgeon general and a native of Puerto Rico, "Puerto Rico, which is such a small island, is sixth [in the nation] in accumulated cases with 20,626, and this is alarming!"[119]

The American Association for World Health has identified several barriers to AIDS prevention and education and offers tips for their resolution:

- A combination of cultural influences such as machismo, familismo (the importance of the family as a unit and source of support), and homophobia may preclude safer sex practices among Latino gay men. Machismo dictates that masculinity can be proved through intercourse. Familismo perceives homosexuality as sinful. Families often instill low self-esteem and personal shame in Latino gay men.
- In a traditionally machista society, women often do not talk to men about sex because it suggests promiscuity. Men often determine the frequency and type of sex.
- According to CAPS, prevention programs targeted at Latinos should consider the cultural characteristics of the population.
- Simpatica refers to the importance of polite social relations that shun assertiveness, negative responses, and criticism. Educators should be aware that Latinos may appear to agree with a message they may not understand or intend to follow.
- Personalismo refers to a preference for relationships that reflect familiarity and warmth. HIV information and service are most effective when workers establish warm relationships and ask questions about family and shared experiences.
- If HIV prevention education is to make an impact on the Latino community, Latinos must address the need to break the silence about sexuality, homophobia, and specific customs that may be detrimental to healthy sexuality, such as disallowing power for women and encouraging men to prove their masculinity through sex. Furthermore, prevention programs should continue to target the two groups most affected by HIV: Latino drug users and men who have sex with other men.[120]

Cultural sensitivity plays a significant role in providing HIV/AIDS education to Latinos, and it is important to remember that regional groups may have unique value systems or religious practices that affect their attitudes toward HIV-AIDS.

These factors are important to note for Latinos and other ethnic minorities. In *Coyote Medicine*, Lewis Mehl-Madrona describes conducting field research with medical students to ascertain why certain clients, mostly ethnic minorities, did not return to California clinics for follow-up treatment. He found that many turned to indigenous healers or shamans for medical treatment. He relates the story of an elderly Mexican woman who did not adhere to her prescribed antibiotic therapy for a respiratory infection but instead received treatment from a *curandera* (a Mexican female shaman) who treated her condition with cleansing, prayer, and sacred herbs. The woman's symptoms subsided, and she felt she was cured, to the consternation of the medical students. Madrona was impressed by the intimacy that developed between healer and patient.

> The striking thing was that most of the patients appreciated their doctor's efforts whether they followed their advice or not. Whatever was prescribed was a small part of the office visit, from the patient's point of view. Most thought the situation, the building, the small talk were all important to their recovery, even when they later ignored the doctor's instructions. In the end, patients felt that the time a doctor spent with them was more important than any medicine.
>
> Our research findings were consistent with the shaman's belief that relationships are the key to healing.[121]

Native Americans

As of June 30, 1997, the CDC recorded 1,677 cases of AIDS among Native Americans, although that number may be misleading. According to the American Association for World Health, because of the absence of a national standard for reporting race or ethnicity in AIDS surveillance, the number of reported AIDS cases among Native Americans, Alaskan Natives, and Native Hawaiians is thought to be low.[122] Further, Native Americans living in urban centers, where there is more access to injection drugs than on a reservation, are likely to be ethnically mislabeled and thus not included as Native American in the CDC surveillance tabulation.

One unique epidemiological trend in the current CDC statistics is that nearly two-thirds of Native American AIDS cases occur among men who have sex with other men. This is not the case with other ethnic minority groups, in which injection drug use is the leading cause of infection. A few possible reasons may explain this pattern among Native Americans. According to a recent report of the National Native American AIDS Prevention Center, "The custom of homosexual inclusion exists in most, if not all, Native American cultural traditions."[123] Therefore, a Native American man who has had sex with other men might be more willing to admit to a homosexual experience than someone from an ethnic/cultural group without a tradition of gay inclusion.

As in any unique cultural group, special factors need to be considered in educating Native Americans about HIV/AIDS. The American Association for World Health has identified two areas. First, collaboration efforts for HIV prevention are often hindered by turf conflicts among tribal government departments and between tribal health departments and nonprofit agencies. These offices often compete for resources and may not communicate or cooperate with each other. Second, HIV education is often provided by people who are perceived as far removed from the Native American populations most affected by HIV/AIDS. In some areas, non-Native heterosexual women provide HIV prevention education from a Western social and clinical perspective without an understanding of the culture.[124]

Hemophiliacs

Hemophiliacs were among the first groups recognized to be at risk for HIV/AIDS. Hemophiliacs have a medical condition characterized by the hereditary absence of one or more of the genes that produce the blood-clotting factors that normally stop bleeding. This defective gene appears almost exclusively in males, as the CDC statistics in the next paragraph underline. A break in the skin or any kind of injury can be life threatening. To avoid problems, hemophiliacs must regularly take clotting factors, which are made from as many as several hundred batches of donated blood. Up until 1986 in the United States (and later in the rest of the world), the companies that made clotting factors did not fully sterilize or screen the blood product they used, which gave HIV a direct vector of infection into many hemophiliacs.[125]

The AIDS epidemic has exacted a heavy toll on hemophiliacs as a group. By June 1997, the CDC reported 38,924 cases of AIDS among adult male hemophiliacs and 189 cases among female hemophiliacs living in the United States. A study of hemophiliacs revealed that the death rate increased from 0.5 to 1.3 per 1,000,000 from 1979 to 1981 through 1987 to 1989.[126] Between 1979 and 1989, the median age of death for hemophiliacs dropped from 57 years to 40 years.[127]

There are unique considerations for hemophiliacs living with HIV disease. Terry Stogell, a hemophiliac, explained in an interview in *Body Positive*:

> Blood products are what generally make our lives a little easier. For instance, today I had an ankle bleed. . . . I infused $3,000 worth of a blood product so I can get around. It's very expensive, and I spend about a quarter of a million dollars a year for blood products. Another issue facing hemophiliacs living with HIV concerns taking protease inhibitors. Since we have prolonged bleeding, we are now not only using a quarter of a million dollars in blood products plus taking all our HIV therapies, but we have to use more blood products than we would normally have to infuse, so paying for blood products is even more expensive. Everybody I talk to who has hemophilia and HIV and is on protease inhibitors is infusing more blood products than they used to. The other issue concerns the fact that 98 percent of us are Hepatitis C+, and when you start taking the antivirals, then your liver count goes up. If you are Hepatitis C+ and you've got HIV and you take all these drugs, then generally, you get liver failure or progressive liver disease. Many people don't want to go on antiviral or protease or cocktail therapy because of their Hepatitis C count or because their liver count is already really high. So they wait and their viral load gets so high, like mine, that it takes forever to get it back down. It's really hard to make decisions about treatments when you add these complications.[128]

Injection Drug Users

As of July 1997, the CDC estimated that a third of all AIDS cases in the United States to date had occurred among injection drug users. At least half of heterosexual cases stemmed from having unprotected sex with an injection drug user.[129]

Of adult and adolescent male AIDS cases in the United States through June 1997, according to the CDC, injection drug users accounted for these percentages of cases according to ethnicity: 9 percent of cases among whites (non-Hispanic), 36 percent among blacks (non-Hispanic), 37 percent among Hispanics, 15 percent among Native American or Alaska Natives, and 5 percent among Asian/Pacific Islanders. Among female injection drug users with AIDS, the percentages were generally higher: 43 percent of cases among whites (non-Hispanic), 46 percent of cases among blacks (non-Hispanic), 46 percent among Hispanics, 48 percent among Native Americans or Alaska Natives, and 17 percent among Asian Pacific Islanders.

Of total AIDS cases, injection drug users represent 22 percent of cases among males, plus another 8 percent of men who have sex with other men and who also inject drugs, and 44 percent of female cases, plus another 17 percent who were infected by having sex with an injection drug user.

Injection drug users constitute a large group with limited access to drug treatment. Conservative estimates indicate that 1.5 million active injection drug users are found in the United States at any given time and that under half a million drug treatment slots are available.[130]

Although substantial evidence shows that needle exchange programs substantially reduce the number of new infections in this population (see the section Needle Exchange in the States in this chapter), the Clinton administration has not approved the use of federal funds for such programs. Because of this stance, the Presidential Commission on AIDS has issued a no-confidence statement on the president's commitment to HIV/AIDS prevention. The April 1998 issue of *Poz* estimated that as of February 28, 1998, the lack of federal funding for needle exchange was responsible for 2,617 new HIV infections for the year to date.[131]

The gravity of the AIDS epidemic among injection drug users is underscored by CDC findings for the last statistical reporting year, July 1996 to June 1997, in the twenty-nine states that track HIV test results (recall that this group excludes New York, California, and Florida, the states with the greatest numbers of AIDS cases). During that period, 15,984 women seroconverted through sex with an injection drug user, and 113,635 men and 41,029 women were infected through injection drug use.

Prisoners

As the HIV/AIDS epidemic has grown to disproportionately affect the poor and racial minorities, it has become crucial to focus on the environments in which those groups are overrepresented. One such environment is the corrections system, represented at the municipal, county, state, and federal levels. This section presents statistics on the extent of the epidemic in prisons and suggestions from the American Association for World Health on how the spread of HIV/AIDS can be curbed. (For a more detailed view of the situation of prisoners with HIV, see "Transmission among Heterosexuals and Prison Inmates" and "HIV/AIDS and the Correctional System" in Chapter 5.)

According to a report in the December 1997 issue of *Alive and Kicking*, a publication for people living with AIDS, more than a million Americans are in prison, and prisoners are six times as likely as the general population to have HIV/AIDS. A 1994 CDC study reported an infection rate in prisons of 5.2 cases per 1,000 inmates, compared with 0.9 per 1,000 people in the general adult population.[132]

A breakdown of the number of AIDS cases per 100,000 people for men and women and for state/federal prisons compared with city/county prisons revealed 464 cases per 100,000 men in state/federal prisons, 705 cases per 100,000 women in state and federal prisons, 342 cases per 100,000 men in city/county prisons, and 201 cases per 100,00 women in city/county prisons.[133]

Given the increasing numbers of prisoners living with HIV and AIDS and expensive treatment advances in the fight against AIDS, the cost of providing medical care for HIV-positive prisoners has risen. A recent study of the situation in Illinois revealed that the cost to the state of AIDS drugs rose from $30,000 a month to $300,000 a month from 1995 to 1997.[134]

The American Association for World Health (AAWH) has listed several factors that contribute to the spread of HIV in prisons:

- Although needles are scarce, illegal, and difficult to hide in prisons, drugs continue to be used. Consequently, needles are almost always shared.
- Sex between men in prisons is common and dangerous, especially since condoms are rarely available.
- Rape exists within prisons and, at times, takes the form of gang rape during institutionalized initiations.

- Tattooing and "blood brotherhood" rites are common practices in prison and present a high risk of HIV infection.
- Prison staff are at risk of contracting HIV. Correctional officers may be pricked by a hidden, infected needle while conducting routine locker searches.
- The incarcerated often lack access to HIV/AIDS information, education, and reasonable medical care. Diseases transmitted in prison, including those transmitted through shared blood, are often treated improperly. In addition to HIV, these diseases include syphilis, hepatitis B and C, and gonorrhea.[135]

The AAWH makes several suggestions for HIV/AIDS prevention in prisons:

- Offer treatment to drug-dependent prisoners.
- Provide liquid bleach with step-by-step instructions on correct use for sterilizing needles and syringes used in drug injection and tattooing. Call the local health department for detailed instructions on disinfection.
- Provide condoms and lubricant to prisoners.
- Prevent violent attacks on prisoners, including sexual abuse and rape.
- Provide health checkups, especially for STDs, and health information.
- Offer comprehensive HIV/AIDS education and prevention programs, especially in conjunction with substance abuse and STD education.
- Offer discharge planning to help the incarcerated develop links with their community.[136]

Health Care Workers

Health care workers do not face a significant risk of HIV exposure on the job. According to the midyear 1997 CDC *HIV/AIDS Surveillance Report*, only 52 occupationally related infections have occurred in the United States during the history of the epidemic; approximately half of those workers developed AIDS. Twenty-seven were physicians, six of whom were infected while performing surgical procedures. This finding underscores the fact that HIV cannot be transmitted through casual contact, although the fact that accidental infections have occurred points to the need for caution when handling HIV-infected blood products.

HIV/AIDS and American Public Opinion

A 1996 ABC News poll revealed the following:

- 37 percent of Americans regarded AIDS as the nation's greatest health problem, down from 70 percent in 1987
- 79 percent thought it was safe to associate with someone who has AIDS, up from 57 percent in 1985
- 39 percent knew someone who has AIDS, compared with 23 percent in 1991
- 17 percent feared contracting HIV, compared with 29 percent in 1991
- 74 percent approved of Magic Johnson's return to professional basketball[137]

A 1995 poll of voters by the Human Rights Campaign Fund on the political ramifications of HIV/AIDS found that:

- 72 percent favored maintaining or increasing levels of Ryan White CARE Act funding
- 56 percent opposed antigay language—such as restrictions on explicit references to homosexuality in federally funded prevention literature—in federal legislation
- 45 percent thought the federal government was not doing enough to address the AIDS crisis
- 59 percent indicated that schools should teach children how to prevent HIV/AIDS, even if that means "exposing children to information about homosexuality"[138]

Notes

1. Lee Hardy. 1996. *ARIC'S Encyclopedic AIDS Medical Glossary*, 2d ed. Baltimore: AIDS Research Information Center, pp. 229–233.

2. American Association for World Health. 1997. "Give Children Hope in a World with AIDS." Washington, D.C.: American Association for World Health, p. 19.

3. Daniel Q. Haney. 1997. "Two Thirds Know They Have AIDS." Associated Press, September 28.

4. American Association for World Health, "Give Children Hope in a World with AIDS," p. 19.

5. Haney, "Two Thirds Know They Have AIDS," p. 17.

6. National Institute for Allergies and Infectious Diseases. 1997. *Fact Sheet: Clinical Research on HIV/AIDS Vaccines.* Bethesda, Maryland: National Institutes of Health.

7. Ibid.

8. Reuters. 1997. "Baltimore Says Effective Vaccine Is Far Away." November 18.

9. Hardy, *ARIC's Encyclopedic AIDS Medical Glossary,* p. 279.

10. UNAIDS. 1997. *Report on the Global HIV/AIDS Epidemic.* HYPERLINK http://www.unaids.org 997.

11. Andrew Purvis. 1996–1997. "The Global Epidemic." *Time,* December 31–January 6: 78.

12. UNAIDS. Report on the Global HIV/AIDS Epidemic (1997.)

13. Ibid.

14. Purvis, "The Global Epidemic," p. 78.

15. UNAIDS, *Report on the Global HIV/AIDS Epidemic.*

16. Purvis, "The Global Epidemic," p. 77.

17. François Chieze. 1995–1996. "Eleven Million Seropositives." *Revue Noire: African Contemporary Art,* December–January–February: 94.

18. Ibid.

19. Quoted in Laurie Fitzpatrick. 1997. "It Takes a Global Village." *A&U—America's AIDs Magazine,* August: 28.

20. Chieze, "Eleven Million Seropositives," p. 94.

21. Ibid.

22. UNAIDS, *Report on the Global HIV/AIDS Epidemic.*

23. Purvis, "The Global Epidemic," p. 78.

24. Chieze, "Eleven Million Seropositives," p. 94.

25. Quoted in Fitzpatrick, "It Takes a Global Village," pp. 27–28.

26. Purvis, "The Global Epidemic," p. 78.

27. UNAIDS, *Report on the Global HIV/AIDS Epidemic.*

28. Ibid.

29. Ibid.

30. Associated Press. 1997. "China: Up to 200,000 Have HIV," November 13.

31. UNAIDS, *Report on the Global HIV/AIDS Epidemic.*

32. Ivan Wolffers. 1997. "Culture, Media, and HIV/AIDS in Asia." *Lancet* 349, no. 9044, January 4: 52.

33. UNAIDS, *Report on the Global HIV/AIDS Epidemic.*

34. Ibid.

35. Michael Smith. "HIV Cases Cut Dramatically in Thailand." United Press International, March 3.

36. UNAIDS, *Report on the Global HIV/AIDS Epidemic.*

37. Ibid.

38. Wolffers, "Culture, Media, and HIV/AIDS in Asia," p. 52.

39. UNAIDS, *Report on the Global HIV/AIDS Epidemic.*

40. Ibid.

41. Ibid.

42. Ibid.

43. Dana Calvo. 1997. "Less Help for Mexicans with AIDS." Associated Press, March 19.

44. UNAIDS, *Report on the Global HIV/AIDS Epidemic.*

45. Ibid.

46. American Association for World Health, "Give Children Hope in a World with AIDS," p. 9.

47. UNAIDS, *Report on the Global HIV/AIDS Epidemic,* p.11.

48. Ibid.

49. Associated Press. 1997. "Haitian Children Inherit AIDS," November 30.

50. UNAIDS, *Report on the Global HIV/AIDS Epidemic.*

51. American Association for World Health, "Give Children Hope in a World with AIDS," p. 9.

52. UNAIDS, *Report on the Global HIV/AIDS Epidemic.*

53. Ibid.

54. Ibid.

55. Ibid.

56. Ibid.

57. Ibid.

58. Ibid.

59. Ibid.

60. Ibid.

61. Ibid.

62. David Gilden. 1998. "Moods Brighten as Statistics Lighten." *GMHC Treatment Issues* 12, no. 3, March: 1.

63. Daniel Q. Haney. "AIDS Deaths Drop in 1997." Associated Press, February 2.

64. Haney, "AIDS Deaths Drop in 1997."

65. Ibid.

66. Ibid.

67. Centers for Disease Control. 1997. "HIV/AIDS Surveillance Report," July.

68. Ibid.

69. Ibid.

70. AIDS Action Council. HYPERLINK http://www.thebody.com/aac/aacpage.html.

71. Arnold Doyle, Richard Jeffreys, and Joseph Kelly. 1998. *National ADAP Monitoring Project: Interim Technical Report, March 1998.* Washington, D.C.: National Alliance of State and Territorial AIDS Directors and AIDS Treatment Data Network, p. 42.

72. Ibid., p. 16.

73. Ibid., p. 9.

74. F. R. Lee. 1994. "Data Show Needle Exchange Curbs HIV among Addicts." *New York Times,* November 24, pp. 1, 9.

75. *Poz* citing Lancet, October 1997, p. 34.

76. Presidential Advisory Council on HIV/AIDS. 1997. *Second Progress Report,* December 7, Washington, D.C.: The White House, p. 3.

77. J. K. Watters, M. J. Estilio, G. L. Clark et al. 1994. "Syringe and Needle Exchange as HIV/AIDS Prevention for Injecting Drug Users." *Journal of the American Medical Association* 271: 115–120.

78. P. Lurie, Al Reingold, B. Bowser et al. 1993. *The Public Health Impact of Needle Exchange Programs in the United States and Abroad.* Atlanta: Centers for Disease Control and Prevention, September.

79. The White House. 1997. *The National AIDS Strategy.* Washington, D.C.: The White House, p. 4.

80. Centers for Disease Control. 1997 *Morbidity and Mortality Weekly* 46, no. 24: 565–568.

81. Ibid.

82. Ibid.

83. Ibid.

84. UNAIDS, *Report on the Global HIV/AIDS Epidemic.*

85. John C. Gonsiorek and Michael Shernoff. 1991. "AIDS Prevention and Public Policy: The Experience of Gay Males," in *Homosexuality: Research Implications for Public Policy,* edited by John C. Gonsiorek and J. D. Weinrich. Sage Publications (HYPERLINK http://www.thebody.com).

86. Ibid.

87. Ibid.

88. Ibid.

89. Ibid.

90. N. Gordon, ed. "Young Gay Men at Increased Risk of AIDS." *Journal of the International Association of Physicians in AIDS Care*, July 9, 1996.

91. Ibid.

92. *Women and HIV Factsheet*. 1997. Bethesda: National Institute of Allergies and Infectious Diseases, April.

93. Ibid.

94. American Association for World Health, *Give Children Hope in a World with AIDS*, p. 16.

95. *Women and HIV Factsheet*, April 1997.

96. Eric Lerner. 1995. "Dr. Jack Lambert on HIV Infection in Children." In *The DIRT on AIDS*, vol. 1, issue 1, February: 1.

97. N. P. Johnson et al. 1997. "Women and Clinical Trials." *Women Alive*, Fall–Winter.

98. Mary Lucey. 1997. "Awareness Is Life—Involvement Is Power." *Women Alive*, Fall–Winter.

99. National Institute of Allergies and Infectious Diseases, *Women and HIV Factsheet*.

100. Lerner, "Dr. Jack Lambert on HIV Infection in Children," p. 1.

101. Ibid., p. 2.

102. Ibid.

103. Centers for Disease Control. 1998. *CDC National Center for HIV, STD, and TB Prevention Daily News*, January. HYPERLINK http://www.cdc.gov.

104. National Institute for Allergies and Infectious Disease, *HIV in Adolescents Factsheet*.

105. Ibid.

106. Ibid.

107. Associated Press. 1998. "AIDS Rising Fastest among Those over 50," January 23.

108. Ibid.

109. C. Thompson. 1996. "AIDS Cases among Blacks Rising." Associated Press, October 22.

110. Funded by the U.S. Government (under the auspices of the U.S. Public Health Service and the Centers for Disease Control), the Tuskeegee Experiment was conducted between 1932 and 1972 in Tuskeegee, Alabama. The study examined syphilis in 399 African-American men,

who were not told that they were infected, to explore how the disease progressed and killed. No one in the study received any treatment, even though penicillin became the standard cure for syphilis in 1947. The Associated Press broke the story in 1972. Since then, many African Americans have expressed their mistrust of the U.S. health care system.

111. American Association for World Health, *Give Children Hope in a World with AIDS*, p. 22.

112. Associated Press. 1996. "Haitian Show Calls AIDS A Myth." October 1.

113. Hardy, *ARIC's Encyclopedic AIDS Medical Glossary*, pp. 175–177.

114. Centers for Disease Control, *HIV/AIDS Surveillance Report.*

115. Kaiser Family Foundation Press Release, March 17, 1998.

116. Ibid.

117. American Foundation for World Health, *Give Children Hope in a World with AIDS*, p. 11.

118. Luis R. Varela. 1997. "Report: Puerto Rico Third in U.S. AIDS Cases." Associated Press, October 18.

119. Ibid.

120. Lewis Mehl-Madrona, M.D. 1997. *Coyote Medicine.* New York: Scribner, pp. 142–143.

121. American Foundation for World Health, *Give Children Hope in a World with AIDS*, p. 22.

122. Ibid., p. 16.

123. National Native American AIDS Prevention Center. 1996. *HIV Prevention for Gay/Bisexual/Two-Spirit Native American Men: A Report of the National Leadership Development Workgroup for Gay/Bisexual/Two-Spirit Native American Men.* Oakland: National Native American AIDS Prevention Center, p. 12.

124. American Association for World Health, *Give Children Hope in a World with AIDS*, p. 22.

125. Hardy, *ARIC's Encyclopedic AIDS Medical Glossary*, p. 134.

126. Centers for Disease Control. 1994. National Center for Injury Prevention and Control, February. HYPERLINK http://www.aegis.com.

127. Ibid.

128. V. M. Hoskins. 1997. "Body Positive Interview." *Body Positive* 10, no. 9, September. http//:www.thebody.com/bp/Sept97/fam.html.

129. Centers for Disease Control, *HIV/AIDS Surveillance Report.*

130. American Association for World Health, *Give Children Hope in a World with AIDS*, p. 17.

131. *Poz.* April 1998: 38.

132. David Acosta. 1997. "Invisible No More: Prisoners Living with HIV/AIDS." *Alive and Kicking,* no. 72, December: 28.

133. Ibid.

134. "Costs Threaten Prison AIDS Care." 1997. *Alive and Kicking,* no. 72, December: 29.

135. American Association for World Health, *Give Children Hope in a World with AIDS,* p. 17.

136. Ibid.

137. Associated Press. 1996. "Poll: AIDS Concern Dropping," February 1.

138. Human Rights Campaign Fund. HYPERLINK http://www.hrc.org.

Documents and Reports

5

This chapter offers a documentary portrait of HIV/AIDS in the United States in two sections. Such a portrait is necessarily complex, but this one has been organized with accessibility and immediacy as the primary goals. The first section gives a detailed look at the development of HIV/AIDS during its first visible years in the United States. Using the most clinical document available, the Centers for Disease Control's (CDC) *Morbidity and Mortality Weekly Report* (MMWR), as a source, excerpts from key public health developments are woven together with historical narrative that offers a setting for understanding the growing epidemic. These texts are followed by excerpts from former U.S. Surgeon General C. Everett Koop's 1986 report on HIV/AIDS. The second section provides a voice for many of those affected by HIV/AIDS through statements and testimony made directly by people with the disease.

The Onset of the Epidemic in the United States

By the time the United States paid attention to HIV/AIDS, it was too late. The virus had already spread to every corner of the North

American continent. The tide of death that would later sweep the United States could perhaps be slowed, but it could not be stopped.

From 1980, when the first gay men began falling ill with strange and exotic ailments, nearly five years passed before medical and public health organizations, the federal and private scientific research establishments, the mass media, and gay community leaders mobilized as they should in a time of threat. The story of the first five years of AIDS in America is a drama of national failure, played out against a background of needless death.[1]

The arrival of AIDS as a recognizable disease in the United States is generally traced to 1981, when epidemiologists first began studying cases of unusual infections and deaths among gay men. Since that time, it has been recognized that other cases of AIDS were present in the United States in the early 1970s. The first published reports in 1981, however, marked the arrival of a new and mysterious malady, unidentified at first as medical experts grappled with clusters of otherwise rare infections and malignancies—some of which had only been seen previously in animals or very small groups of humans.

The material in this section has been chosen to illustrate the growth of the epidemic, as chronicled in official public health documents. The following edited excerpts from published reports of the CDC in its MMWR convey what was known about the early AIDS cases and give a clear indication of why the early manifestations of AIDS were quickly labeled for the public as a gay disease. The relative frequency of the reports also shows how rapidly the disease was spreading.

Opportunistic Infections

Pneumocystis Pneumonia, Los Angeles

In the period October 1980–May 1981, five young men, all active homosexuals, were treated for biopsy-confirmed *Pneumocystis carinii* (PC) pneumonia at three different hospitals in Los Angeles, California. Two of the patients died. All five patients had laboratory-confirmed previous or current cytomegalovirus (CMV) infection and candidal mucosal infection.

The patients did not know each other and had no known common contacts or knowledge of sexual partners who had similar illnesses. The five did not have comparable histories of sexually transmitted diseases. Two of the five reported having frequent homosexual contacts with various partners. All five reported using inhalant drugs, and one reported parental drug abuse.

Source: MMWR 30 (June 5, 1981): 250–252.

Editorial note: *Pneumocystis* pneumonia in the United States is almost exclusively limited to severely immunosuppressed patients. The occurrence of *Pneumocystosis* in these five previously healthy individuals with no clinically apparent underlying immunodeficiency is unusual. The fact that the patients were homosexuals suggests an association between some aspect of a homosexual lifestyle or disease acquired through sexual contact and *Pneumocystis* pneumonia in this population. All of these observations suggest the possibility of a cellular-immune dysfunction related to a common exposure that predisposes individuals to opportunistic infections such as *Pneumocystosis* and candidiasis.

Just one month later, the CDC reported on another rarely reported ailment that had been found among gay men over two years earlier. Some patients had died. The CDC pointed out that these cases mean the previous report did not describe an isolated circumstance and that it could not be certain of a link to the gay community in these cases.

Kaposi's Sarcoma and *Pneumocystis* Pneumonia among Homosexual Men, New York City and California

During the past 30 months, Kaposi's sarcoma (KS), an uncommonly reported malignancy in the United States, has been diagnosed in 26 homosexual men (20 in New York City [NYC], 6 in California). The 26 patients range in age from 26–51 years (mean: 39 years). Eight of these patients died (7 in NYC, 1 in California)—all within 24 months after KS was diagnosed.

A review of the New York University Coordinated Cancer Registry for KS in men under age 50 revealed no cases from 1970 to 1979 at Bellevue Hospital and 3 cases in this age group at the New York University Hospital from 1961 to 1979.

Since the previous report of 5 cases of *Pneumocystis* pneumonia in homosexual men from Los Angeles, 10 additional cases (4 in Los Angeles and 6 in the San Francisco Bay area) of biopsy-confirmed PC pneumonia have been identified in homosexual men in the state. Two of the 10 patients also have KS. This brings the total number of *Pneumocystis* cases among homosexual men in California to 15 since September 1979. Patients range in age from 25 to 46 years.

Source: MMWR 30 (July 4, 1981): 305–308.

Editorial note: KS affects primarily elderly men. The occurrence of this number of KS cases during a 30-month period among young, homosexual men is highly unusual. No previous association between KS and sexual preference has been reported. The fact that 10 new cases of *Pneumocystis* pneumonia have been identified in homosexual men suggests that the 5 previously reported cases were not an isolated phenomenon.

Although it is not certain that the increase in KS and PC pneumonia is restricted to homosexual men, the vast majority of recent cases have been reported from this group. Physicians should be alert for Kaposi's sarcoma, PC pneumonia, and other opportunistic infections associated with immunosuppression in homosexual men.

Just eight weeks later, the CDC had received reports of more than twice as many new cases of PCP and KS, the majority among gay white men.

Follow-up on Kaposi's Sarcoma and *Pneumocystis* Pneumonia

Twenty-six cases of Kaposi's sarcoma and 15 cases of *Pneumocystis carinii* pneumonia (PCP) among previously healthy homosexual men were recently reported. Since July 3, 1981, CDC received reports of an additional 70 cases of these two conditions in persons without known underlying disease. . . .

The majority of the reported cases of KS and/or PCP have occurred in white men. Patients ranged in age from 15–52 years; over 95 percent were men 25–49 years of age. Ninety-four percent (95/101) of the men for whom sexual preference was known were homosexual or bisexual. Forty percent of the cases were fatal.

Source: MMWR 30 (August 28, 1981): 409–410.

As researchers worked to identify the still unnamed disease, they focused on possible links to the sexual preference of those affected. Sexual practices, frequency and number of sexual partners, and drug use were examined.

Persistent, Generalized Lymphadenopathy among Homosexual Males

Since October 1981, [57] cases of persistent, generalized lymph-adenopathy—not attributable to previously identified cases among homosexual males—have been reported to CDC by physicians in several major metropolitan areas in the United States. These reports were prompted by an awareness generated by ongoing CDC and state investigations of other emerging health problems among homosexual males. . . .

Recorded medical histories for the 57 patients suggested that the use of drugs such as nitrite inhalants, marijuana, hallucinogens, and cocaine was common. Many of these patients have a history of sexually transmitted infections.

Source: MMWR 31 (May 21, 1982): 249–252.

The following CDC report, published less than a month later, shows that what the CDC refers to as an epidemic is more diversified in several ways than previously thought: by the sexual orientation of those affected, race, and geography. According to the report, similar opportunistic infections have been reported in 20 states.

Update on Kaposi's Sarcoma and Opportunistic Infections in Previously Healthy Persons, United States

Between June 1, 1981, and May 28, 1982, CDC received reports of 355 cases of Kaposi's sarcoma (KS) and/or serious opportunistic infections (OI), especially *Pneumocystis carinii* pneumonia (PCP), occurring in previously healthy persons between 15 and 60 years of age. Of the 355, 281 (79 percent) were homosexual or bisexual men, 41 (12 percent) were heterosexual men, 20 (6 percent) were men of unknown sexual orientation, and 13 (4 percent) were heterosexual women. This proportion of heterosexuals (16 percent) is higher than previously described.

Five states—California, Florida, New Jersey, New York, and Texas—accounted for 86 percent of the reported cases. The rest were reported by 15 other states. . . .

Both male and female heterosexual PCP patients were more likely than homosexual patients to be black or Hispanic.

Source: MMWR 31 (June 11, 1982): 294–301.

Editorial note: Sexual orientation information was obtained from patients by their physicians, and the accuracy of reporting cannot be determined; therefore, comparisons between KSOI cases made on the basis of sexual orientation must be interpreted cautiously. Similarities between homosexual and heterosexual cases in diagnoses and geographic and temporal distribution suggest that all are part of the same epidemic. . . . Differences in race, proportion of PCP cases, and intravenous drug use, however, suggest that risk factors may be different for these groups.

One week later, the CDC reported on what became known as the Orange County Connection, an interconnected series of KS and PCP cases that included the same non-Californian as a sexual contact in an improbable fashion. Air Canada steward Gaetan Dugas, sometimes referred to as Patient Zero, was one of the first North Americans diagnosed with AIDS, although his case was not followed clinically in the United States because of his nationality. Dugas had a KS lesion removed from his face in spring 1980.

According to CDC researcher William Darrow, as of April 12, 1982, Dugas or one of his partners had had sex with 40 of the first 248 gay men who were diagnosed with the disease. This network of contacts involved people in 10 cities and created further generations of sexual contacts. This clustering of cases from a string of identifiable sexual contacts offered strong proof that a lone infectious agent was responsible for the transmission of the disease.[2]

In addition, Darrow found that all of the early New York City cases that involved gay men could be traced to a similar string of common sexual contacts during summer 1976. It was not until 1978 and 1979, however, that these men first became ill, lending credence to a theory that the causative agent of the disease could maintain a prolonged latency period.[3]

A Cluster of Kaposi's Sarcoma and *Pneumocystis Carinii* Pneumonia among Homosexual Male Residents of Los Angeles and Orange Counties, California

In the period June 1, 1981, to April 12, 1982, CDC received reports of 19 cases of biopsy-confirmed Kaposi's sarcoma (KS) and/or *Pneumocystis carinii* pneumonia (PCP) among previously healthy homosexual male residents of Los Angeles and Orange Counties, California. Following an unconfirmed report of possible associations among cases in southern California, interviews were conducted with all 8 of the patients still living and with the close friends of 7 of the 11 patients who had died.

Within 5 years of the onset of symptoms, 9 patients (6 with KS and 3 with PCP) had sexual contact with other patients with KS or PCP. Seven patients from Los Angeles County had sexual contact with other patients from Los Angeles County, and 2 from Orange County had sexual contact with 1 patient who was not a resident of California. Four of the 9 patients had been exposed to more than 1 patient who had KS or PCP.

The other 4 patients in the group of 13 had no known sexual contact with reported cases. However, 1 patient with KS had an apparently healthy sexual partner in common with 2 persons with PCP; 1 patient with KS reported having had sexual contact with 2 friends of the non-Californian with KS; and 2 patients with PCP had most of their anonymous contacts (>80 percent) with persons in bathhouses attended frequently by other persons in Los Angeles with KS or PCP.

The 9 patients from Los Angeles and Orange Counties directly linked to other patients are part of an interconnected series of cases that may include 15 additional patients (11 with KS and 4 with PCP) from 8 other cities. The non-Californian with KS mentioned earlier is part of this series.

Source: MMWR 31 (June 18, 1982): 305–307.

Editorial note: The probability that 7 of 11 patients with KS or PCP would have sexual contact with any one of the other 16 reported patients in Los Angeles County would seem remote. The probability that 2 patients with KS living in different parts of Orange County would have sexual contact with the same non-Californian with KS would appear to be even lower.

Naming the Disease

In September 1982, the CDC reported on the rapid growth of the disease now christened Acquired Immune Deficiency Syndrome, or AIDS. Just a few months earlier, scientists had finally come to agreement on a name for what was killing people, discarding GRID (Gay Related Immune Deficiency), CAIDS (Community Acquired Immune Deficiency Syndrome), and ACIS (Acquired Community Immune Syndrome). Kaposi's sarcoma alone had frequently been referred to as gay cancer. At this time, the CDC also published its first definition of the disease.

Update on Acquired Immune Deficiency Syndrome (AIDS)—United States

Between June 1, 1981, and September 15, 1982, CDC received reports of 593 cases of Acquired Immune Deficiency Syndrome (AIDS). Death occurred in 243 cases (41 percent).

The incidence of AIDS by date of diagnosis (assuming an almost constant population at risk) has roughly doubled every half-year since the second half of 1979. An average of one to two cases are now diagnosed every day. Although the overall case-mortality rate for the current total of 593 is 41 percent, the rate exceeds 60 percent for cases diagnosed over a year ago.

Source: MMWR 31 (September 24, 1982): 507–514.

Editor's note: Two points in this update deserve emphasis. First, the eventual case-mortality rate of AIDS, a few years after diagnosis, may be far greater that the 41 percent overall case-mortality rate noted earlier. Second, the reported incidence of AIDS has continued to increase rapidly. Only a small percentage of cases have none of the identified risk factors (male homosexuality, intravenous drug abuse, Haitian origin, and perhaps hemophilia A). To avoid a reporting bias, physicians should report cases regardless of the absence of these factors.

Blood and Blood Products

In July 1982, the CDC released information on the first cases of opportunistic infection among hemophiliacs. Hemophilia A is an inherited disorder, linked to gender, and characterized by a deficiency in Factor VIII, a clotting component of the blood. Approximately 20,000 people in the United States have this form of hemophilia; about 60 percent are classified as severe. They are treated intravenously with Factor VIII products, often made with a concentrate from blood donated by over a thousand people. These blood products, produced commercially and from donations, are regulated by the federal Food and Drug Administration (FDA).

Pneumocystis Carinii Pneumonia (PCP) among Persons with Hemophilia A

CDC recently received reports of three cases of *Pneumocystis carinii* pneumonia among patients with hemophilia A and without other underlying diseases. Two have died; one remains critically ill. All three were heterosexual males; none had a history of intravenous (IV) drug abuse.

For each patient, records of the administration of Factor VIII concentrate were reviewed to determine manufacturer and lot numbers. No two of the patients are known to have received concentrate from the same lots.

Source: MMWR 31 (July 16, 1982): 365–367.

Just four months after its first report on OIs among hemophiliacs, the CDC updated the report with the news that the first three patients had died and four others cases had been reported.

Update on Acquired Immune Deficiency Syndrome (AIDS) among Patients with Hemophilia A

In most cases, these patients have been the first AIDS cases in their cities, states, or regions. They have had no common medications, occupations, habits, types of pets, or any uniform antecedent history of personal or family illnesses with immunological relevance.

Two of the patients described here are 10 years of age or less, and children with hemophilia must now be considered at risk for the disease. In addition, the number of cases continues to increase, and the illness may pose a significant risk for patients with hemophilia.

The National Hemophilia Foundation and CDC are now conducting a national survey of hemophilia treatment centers to estimate the prevalence of AIDS-associated diseases during the past 5 years and to provide active surveillance of AIDS among patients with hemophilia.

Source: MMWR 31 (December 10, 1982): 644–652.

As early as mid-1981, CDC epidemiologist Dr. Mary Guinan had thought that if this disease was spread like Hepatitis B, through contact with the blood of intravenous drug users, then hemophiliacs and blood transfusion recipients—frequently affected by hepatitis—were another likely group to show signs of the new disease.[4] Yet, the advent of the first hemophilia cases described earlier did not prompt action by the voluntary blood banks, for-profit blood-products manufacturers, or the government. Instead, even though each use of Factor VIII exposed a recipient hemophiliac to many individual donors, Assistant Secretary for Health and Human Services (HHS) Dr. Edward N. Brandt Jr. did not stray from the Food and Drug Administration's (FDA) official policy on the nation's blood supply, stating at an August 1982 conference, "We can't be sure there is a connection between blood products used by these patients and AIDS."

In the same December issue of MMWR, the CDC reported on a case identified in August of that year by prominent pediatric immunologist Dr. Art Ammann in San Francisco: a transfusion-related case of AIDS in an infant. Even this report was insufficient to convince blood-industry officials to take action.

Possible Transfusion-Associated Acquired Immune Deficiency Syndrome (AIDS), California

CDC has received a report of a 20-month-old infant from the San Francisco area who developed unexplained cellular immunodeficiency and opportunistic infection. This occurred after multiple transfusions, including a transfusion of platelets from the blood of a male subsequently found to have the Acquired Immune Deficiency Syndrome (AIDS.)

The parents and brother of the infant are in good health. The parents are heterosexual non-Haitians and do not have a history of intravenous drug abuse. The infant had no known personal contact with an AIDS patient.

Source: MMWR 31 (December 10, 1982): 652–654.

Editorial note: This report and continuing reports of AIDS among persons with hemophilia A raise serious questions about the possible transmission of AIDS through blood and blood products. The assistant secretary for health is convening an advisory committee to address these questions.

The advisory group convened in January 1983 and included representatives from the National Institutes of Health (NIH), the FDA, the National Gay Task Force, the American Red Cross, the American Association of Blood Banks, and the Pharmaceutical Manufacturers Association, which represents commercial blood-products makers. The group discussed the relatively small number of cases that had appeared so far, possible future impact given the apparent latency of the disease for long periods, the cost burden of testing blood for hepatitis B antibodies, the discouraging effect of screening questionnaires on the donor base among urban gay men, and other issues. The participants could not agree on any plan of action.

Perinatal Transmission

Just one week later, the CDC published another important report supporting the theory that a new infectious agent was behind the epidemic.

CDC has received reports of four infants (under 2 years of age) with unexplained cellular immunodeficiency and opportunistic infections. None of the four infants described in the case reports was known to have received blood or blood products before onset of illness.

Source: MMWR 31 (December 17, 1982): 665–667.

Editorial note: Although the etiology of AIDS remains unknown, a series of epidemiological observations suggests it is caused by an infectious agent. If the infants described in the four case reports had AIDS, exposure to the putative AIDS agent must have occurred very early. . . . Transmission of an AIDS agent from mother to child, either in utero or shortly after birth, could account for the early onset of immunodeficiency in these infants.

Transmission among Heterosexuals and Prison Inmates

The first CDC report in 1983 contained news of the further spread of the epidemic into two new groups: heterosexuals and prison inmates. With the addition of heterosexuals to a list that only recently had included recipients of blood transfusions, virtually anyone was at risk for AIDS.

Immunodeficiency among Female Sexual Partners of Males with Acquired Immune Deficiency Syndrome (AIDS), New York

CDC has received reports of two females with cellular immunodeficiency who have been steady sexual partners of males with the Acquired Immune Deficiency Syndrome.

Source: MMWR 31 (January 7, 1983): 697–698.

Editorial note: Epidemiological observations increasingly suggest that AIDS is caused by an infectious agent. The description of a cluster of sexually related AIDS patients among homosexual males in southern California suggested such an agent could be transmitted sexually or through other intimate contact. . . . The present report suggests the infectious agent hypothesis and the possibility that transmission of the putative AIDS agent may occur among both heterosexual and male homosexual couples.

Acquired Immune Deficiency Syndrome (AIDS) in Prison Inmates—New York, New Jersey

CDC has received reports from New York and New Jersey of 16 prison inmates with the Acquired Immune Deficiency Syndrome (AIDS).

New York: Between November 1981 and October 1982, 10 AIDS cases were reported among inmates of New York state correctional facilities. The patients had been imprisoned from 3 to 36 months before developing symptoms. . . .

All 10 patients reported that they were heterosexual before imprisonment; one is known to have had homosexual contacts since confinement. However, the other 9 patients were regular users of intravenous drugs before imprisonment. . . . The 19 patients were housed in seven different prisons when they first developed PCP or KS.

New Jersey: Of the 48 AIDS cases reported in New Jersey since June 1981, six have involved inmates of New Jersey state correctional facilities. They were imprisoned from 1 to 36 months before onset of symptoms.

All six patients have histories of chronic IV drug abuse. . . . Four were heterosexual, and one was homosexual. The two living patients have denied both IV drug use and homosexual activity since imprisonment. No two of the six patients had been confined in the same facility at the same time.

Source: MMWR 31 (January 7, 1983): 700–701.

Risk Reduction

The CDC published its first guidelines on risk reduction in March 1983. The guidelines were the federal government's only effort to date to stop the spread of the disease.

Prevention of Acquired Immune Deficiency Syndrome (AIDS): Report of Inter-Agency Recommendations

No AIDS cases have been documented among health care or laboratory personnel caring for AIDS patients or processing laboratory specimens. To date, no person-to-person transmission has been identified other than through intimate contact or blood transfusion.

Several factors indicate that individuals at risk for transmitting AIDS may be difficult to identify. The pool of persons potentially capable of transmitting an AIDS agent may be considerably larger than the presently known number of AIDS cases. Furthermore, the California cluster investigation and other epidemiologic findings suggest a latent period of several months to 2 years between exposure and recognizable clinical illness and imply that transmissibility may precede recognizable clinical illness. Thus, careful histories and physical examinations alone will not identify all persons capable of transmitting AIDS but should be useful in identifying persons with definite AIDS diagnoses or related symptoms. . . . Persons who may be considered at increased risk of AIDS include those with symptoms and signs suggestive of AIDS, sexual partners of AIDS patients, sexually active homosexual or bisexual men with multiple partners, Haitian entrants to the United States, present or past abusers of IV drugs, patients with hemophilia, and sexual partners of individuals at increased risk for AIDS.

Although the cause of AIDS remains unknown, the Public Health Service recommends the following actions:

1. Sexual contact should be avoided with persons known or suspected to have AIDS. Members of high-risk groups should be aware that multiple sexual partners increases the probability of developing AIDS.
2. As a temporary measure, members of groups at increased risk for AIDS should refrain from donating plasma and/or blood. The recommendation includes all individuals belonging to such groups, even though many individuals are at little risk of AIDS. Centers collecting plasma and/or blood should inform potential donors of this recommendation. The Food and Drug Administration (FDA) is preparing new recommendations for manufacturers of plasma derivatives and for establishments collecting plasma or blood. This is an interim

measure to protect recipients of blood products and blood until specific laboratory results are available.

3. Studies should be conducted to evaluate screening procedures for their effectiveness in identifying and excluding plasma and blood with a high probability of transmitting AIDS. These procedures should include specific laboratory tests as well as careful histories and physical examinations.

4. Physicians should adhere strictly to medical indications for transfusions, and autologous blood transfusions are encouraged.

5. Work should continue toward safer blood products for use by hemophilia patients. . . .

As long as the cause remains unknown, the ability to understand the natural history of AIDS and to undertake preventive measures is somewhat compromised. However, the above recommendations are prudent measures that should reduce the risk of acquiring and transmitting AIDS.

Source: MMWR 32 (March 4, 1983): 101–104.

Government Responses to the Epidemic

The Surgeon General's Report

In October 1986, U.S. Surgeon General Dr. C. Everett Koop issued a report on HIV/AIDS in the United States. The frank nature of the report, as well as its emphasis on the epidemic as a public health problem rather than a political issue, took both conservatives and liberals by surprise. The following excerpt from Koop's introductory letter to the report is followed by some sections of the report itself.

Acquired Immune Deficiency Syndrome is an epidemic that has already killed thousands of people, mostly young, productive Americans. In addition to illness, disability, and death, AIDS has brought fear to the hearts of most Americans—fear of disease and fear of the unknown. . . .

My report will inform you about AIDS, how it is transmitted, the relative risks of infection, and how to prevent it. It will help you understand your fears. Fear can be useful when it helps people avoid behavior that puts them at risk for AIDS. On the other hand, unreasonable fear can be as crippling as the disease itself. . . .

In preparing this report, I consulted with the best medical and scientific experts this country can offer. I met with leaders of organizations concerned with health, education, and other aspects of our society to gain their views of the problems associated with AIDS. This report was written personally by me to provide the necessary understanding of AIDS. . . .

The vast majority of Americans are against illicit drugs. As a health officer I am opposed to the use of illicit drugs. As a practicing physician for more than forty years, I have seen the devastation that follows the use of illicit drugs—addiction, poor health, family disruption, emotional disturbances, and death. I applaud the President's initiative to rid this nation of the curse of illicit drug use and addiction. The success of his initiative is critical to the health of the American people and will also help reduce the number of persons exposed to HIV.

Some Americans have difficulties dealing with the subjects of sex, sexual practices, and alternate lifestyles. Many Americans are opposed to homosexuality, promiscuity of any kind, and prostitution. This report must deal with all of these issues but does so with the intent that information and education can change individual behavior, since this is the primary way to stop the epidemic of AIDS. This report deals with the positive and negative consequences of activities and behaviors from a health and medical point of view.

Adolescents and pre-adolescents are those whose behavior we wish to especially influence because of their vulnerability when they are exploring their own sexuality (heterosexual and homosexual) and perhaps experimenting with drugs. Teenagers often consider themselves immortal, and these young people may be putting themselves at great risk.

Education about AIDS should start in early elementary school and at home so that children can grow up knowing the behavior to avoid to protect themselves from exposure to HIV. The threat of AIDS can provide an opportunity for parents to instill in their children their own moral and ethical standards.

Those of us who are parents, educators, and community leaders, indeed all adults, cannot disregard this responsibility to educate our young. The need is critical, and the price of neglect is high. The lives of our young people depend on our fulfilling our responsibility.

AIDS is an infectious disease. It is contagious, but it cannot be spread in the same manner as a common cold or measles or chicken pox. It is contagious in the same way that sexually transmitted diseases, such as syphilis and gonorrhea, are contagious. AIDS can also be spread through the sharing of intravenous drug needles and syringes used for injecting illicit drugs.

AIDS is not spread by everyday contact but by sexual contact (penis-vagina, penis-rectum, mouth-rectum, mouth-vagina, mouth-penis). Yet, there is great misunderstanding resulting in unfounded fear that AIDS can be spread by casual, nonsexual contact. The first cases of AIDS were reported in this country in 1981. We would know by now if AIDS were passed by casual, nonsexual contact.

At the beginning of the AIDS epidemic, many Americans had little sympathy for people with AIDS. The feeling was that somehow people from certain groups deserved their illness. Let us put those feelings behind us. We are fighting a disease, not people. Those who are already afflicted are sick people and need our care, as do all sick patients. The country must face this epidemic as a unified society. We must prevent the spread of AIDS while at the same time preserving our humanity and intimacy.

AIDS is a life-threatening disease and a major public health issue. Its impact on our society is and will continue to be devastating. By the end of 1991, an estimated 270,000 cases of AIDS will have occurred, with 179,000 deaths within the decade since the disease was first recognized. In the year 1991, an estimated 145,000 patients with AIDS will need health and supportive services at a total cost of between $8 and $16 billion. However, AIDS is preventable. It can be controlled by changes in personal behavior. It is the responsibility of every citizen to be informed about AIDS and to exercise the appropriate preventive measures. This report will tell you how.

The spread of AIDS can and must be stopped.

The following are excerpts from Dr. Koop's report.

The Challenge of the Future

An enormous challenge to public health lies ahead of us, and we would do well to take a look at the future. We must be prepared to manage those things we can predict, as well as those we cannot.

At the present time, there is no vaccine to prevent AIDS.

There is no cure. AIDS, which can be transmitted sexually and by sharing needles and syringes among illicit intravenous drug users, is bound to produce profound changes in our society, changes that will affect us all.

Information and Education Only Weapons against AIDS

It is estimated that in 1991, 54,000 people will die from AIDS. At this moment, many of them are not infected with HIV. With proper information and education, as many as 12,000 to 14,000 people could be saved in 1991 from death by AIDS.

AIDS Will Impact All

The changes in our society will be economic and political and will affect our social institutions, our educational practices, and our health care. Although AIDS may never touch you personally, the societal impact certainly will.

Be Educated, Be Prepared

Be prepared. Learn as much about AIDS as you can. Learn to separate scientific information from rumor and myth. The Public Health Service, your local public health officials, and your family physician will be able to help you.

Special Educational Concerns

There are a number of people, primarily adolescents, that do not yet know they will be homosexual or become drug abusers and will not heed this message; there are others who are illiterate and cannot heed this message. They must be reached and taught the risk behaviors that expose them to infection with HIV.

Anger and Guilt

Some people afflicted with AIDS will feel a sense of anger and others a sense of guilt. In spite of these understandable reactions, everyone must join the effort to control the epidemic, to provide for the care of those with AIDS, and to do all we can to inform and educate others about AIDS and how to prevent it.

Confidentiality

Because of the stigma that has been associated with AIDS, many afflicted with the disease or who are infected with the virus are reluctant to be identified with AIDS. Because there is no vaccine to prevent AIDS and no cure, many feel there is nothing to be gained by revealing sexual contacts that might also be infected with the AIDS virus. When a community or a state requires reporting of those infected to public health authorities in order to trace sexual and intravenous drug contacts, as is the practice with other sexually transmitted diseases, those infected with the AIDS virus go underground out of the mainstream of health care and education. For this reason, current public health practice is to protect the privacy of the individual infected with the AIDS virus and to maintain the strictest confidentiality concerning his/her health records.

Schools

Schools will have special problems in the future. In addition to the guidelines already mentioned in this pamphlet, there are other things that should be considered such as sex education and education of the handicapped.

Sex Education

Education concerning AIDS must start at the lowest grade possible as part of any health and hygiene program. The appearance of AIDS could bring together diverse groups of parents and educators with opposing views on inclusion of sex education in the curricula. There is now no doubt that we need sex education in schools and that it must include information on heterosexual and homosexual relationships. The threat of AIDS should be sufficient to permit a sex education curriculum with a heavy emphasis on prevention of AIDS and other sexually transmitted diseases.

Handicapped and Special Education

Children with AIDS will be attending school along with others who carry the AIDS virus. Some children will develop brain disease, which will produce changes in mental behavior. Because of the right to special education of the handicapped and the mentally retarded, school boards and higher authorities will have to provide guidelines for the management of such children on a case-by-case basis.

Labor and Management

Labor and management can do much to prepare for AIDS so that misinformation is kept to a minimum. Unions should issue preventive health messages because many employees will listen more carefully to a union message than they will to one from public health authorities.

AIDS Education and the Work Site

Offices, factories, and other work sites should have a plan in operation for education of the workforce and accommodation of AIDS patients before the first such case appears at the work site. Employees with AIDS should be dealt with as are any workers with a chronic illness. In-house video programs provide an excellent source of education and can be individualized to the needs of a specific work group.

Strain on the Health Care Delivery System

The health care system in many places will be overburdened, as it is now in urban areas with large numbers of AIDS patients. It is predicted that during 1991 there will be 145,000 patients requiring hospitalization at least once and 54,000 patients who will die of AIDS. Mental disease (dementia) will occur in some patients who have the AIDS virus before they have any other manifestation.

State and local task forces will have to plan for these patients by utilizing conventional and time-honored systems but will also have to investigate alternate methods of treatment and alternate sites for care, including home care.

The strain on the health system can be lessened by family, social, and psychological support mechanisms in the community. Programs are needed to train chaplains, clergy, social workers, and volunteers to deal with AIDS. Such support is particularly critical to the minority communities.

Mental Health

Our society will also face an additional burden as we better understand the mental health implications of infection by the AIDS virus. Upon being informed of infection with the AIDS virus, a young, active, vigorous person faces anxiety and depression brought on by fears associated with social isolation, illness, and dying. Dealing with these individual and family concerns will require the best efforts of mental health professionals.

Controversial Issues

A number of controversial AIDS issues have arisen and will continue to be debated largely because of lack of knowledge about AIDS, how it is spread, and how it can be prevented. Among these are the issues of compulsory blood testing, quarantine, and identification of AIDS carriers by some visible sign.

Compulsory Blood Testing

Compulsory blood testing of individuals is not necessary. The procedure could be unmanageable and cost-prohibitive. It can be expected that many who test negatively might actually be positive due to recent exposure to the AIDS virus and give a false sense of security to the individual and his/her sexual partners concerning necessary protective behavior. The prevention behavior described in this report, if adopted, will protect the American public and contain the AIDS epidemic. Voluntary testing will be available to those who have been involved in high-risk behavior.

Quarantine

Quarantine has no role in the management of AIDS because AIDS is not spread by casual contact. The only time some form of quarantine might be indicated is in a situation where an individual carrying the AIDS virus knowingly and willingly continues to expose others through sexual contact or sharing drug equipment. Such circumstances should be managed on a case-by-case basis by local authorities.

Identification of AIDS Carriers by Some Visible Sign

Those who suggest the marking of carriers of the AIDS virus by some visible sign have not thought the matter through thoroughly. It would require testing of the entire population, which is unnecessary, unmanageable, and costly. It would miss those recently infected individuals who would test negatively but be infected. The entire procedure would give a false sense of security. AIDS must and will be treated as a disease that can infect anyone. AIDS should not be used as an excuse to discriminate against any group or individual.

Source: Dr. C. Everett Koop. 1986. *Surgeon General's Report on Acquired Immune Deficiency Syndrome.* Washington, D.C.: U.S. Department of Health and Human Services.

Needle exchange has been a source of contention between the Clinton administration and scores of public health professionals. Even though sustained evidence indicates that needle exchange programs dramatically lower the transmission rate among injection drug users and their sexual contacts, Clinton and Health and Human Services Director Donna Shalala have refused to commit federal funds to this life-saving endeavor. What follows is Clinton's Advisory Council on HIV/AIDS's no-confidence statement.

Presidential Advisory Council on HIV/AIDs Resolution on Needle Exchange Programs

March 17, 1998

WHEREAS we the members of the Presidential Advisory Council on HIV/AIDS have on several occasions advised the President and Health and Human Services Secretary Donna Shalala that the Administration's current policy on needle exchange programs threatens the public health and directly contradicts current scientific evidence regarding the efficacy of such programs; and

WHEREAS this Administration has yet to put forward a coherent plan to increase access to substance abuse treatment or to combat the spread of HIV among injection drug users and their partners; and

WHEREAS nearly 50 percent of all new HIV infections, and 44 percent, 44 percent, and 61 percent of all reported AIDS cases among African Americans, Latinos, and women, respectively, are related to injection drug use; and

WHEREAS the Congress in 1997 reaffirmed Secretary Shalala's authority to make federal funds available for needle exchange programs, provided that she first determine that needle exchange programs reduce HIV transmission and do not encourage drug use; and

WHEREAS no fewer that six federally funded reports (including a 1997 Consensus Report prepared by the National Institutes of Health) and numerous other scientific studies have concluded that the above two criteria have been met; and

WHEREAS the nation's leading public health groups, including the American Medical Association, the American Public Health Association, the National Academy of Sciences, and the Association of State and Territorial Health Officers, support needle exchange programs and the elimination of federal funding restrictions; and

WHEREAS 61 percent of Americans surveyed believe that decisions regarding the use of federal funds for needle exchange programs should be made by local communities and not the federal government; and

WHEREAS it is essential that the nation's health policies be based on sound, scientific evidence rather that on unsubstantiated fears or politics; and

WHEREAS in light of the disproportionate impact of injection drug-related HIV on communities of color in the United States, the Secretary's continuing inaction undermines the credibility of the Administration's stated goal of reducing racial and ethnic health disparities; therefore

BE IT RESOLVED that, in the interest of the public health and in our capacity as independent advisors to the Administration, we unanimously express "no confidence" in the Administration's commitment and willingness to achieve the President's stated goal of "reducing the number of new infections annually until there are no new infections"; and

BE IT FURTHER RESOLVED that the Council urges Secretary Shalala to issue an immediate determination declaring the efficacy of needle exchange programs in preventing the spread of HIV while not encouraging the use of illegal drugs.

Firsthand Perspectives on the Epidemic

People with AIDS (PWAs) Take a Stand

In 1987, the founding meeting of People with AIDS/ARC (AIDS Related Complex) was held in Denver at the Second International AIDS Forum. The National Association of People with AIDS was organized at the forum and became the catalyst for self-empowerment among PWAs. Although it was later pointed out that the following document excluded women with HIV/AIDS, it is nevertheless considered a milestone.

The Denver Principles

We condemn attempts to label us as victims, which implies defeat, and we are only occasionally patients, which implies passivity, helplessness, and dependence upon the care of others. We are people with AIDS.

We recommend that health care professionals who are gay

1. Come out, especially to their patients who have AIDS.
2. Always clearly identify and discuss the theory they favor as to the cause of AIDS, since this bias affects the treatment and advice they give.
3. Get in touch with their feelings (fears, anxieties, hopes, etc.) about AIDS and not simply deal with AIDS intellectually.
4. Take a thorough personal inventory and identify and examine their own agendas around AIDS.
5. Treat people with AIDS as whole people and address psychosocial issues as well as biophysical ones.
6. Address the question of sexuality in people with AIDS specifically, sensitively, and with information about gay male sexuality in general and the sexuality of people with AIDS in particular.

We recommend that all people

1. Support us in our struggle against those who would fire us from our jobs, evict us from our homes, refuse to touch us, separate us from our loved ones, our community, or our peers, since there is no evidence that AIDS can be spread by casual social contact.
2. Do not scapegoat people with AIDS, blame us for the epidemic, or generalize about our lifestyles.

We recommend that people with AIDS

1. Form caucuses to choose their own representatives, to deal with the media, to choose their own agenda, and to plan their own strategies.

2. Be involved at every level of AIDS decisionmaking and specifically serve on the boards of directors of provider organizations.
3. Be included in all AIDS forums with equal credibility as other participants to share their own experiences and knowledge.
4. Substitute low-risk sexual behaviors for those that could endanger themselves or their partners, and we feel that people with AIDS have an ethical responsibility to inform their potential sexual partners of their health status.

People with AIDS have the right

1. To as full and satisfying sexual and emotional lives as anyone else.
2. To quality medical treatment and quality social service provision without discrimination in any form, including sexual orientation, gender, diagnosis, economic status, age, or race.
3. To full explanations of all medical procedures and risks, to choose or refuse their treatment modalities, to refuse to participate in research without jeopardizing their treatment, and to make informed decisions about their lives.
4. To privacy, to confidentiality of medical records, to human respect, and to choose who their significant others are.
5. To die and live in dignity.

The following excerpts are testimony from three economically disadvantaged PWAs: a woman, an injection drug user, and a homeless man. Although their testimony was given early in the AIDS epidemic, the social realities they portray are consistent with contemporary findings about the problems faced by the respective groups they represent.

Women and HIV/AIDS

The National Conference on AIDS and HIV Infection in Ethnic and Racial Minorities was held in Washington, D.C., in August 1989. Phyllis Sharpe, a New York City mother and former drug user, testified at the conference about some of the unique problems facing minority women. In May 1990, Sharpe also spoke at a demonstration at the National Institutes of Health in Bethesda, Maryland, about the lack of access to drug trials for women in her situation. The following excerpts are taken from those two statements.

My name is Phyllis Sharpe of Brooklyn, New York. I am a victim of years of drug abuse. I have six children and two grandchildren. I am single, black, and have very little means of finance. In February 1988, I discovered I was HIV positive. At that time, I was still a user. The Bureau of Child Welfare was called by a family member, and my youngest daughter was taken from me. This happened ten months ago. She is now two years old and is HIV positive also. . . . I have been drug-free since November 1988. . . . I joined a women's support group to accept both my daughter's and my own illnesses. This group helped me put things in motion to get funds, medical care, and housing. . . . Without an apartment, the Bureau of Child Welfare wouldn't even think of returning my daughter to me. . . .

Being a PWA and living on a fixed income, I've been forced to experience nontreatment and poor treatment. Seeing a different doctor each appointment who asks the same questions as the one before. Never being asked or told of a drug trial for women or children. I learned of trials in a support group, but it seems as though women and children aren't included. The only medications that are offered are AZT and Bactrim. . . . Why are these the only drugs offered? . . .

I have a home now, but just 10 months ago I was still homeless. Many people who are here today are homeless right now. One thing I can tell you about the NIH—they don't have any homeless people in their trials. And they don't have trials for people who use drugs either.

Source: "Statements of Phyllis Sharpe," in *Ending the Silence: Voices of Homeless People Living with AIDS*. 1990. New York: National Coalition for the Homeless, June, pp. 43–44, 51.

Injection Drug Users

The National Commission on AIDS, formed by the U.S. Congress in 1989, heard testimony in Washington, D.C., on November 2, 1989. One witness was Ralph Hernandez, a New York City veteran and IV drug user. The following is excerpted from his testimony.

My name is Ralph Hernandez. I am a Vietnam vet. I am homeless, and I am living with AIDS. When I went to Nam, the government told me I was putting my life at risk for my country. . . . I became disabled and finally I got AIDS. . . .

I was honorably discharged from the United States Army in 1974 with a service-connected disability. But I had another illness, too. In Nam, I had become addicted to drugs. Even with my handicaps I went to school, I got a job with the 'phone company, and I supported my wife and children. The whole time I was still using drugs.

In 1987, I started getting sores on my skin, and my physical appearance started deteriorating. I left my wife and started shooting up more and more. I felt too weak to go to work. Soon I lost my apartment and then my job. I tried to get into the VA hospital, but they wouldn't see me because I was homeless. They wouldn't even let me into the detox program. They told me to just stop shooting. . . .

I went to the Washington Heights Shelter. When I took my clothes off in the shower, the other homeless people kicked . . . me. Then they called the guards and the guards threw me out. I went to another shelter, but I was afraid to stay there. So I started living in the tunnels under Grand Central Station. Even there I had to hide so no one would see the condition I was in. . . .

The VA had lost all my papers. I had been tested there for AIDS three times, but because I am homeless they have lost my records each time. . . .

For six months I have been in a methadone program and I try not to use drugs any more. But the VA is still not giving me any medical treatment. I still do not have a place to live.

I wish you knew how I feel when I go on the subway and see people move away from me. . . . I served my country in time of crisis. Now that I'm in crisis, where is my country?

I am not the only one who has experienced this. There are thousands of homeless men and women with AIDS struggling to survive. . . . Like me, they have no place to turn to.

Source: "Statement of Ralph Hernandez," in *Ending the Silence: Voices of Homeless People Living with AIDS*. 1990. New York: National Coalition for the Homeless, June, pp. 11–13.

Homeless People with HIV/AIDS

On March 21, 1990, the House Subcommittee on Housing and Community Development held hearings in Washington, D.C., on a bill introduced by Congressman Jim McDermott (D-WA), a physician from Seattle. The bill was designed to provide housing relief for homeless people with AIDS. Irving Porter of New York City testified at that hearing and provided a dramatic statement of the problems facing drug users seeking treatment. Porter explained how he intentionally became homeless to get what little treatment was available.

Approximately twelve years ago, my life began to fall out of control. I found myself addicted to cocaine and alcohol. . . . In 1985, I decided to do something about my drug problems. I knew I needed residential treatment if I was going to kick my addiction, but all the drug treatment slots were full. In October of that year, I learned that a few designated drug treatment slots were available for people who were homeless. I know it sounds crazy, but the only way I knew to get the treatment I needed was to become homeless myself.

So I gave up my job as a bookkeeper and gave up my apartment as well. I then entered the New York City shelter system. Little did I know I was only compounding my problems. I was entering a system that was easy to get into but almost impossible to ever get out of. . . .

All I wanted at this time was to be interviewed and placed in a drug program. The sooner I got the hell out of the shelter, the happier I would be. After a few days, I was sent to Daytop Village . . . one of the oldest drug treatment programs in the country. . . .

While I was in drug treatment, I revealed that I was bisexual. They then tested me for HIV without my knowledge. I was told by the nurse that my immune system was shot, but I was never told that I was HIV positive. . . . After 21 months . . . I decided to leave the program. . . . I wound up in Greenpoint Men's Shelter in Brooklyn, New York. . . .

As time moved on, I started losing weight. I became very weak. I would lose my breath just from walking. I went to Beth Israel Hospital. I was diagnosed as having pneumonia. . . . I signed myself out of that hospital and immediately went to Beekman Hospital, where I was diagnosed as having active tuberculosis. I was advised by the doctor to be tested for AIDS. I was tested, and the results were positive. When I was given the news, I just wanted to DIE. I was put into isolation and treated for TB. . . . Again I found myself living on the streets. . . . I collapsed while standing in line for a meal and was taken to New York Hospital. . . .

The city put me in a "welfare hotel." My hotel room is certainly better than a shelter or the streets, but it is still not the proper living situation for a person with AIDS. I have been in that same room for almost a year. I am still waiting for proper housing. I presently have to share my bathroom with about 20 people. I have to be very careful not to pick up any infections. Also, there are drugs throughout the hotel, so I have to deal with a lot of temptation. . . .

If you take a look at the statistics on homeless people who are now HIV infected, you will see that my experience as a homeless black male has been and will be the NEW TREND OF AIDS. . . . Even now, the city, state, and federal governments would like to pretend that we don't exist.

When I first gave up my home to enter the shelter system, I didn't realize I had gotten on a merry-go-round that I couldn't stop. The people I saw trying to get into drug treatment back then are the same ones I later saw in the shelter system. The ones I saw who finally got drug treatment are the same people I see today in the hospital and in my infectious disease clinic.

When I die, my death certificate will probably say I died of AIDS. But I want the world to know the real cause: a government that saw AIDS and left it unchecked. . . . You think AIDS will stop with us. But HIV doesn't see skin color, and it can't tell a person's sexual orientation. Because you didn't care, AIDS will continue to spread.

Source: "Statement by Irving Porter," in *Ending the Silence: Voices of Homeless People Living with AIDS.* 1990. New York: National Coalition for the Homeless, June, pp. 36–42.

Hemophiliacs

Hemophiliacs were among the first groups of people to be devastated by the HIV/AIDS epidemic. Their plight is often overlooked, as they no longer constitute a statistically large portion of cases, but the impact of the epidemic on their community has been profound.

[The term *innocent victim*] is used a lot in Japan. Five or ten years ago, people in the United States used it a great deal. No, I don't think that we look at ourselves as innocent victims. To me, to say "I got it the good way and my other buddy at ACT UP, he got it the bad way" is ridiculous. No, I can't buy into that. I'm not a victim. True, I got HIV through negligence on a lot of people's part, but if I was a victim I would be under this little rock somewhere saying, "Help me, feel sorry for me." I'm empowered. I'm not a victim. I'm an activist. At one point I probably felt like I was a victim.

Source: Terry Stodgell, AIDS activist and hemophiliac living with HIV disease. Quoted in V. M. Hoskins. "Body Positive Interview." *Body Positive* 10 no. 9. http//:www.thebody.com/bp/Sept97/fam/html.

Testimony of Ryan White before the Presidential Commission on AIDS, March 1988

I came face-to-face with death at 13 years old. I was diagnosed with AIDS—a killer. Doctors told me I'm not contagious. Given six months to live and being the fighter that I am, I set high goals for myself. It was my decision to live a normal life, go to school, be with my friends, and enjoy day-to-day activities. It was not going to be easy.

The school I was going to said they had no guidelines for a person with AIDS. . . . We began a series of court battles for nine months while I was attending classes by telephone. Eventually, I won the right to attend school, but the prejudice was still there. Listening to medical facts was not enough. People wanted 100 percent guarantees. There are no 100 percent guarantees in life, but concessions were made by Mom and me to help ease the fear. We decided to meet everyone halfway. . . . Because of the lack of education on AIDS, discrimination, fear, panic, and lies surrounded me. (1) I became the target of Ryan White jokes. (2) Lies [were told] about me biting people, (3) spitting on vegetables and cookies, [and] (4) urinating on bathroom walls. (5) Some restaurants threw away my dishes. (6) My school locker was vandalized inside, and folders were marked FAG and other obscenities.

I was labeled a troublemaker, my mom an unfit mother, and I was not welcome anywhere. People would get up and leave so they would not have to sit anywhere near me. Even at church, people would not shake my hand.

This brought in the news media, TV crews, interviews, and numerous public appearances. I became known as the AIDS boy. I received thousands of letters of support from all around the world, all because I wanted to go to school. It was difficult, at times, to handle, but I tried to ignore the injustice because I knew the people were wrong. My family and I held no hatred for those people because we realized they were victims of their own ignorance. We had great faith that with patience, under-standing, and education, my family and I could be helpful in changing their minds and attitudes.

Financial hardships were rough on us, even though Mom had a good job at G.M. [General Motors]. The more I was sick, the more work she had to miss. Bills became impossible to pay. My sister, Andrea, was a championship roller skater who had to sacrifice, too. There was no money for her lessons and travel. AIDS can destroy a family if you let it, but luckily for my sister and me, Mom taught us to keep going: Don't give up, be proud of who you are, and never feel sorry for yourself.

Source: Presidential Commission on AIDS, March 1988

The Impact of HIV/AIDS on Other Aspects of Society

HIV/AIDS and the Correctional System

HIV Disease in Correctional Facilities: A Model Response

General Principles

The National Commission on AIDS recommends that policies with respect to HIV disease in prison be guided by the following basic principles:

1. The HIV epidemic in correctional facilities is part of the same epidemic the nation is experiencing outside prison walls. Interventions among prisoners will save lives and will have a significant impact upon the course of the epi-demic in communities to which prisoners will return.
2. Society has a moral and legal obligation to provide pris-oners with the means to prevent HIV infection and to provide adequate medical care to infected prisoners at all stages of HIV disease.
3. Decisions regarding HIV policies should be based on sound medical and public health principles. Interven-

tions employed in the correctional setting should be guided by the same standards of care employed in interventions targeting the general community.

4. Control and prevention of HIV infection must be viewed in the context of the need to improve significantly overall hygiene and health facilities in prisons.

Recommended Guidelines

I. Medical Care

Asymptomatic HIV infection is a serious medical condition requiring regular medical attention and in many cases aggressive treatment.

Medical, nursing, inpatient, and outpatient services for prisoners with HIV disease should, at a minimum, be equal to prevailing standards of care for people with HIV disease in the community at large.

Correctional facilities should immediately address the controllable subsidiary epidemics of sexually transmitted diseases and tuberculosis. Infection control protocols established by the U.S. Public Health Service/Centers for Disease Control should be strictly followed.

Because of the complex and rapidly changing nature of HIV treatment protocols, quality assurance mechanisms should be implemented to review periodically the adequacy and efficacy of prison medical care.

Medical information revealed in the course of treatment should be rigorously protected from disclosure to nontreating personnel.

Treatment of drug addiction should be expanded until all prisoners who request such treatment are able to receive it.

Adequate care includes, but is not limited to:

- Meaningful access to HIV testing
- Regular examinations by physicians with sufficient training to diagnose and treat HIV infection and HIV-related illnesses
- A full physical examination at the time the infection is diagnosed and subsequently as medically indicated
- Access to necessary specialist care where appropriate
- T cell monitoring at the intervals prescribed by the U.S. Public Health Service

- Timely, consistent, and appropriate access to necessary medications, including prophylactic drug therapies approved by the Food and Drug Administration or recommended by federal health authorities
- Access to dental care
- Access to mental health care
- Access to meaningful drug treatment on demand
- Clean, hygienic housing facilities
- Appropriate diets.

II. Identification

Voluntary HIV testing and counseling should be available to all prisoners who request it on a confidential and/or anonymous basis. All HIV tests should be accompanied by individual pre- and post-test counseling conducted by a trained AIDS counselor observing U.S. Public Health Service/Centers for Disease Control guidelines. Test results should never be made available to any prison employee, even a prison medical employee, without the specific, written informed consent of the prisoner.

Mandatory testing or screening should not be employed.

III. Information and Education

HIV education should be a high priority for all correctional facilities. Educational programs should include components targeted at reducing behaviors that place individuals at risk, alleviating fear of HIV infection and people with HIV disease, and informing everyone in the correctional setting of available medical care.

Both inmates and staff need live, interactive HIV education from a credible, properly trained educator at regular intervals. Distribution of written materials and exclusive reliance in video-taped educational presentations are not sufficient. All education should be culturally sensitive and linguistically appropriate.

Education to reduce the risk of HIV infection from intravenous drug use and sexual activity should be explicit and include clear advice about resources available in the prison setting that may be employed to reduce the risk of infection, even where these behaviors occur in violation of prison regulations or applicable law.

Condom distribution should be part of overall health promotion and HIV prevention efforts in all correctional systems.

Because prisoners may discount information provided by prison authorities, outside organizations, including health departments and AIDS service agencies, should be involved in the preparation and presentation of HIV education programs wherever possible. Inmates themselves should be trained and equipped to serve as HIV educators among their peers, with adequate supervision and support from trained HIV educators.

HIV continuing education programs developed specifically for correctional social service and medical staff should be mandatory and regularly updated. Updated HIV education should be regularly provided for staff of departments of probation and parole as well.

Support groups for prisoners living with HIV disease should be promoted and encouraged. Correctional systems should work cooperatively with community-based AIDS service organizations in providing support services and counseling to bridge the gap between institutions and the community and to provide follow-up services as inmates return to the community.

IV. Management

Discrimination and punitive treatment of people living with HIV disease discourage them from seeking education, testing, and treatment, thus compromising efforts to prevent new HIV infections and to treat persons living with HIV disease.

Prisoners should not be isolated or housed in special units solely because of their HIV serostatus.

Prisoners with HIV disease should be permitted to participate in all prison programs and jobs for which they are otherwise qualified, including positions in food or health services, in keeping with U.S. Public Health Service/Centers for Disease Control guidelines.

HIV-related information in the possession of medical providers should be released only under extraordinary circumstances to prison authorities for the benefit of the patient. Staff should be trained to protect the privacy of inmate medical data. Work rules prohibiting release of HIV-related information should be strictly enforced.

Jails and prisons should have written HIV management policies and treatment protocols that reflect the most up-to-date medical and scientific information. These policies should be reviewed frequently.

Universal precautions should be integrated into institutional procedures to limit the health risk to staff and inmates.

V. Release

HIV disease should not be a reason to punish further any prisoner. Release should not be capriciously denied merely because of HIV status.

To maintain continuity of care during the transition from prison to the community, every inmate with HIV disease should be assisted in finding medical care and support services within the community. This should include assisting prisoners to register with community-based case management services prior to release where such services are available and if the prisoner so desires.

Prisons and jails should have workable early-discharge and medical furlough programs providing for the timely release of inmates whose incarceration is no longer medically appropriate.

VI. The Role of Public Health Authorities

Public health authorities must recognize that even though legal and architectural barriers have been erected between institutionalized populations and the community at large, such barriers are often illusory. Individuals move to and from institutions, return to their communities and loved ones, as new waves of entrants await confinement. We must learn that we cannot speak of the health of the nation without also addressing the health of individuals in prisons, jails, and other institutions.

Prisons contain a disproportionate number of people at risk of, or infected with, HIV. Public health agencies should make intervention in this setting a high priority and should work closely with corrections officials to bring successful public health strategies—for example, education, voluntary testing and counseling, health care—to bear in prisons.

Recommendations

In addition to the model guidelines outlined above, the National Commission on AIDS makes the following specific recommendations:

The U.S. Public Health Service should develop guidelines for the prevention and treatment of HIV disease in all federal, state, and local correctional facilities. Immediate steps should be taken to control the subsidiary epidemics of tuberculosis and sexually transmitted diseases. Particular attention should be given to the specific needs of women and youth within all policies.

1. Given the dearth of anecdotal and research information on incarcerated women, incarcerated youth, and children born in custody, federal and state correctional officials should immediately assess and address conditions of confinement, adequacy of health care delivery systems, HIV education programs, and the availability of HIV testing and counseling for these populations.
2. To combat the overwhelming effects which drug addiction, overcrowding, and HIV disease are having on the already severely inadequate health care services of correctional systems nationwide, a program such as the National Health Service Corps should be created to attract health care providers to work in correctional systems.
3. The Department of Health and Human Services should issue a statement clarifying the federal policies on prisoners' access to clinical trials and investigational new drugs. In addition, the Food and Drug Administration, in conjunction with the Health Resources and Services Administration and the National Institutes of Health, should initiate an educational program directed toward informing inmates and health care professionals working in correctional facilities of the availability of investigational new drugs, expanded access programs, and applicable criteria for eligibility of prisoners in prophylactic and therapeutic research protocols.
4. Meaningful drug treatment must be made available on demand inside and outside correctional facilities. Access to family social services and nondirective reproductive counseling should also be made available, with special emphasis on the populations of incarcerated women, youth, and children born in custody.
5. Prison officials should ensure that both inmates and correctional staff have access to comprehensive HIV education and prevention programs. Particular attention should be paid to staff training on confidentiality and educating inmates about the resources available in the

prison setting that may be employed to reduce the risk
of infection.
6. The burden of determining and assuring standards of
care has largely fallen to the courts due, in part, to the
failure of public health authorities to take a leadership
role in assuring appropriate standards of health care and
disease prevention for our incarcerated populations. Bar
associations and entities such as the Federal Judicial
Center must, therefore, establish programs to educate
judges, judicial clerks, and court officers about HIV disease.

Source: *Report of the National Commission on AIDS.* 1991. Washington,
D.C.: National Commission on AIDS, pp. 33–37.

HIV/AIDS and the Workplace

Responding to AIDS: Ten Principles for the Workplace

1. People with AIDS or HIV (Human Immunodeficiency
Virus) infection are entitled to the same rights and opportunities as people with other serious or life-threatening illnesses.
2. Employment policies must, at a minimum, comply
with federal, state, and local laws and regulations.
3. Employment policies should be based on the scientific
and epidemiological evidence that people with AIDS or
HIV infection do not pose a risk of transmission of the
virus to coworkers through ordinary workplace contact.
4. The highest levels of management and union leadership should unequivocally endorse nondiscriminatory
employment policies and educational programs about
AIDS.
5. Employers and unions should communicate their support of these policies to workers in simple, clear, and
unambiguous terms.
6. Employers should provide employees with sensitive,
accurate, and up-to-date education about risk reduction
in their personal lives.
7. Employers have a duty to protect the confidentiality of
employees' medical information.
8. To prevent work disruption and rejection by coworkers

of an employee with AIDS or HIV infection, employers and unions should undertake education for all employees before such an incident occurs and as needed thereafter.

9. Employers should not require HIV screening as part of pre-employment or general workplace physical examinations.

10. In those special occupational settings where there may be a potential risk of exposure to HIV (for example, in health care, where workers may be exposed to blood or blood products), employers should provide specific, ongoing education and training, as well as the necessary equipment, to reinforce appropriate infection control procedures and ensure that they are implemented.

Source: National Leadership Coalition on AIDS

Notes

1. Randy Shilts. 1987. *And the Band Played On: Politics, People, and the AIDS Epidemic.* New York: St. Martin's Press, pp. xxi, xxii.

2. Ibid., p. 147.

3. Ibid., p. 142.

4. Ibid., p. 83.

HIV/AIDS and the Law

6

Significant Legislation since 1982

Following is a chronological summary of federal legislation on HIV/AIDS from 1982 to 1996.

1982   The first federal funds for HIV/AIDS—$5.6 million—are allocated to research.

1984   Community-based organizations receive $150,000 in targeted funds for AIDS work.

1985   The National Institutes of Health (NIH) receives a major increase in AIDS research funding.

1986   Federal spending on AIDS is increased by $47 million to create what will become the AIDS Clinical Trials Groups.

1987   The Helms Amendment, which prohibits federal funding for HIV/

AIDS education that encourages or promotes homosexual activity, passes the U.S. Senate 94 to 2.

Also in 1987, $30 million is appropriated to help poor Americans purchase AZT.

1988   HIV/AIDS prevention and research programs are established with the passage of the Health Omnibus Programs Extension (HOPE) Act.

1989   The Helms Amendment barring persons with HIV from entering the United States is added to an appropriations bill.

1990   The Americans with Disabilities Act is passed. The act becomes effective in stages beginning in January 1992, and the law has an important impact on HIV-infected people. The law prohibits discrimination against persons with disabilities—including persons infected with HIV—in all employment practices, including job application procedures, hiring, firing, advancement, compensation, and training. The act also prohibits discrimination based on a relationship or an association, which protects individuals in situations in which they are threatened because of unfounded assumptions about their relationship to a person with a disability. It also protects a person from action resulting from bias about certain disabilities. For instance, a person's hiring or continued employment cannot be threatened because a spouse's illness may require that the employee take frequent time off. Also, individuals are protected from discrimination resulting from the knowledge that nonwork time is spent being a buddy to a person with AIDS (PWA).

Also in 1990, the Ryan White Comprehensive AIDS Resources Act (CARE, PL 101-381) is passed. This $350 million measure provides the first direct federal grants to 16 cities hit hardest by the HIV/AIDS epidemic. About $200 million of the funds represent level funding for programs that already exist. Previously, federal funds were targeted largely to preventive measures rather than to health care services. Title I of CARE provides direct funding to cities that have more than 2,000 reported cases of AIDS or an incidence higher than 0.0025 per capita. Title I is authorized at $275 million for FY1991 but is funded at $87.8 million. In FY1992, 18 cities are eligible for Title I funds. The 1992 revision of the CDC AIDS definition may also affect funding eligibility. Title II of CARE funds the establishment of statewide care consortia, home-based and community-based care, health insurance coverage continuation, and treatment. It is funded at 32 percent of the authorized level. Title III funds counseling, testing, and early intervention, administered jointly by the CDC and the Health Resources Services Administration (HRSA). Title IV provides for pediatric demonstration projects, the establishment of research priorities, and emergency response employee notification. Title IV is not funded for FY1991.

Also in 1990, $156 million is authorized as part of the AIDS Housing Opportunities Act to improve housing choices for people with HIV.

The 1990 Immigration Reform Act makes the secretary of Health and Human Services responsible for listing illnesses that would exclude immigrants, reversing the Helms Amendment. (In 1991, HIV is kept on the list despite massive protest; as a result; the next international AIDS conference, planned for Boston in 1992, is canceled.)

Source: AIDS Action Council, 1991.

1994   On September 13, 1994, Congress amends the Violence Against Women Act to give district courts the authority to order a criminal defendant charged with "an offense of the type referred to in subsection (a) [violent offenses against women in which there is a possibility of HIV transmission]" of the amendment to be tested for HIV under certain circumstances, with the test results to be disclosed to the victim and, with court permission, a limited number of other persons.

1996   The Health Insurance Portability and Accountability Act (Section 101[g] of the Tax Code) repeals the imposition of income tax on money individuals receive from

1996
cont.

viatical settlements, which also removes state and local tax liability. The federal action goes into effect January 1997. Since many PWAs cash in their life insurance policies for viatical settlements, the repeal has special significance for those living with AIDS.

Legal Aspects of HIV/AIDS

Discrimination

As the HIV/AIDS epidemic has grown, it has strained major U.S. social institutions, including the nation's health care system, schools, prison system, blood supply, and insurance industry. In the process, the pandemic has opened the gate to a flood of litigation focused on discrimination. Because HIV/AIDS infects mostly those who are members of traditionally disenfranchised groups, such as gay men and people of color, discrimination is not a new threat to those HIV sufferers.

According to the National AIDS Strategy (1997):

> Discrimination against people living with HIV or AIDS violates the human rights of individual Americans and undermines our efforts to prevent and treat HIV infection. The extraordinary stigma that has been attached to HIV disease hampers the ability of people living with HIV and AIDS to live full lives free of fear.
>
> Discrimination also undermines efforts to prevent and treat HIV infection and bring the epidemic under control.
>
> The Strategy recognizes two principal laws used to protect HIV positives against discrimination:
>
> - Enactment of the Harkin-Humphrey Amendment to the Civil Rights Restoration Act, clarifying that Section 50 of the Rehabilitation Action of 1973 applied to people with contagious diseases, including HIV; and
> - Enactment of the Americans with Disabilities Act of 1990 (AD), which protects individuals living with HIV and AIDS and people perceived to be at risk for HIV from discrimination in housing, employment, and public access.[1]

Discrimination cases that involve HIV/AIDS have occurred at all levels of the judicial system, as well as in other public agencies. Federal, state, and local courts hear these cases, as do state and local human rights commissions and other administrative agencies.

Criminal Prosecution for HIV Transmission

By 1998, twenty-seven states had criminal statutes regarding HIV transmission.[2] The most recent addition is a Pennsylvania law, PA S 635, which was signed into law on February 18, 1998. The law specifically deals with prisoners and reads:

> For every person who has been sentenced to death or life imprisonment in any penal institution in the state, adds the following to the offenses warranting penalty of murder in the second degree: intentionally or knowingly causing another to come into contact with blood, seminal fluid, saliva, urine, or feces by throwing, tossing, spitting, or expelling such fluid or material when, at the time of the offense, the person knew, had reason to know, should have known, or believed such fluid or material to have been obtained from an individual, including the person charged under this section, infected by a communicable disease, including, but not limited to, human immunodeficiency virus (HIV) or hepatitis B.

(Note that the bill equates spitting and contact with urine with sexual contact, even though it has been proven that the former are not vectors for HIV infection. The ramifications of this issue will be discussed later in this section.)

There is a growing trend toward criminalizing HIV transmission. At any given moment, bills regarding the criminalization of HIV transmission are pending in virtually every state legislature. Most of these bills contain language specifying mandatory names reporting, partner notification, or both. The bills and laws cause anxiety among people living with HIV and their advocates.[3]

The question is whether to approach HIV transmission as a health issue or a legal one. An underlying rationale for such legislation appears to be HIV prevention, but does criminalizing

HIV transmission really curb the spread of the disease? According to Stephen Gendin, president of the Community Prescription Service:

> What I'm afraid of in terms of HIV education is that first we're criminalizing and then we're moralizing and only after that are we educating. Or we're never educating—we don't get to that. And in an environment where people are either being locked up or being told they're evil, it's very hard to teach effective prevention. It's awful to imagine, but there will be more and more talk shows where people who bareback are yelled at onstage by hundreds of people. And that will pass as HIV education.[4]

Meurig Hotron, a PWA and a former member of the World Health Global AIDS Program, adds:

> Safe-sex negotiations are based on an assumption of equality—that each person is responsible for their own protection. The view that transmission is—alone or primarily—the responsibility of the positive person is wrong-headed. It creates a demand for prevention strategies that assume both that the presumed negative has a right to know their partner's status and that the presumed positive has a responsibility to know and a duty to protect. This has been shown, time and again, to be unworkable.[5]

In spite of the debate over individual responsibility in sexual behavior, HIV transmission prosecutions have been a fact in the United States for a number of years. In December 1992, Salvadore Gamberella was sentenced to 10 years in prison for knowingly exposing a woman to HIV. He was convicted under a 1987 Louisiana law that reads: "No person shall intentionally expose another to Acquired Immune Deficiency Syndrome through sexual contact without the knowing and lawful consent of the victim."[6] Six years later, James Wallace Jones was sentenced to 15–22½ years in prison for having sex with women whom he did not inform of his HIV status, although none of the women tested positive.

As these prosecutions continue, wide latitude has been revealed in judicial initiative. Consider the case of Jerrime Day.

According to a January 1998 Associated Press report, a Florida court devised an interesting way to prevent an HIV-positive man from having sex without disclosing his HIV status to prospective partners. Jerrime Day, age 20, had been charged with infecting a sixteen-year-old sex partner with HIV in 1996 without informing the girl of his HIV-positive status. Day could have faced four years in prison had he been convicted, but instead he pleaded no contest to a misdemeanor in a plea-bargain agreement. Orange County Judge Deb Blechman ordered Day to secure a written consent form from anyone with whom he was going to have sexual intercourse; the form had to be signed in front of a witness prior to the sex act as part of Day's probation. Judge Blechman said she wanted to make sure others would not be unknowingly exposed to HIV by Day: "If the consequences were not so severe, none of this would be necessary. Day will not be obligated to continue securing written consent once his 9-month probation ends."

Although any HIV-positive man can be successfully prosecuted for having unprotected sex, he may not be charged with attempted murder if he rapes someone. Recently, the courts have been rejecting attempted murder charges brought against HIV-positive rapists. According to the Associated Press, in July 1996, attempted first degree murder charges were thrown out against Andrew Lee Monk, age 27, a man who knew he was HIV positive and was accused of raping a twelve-year-old girl. The judge's ruling was based on the fact that the prosecution was unable to show that Monk intended to commit murder by having sex with the girl, who had since tested HIV negative. Similar verdicts have been rendered in other rape cases. (See *Smallwood v. State of Maryland* later in this chapter. Also see *People v. Jensen*, 564 N.W. 192 [1997], for a case involving a mentally incapacitated woman who was successfully prosecuted under an HIV transmission law even though the liaison may have been involuntary on her part.)

Other cases involving HIV transmission and attempted transmission have not required that the prosecution prove a genuine threat of HIV exposure. For example, when sentencing Gregory Smith, a seropositive gay black man, on charges of attempted murder for biting a prison guard in 1990, a New Jersey Supreme Court judge openly acknowledged that HIV cannot be transmitted by a bite but stated that he wanted to issue a clear message that "criminal behavior of this nature will be met with swift and severe punishment."[7]

In such cases, the messages the courts send are confusing and questionable because they obfuscate what constitutes public health policy versus jurisprudence. Many successful HIV transmission prosecutions (based on either HIV-specific laws or preexisting laws that pertain to attempted murder, assault, and so on) have involved only spitting and biting. Lawyer Margaret Fine, who worked for an AIDS organization in 1993, stated: "Prosecutors should not be bringing charges for these offenses [spitting and biting] because there is no significant risk of transmission. What is happening is that prosecutors and courts are making an AIDS policy that is sharply contradictory to that of public health policies on AIDS."[8]

Another issue raised by activists that may have a major impact on such prosecutions in the future is that of what will happen if HIV becomes perceived as a chronic yet manageable infection.[9] How can society justify lengthy prison sentences if there is no immediate threat of death from HIV transmission?

Legal Considerations for HIV-Infected Persons

When individuals become aware that they are infected with HIV, they must inform themselves not only about the medical issues affecting them but about legal considerations as well. Since HIV/AIDS is likely to both significantly shorten an infected person's life and result in frequent hospitalizations, infected individuals must address legal issues members of their age group rarely face.

According to Kathleen C. Buckley, an attorney who counsels HIV-infected clients at the Health Education Resource Organization, a Maryland AIDS service organization: "Since many of our clients are aware of the loss of control that often occurs at the end stage of AIDS, it is important that they know that they can exercise some control over decisions regarding health care, medical care, financial concerns, and future planning for their minor children prior to their possible loss of mental capacity to make such decisions."[10] Although Buckley's clients are covered by Maryland law, and legal terminology and minute points of law vary from state to state, the types of legal documents she recommends for her clients apply to all HIV-infected people in the United States: a Living Will, Health Care Power of Attorney, Financial Power of Attorney, Last Will and Testament, Standby Guardianship, and Limited Power of Attorney. She explains these documents as follows:

> The Living Will allows the individual to state his [or her] wish in the event that he [or she] has a terminal

condition (which the State of Maryland defines as death expected usually within 6 months) or is in a persistent vegetative state (the Karen Quinlan situation—irreversible coma). Three choices are available for either condition: do nothing to prolong life, do everything to keep the person alive, or a compromise position—no machine or heroic measures but do provide nutrition artificially. This last choice would usually involve insertion of intravenous lines, Hickman catheter, a nasal tube, or a gastrostomy tube (a feeding tube inserted through the abdominal wall into the stomach).

Because our clients usually fall into a third category not covered by the Living Will, we provide a document—Health Care Power of Attorney—that allows the client to name a trusted party (agent) to speak for him [or her] in the event that he [or she] is incapable of making medical decisions or communicating with his [or her] health care providers. Two doctors would certify to the client's incapacity before this document would confer any authority on the agent. Because many of our clients have frequent hospitalizations due to opportunistic infections and would not necessarily be terminally ill or in a persistent vegetative state (conditions covered under the Living Will), this document is necessary for virtually all of our clients. In addition to designating a trusted person to communicate with medical personnel and institutions, the client names a guardian of his [or her] person should that become necessary. The Health Care Power of Attorney allows the individual to make the same choices as the Living Will for "end-stage" condition: do nothing, do everything, no heroics but provide nutrition. An "end-stage" condition is defined in the state as an advanced, progressive, irreversible condition caused by injury, disease, or illness that has caused severe and permanent deterioration indicated by incompetence and complete physical dependency and for which, to a reasonable degree of medical certainty, treatment of the irreversible condition would be medically ineffective.

The durable Power of Attorney (for financial affairs) is important for our clients in the event that they lose mental capacity because of dementia caused by the virus, and also it could come into play when they are hospitalized for extended periods and are unable to handle their financial affairs for that reason. This document also allows the client to name a guardian of the person.

Clients also need a Last Will and Testament. This document allows the client to name those persons to whom he [or she] wishes to leave his [or her] property following his [or her] death. This can be especially important where the client wishes to bequeath his [or her] property to friends and not family. If there are minor children surviving, the client can also make his [or her] wishes known as to who is his/her choice of guardian for those children. The client also names a Personal Representative (called Executor in many states) to handle the estate. The Personal Representative distributes any bequests to those persons the client names in his [or her] Will. The Personal Representative also handles all the financial affairs of the estate: income taxes, bills, bank accounts, sale of assets, etc.

Planning for the future care of minor children is also a concern for many of our clients. The Standby Guardianship statute allows a custodial parent, who is at risk of becoming incapacitated or dying within two years from a life-threatening or chronic illness, to name a person to step into his/her shoes when the parent is unable to care for the children. As the patient's health warrants, the care of the children can be transferred back and forth between the parent and the standby guardian. The other parent (if living) must consent to the custodial parent's designation of a standby guardian. If consent is withheld, a court may make a determination that it is in the best interest of the child that the custodial parent's designation be affirmed. If the court has approved the designation, then even upon the death of the parent the future care of the children has been arranged.

A limited Power of Attorney can also be used to arrange for someone other than the parent to assume many of the parent's responsibilities. This is a simple one-page document that enables the agent (named by the parent) to act on the child's behalf: enrolling the child in school, taking the child for medical care, applying for entitlement for the child, etc. This document is no longer effective when the parent dies. Therefore, it is important that the standby guardianship be established also.[10]

Selected Cases

The rest of the chapter presents summaries of a few of the legal cases involving HIV/AIDS that are significant because of either the issues addressed or the outcome of the case. An attempt has been made to group the cases according to their relevant issues, but some of the cases clearly involve more than one issue. Many other cases can be found on other aspects of the law. Complex cases can remain in the judicial system for years before a final decision is rendered. The cases included here give an idea of the broad range of topics covered on the subject of HIV/AIDS and the types of complaints heard by human rights agencies and the courts.

Americans with Disabilities Act Cases

Randon Bragdon, Petitioner v. Sidney Abbott, U.S. Supreme Court, No. 97-157 (1998)

On June 25, 1998, the Supreme Court of the United States ruled 5–4 that the 1990 Americans with Disabilities Act applied to asymptomatic HIV-positive individuals in *Randon Bragdon, Petitioner v. Sidney Abbott (et al. on Writ of Certiorari to the United States Court of Appeals for the First Circuit.*) It marked the first time in history that the Supreme Court ruled on an HIV-specific issue.

The judgment was rendered in favor of Sidney Abbott, an HIV-positive woman, on her claim that Randon Bragdon, a dentist, acted in violation of the Americans with Disabilities Act (the ADA), 104 Stat. 327, 42 U.S.C. § 12101 et seq., by refusing to treat her in his dental office. The case stemmed from an incident in September 16, 1994, when Ms. Abbott visited Dr. Bragdon's Bangor, Maine, office for an examination. On her patient registration, she indicated that she was HIV-positive. At the time, she was asymptomatic. Dr. Bragdon examined her and discovered a cavity which he refused to treat in his office, stating that it was his infectious disease policy to treat such matters in a hospital setting.

Ms. Abbott would have to shoulder the additional costs the hospital charged for its use of facilities.

Ms. Abbott sued on the grounds that she was protected against such undue hardship by the Section 302 of ADA , which states: "No individual shall be discriminated against on the basis of disability in the full and equal enjoyment of the goods, services, facilities, privileges, advantages, or accommodations of any place of public accommodation by any person who . . . operates a place of public accommodation."

Lower Courts had consistently ruled that the ADA applied to individuals with full-blown AIDS. However, there was dissent among courts as to whether asymptomatic HIV infection met the criteria of a real or perceived disability.

In the majority opinion, Justice Anthony M. Kennedy wrote:

> In light of the immediacy with which the virus begins to damage the infected person's white blood cells and the severity of the disease, we hold it is an impairment from the moment of infection. As noted earlier, infection with HIV causes immediate abnormalities in a person's blood, and the infected person's white cell count continues to drop throughout the course of the disease, even when the attack is concentrated in the lymph nodes. In light of these facts, HIV infection must be regarded as a physiological disorder with a constant and detrimental effect on the infected person's hemic and lymphatic systems from the moment of infection. HIV infection satisfies the statutory and regulatory definition of a physical impairment during every stage of the disease.

The decision supported the lower court's ruling that Ms. Abbott was disabled because she was substantially limited in a major life activity—the ability to have children. Justice Kennedy's decision explains the rationale used to determine this:

> Our evaluation of the medical evidence leads us to conclude that respondent's infection substantially limited her ability to reproduce in two independent ways. First, a woman infected with HIV who tries to conceive a child imposes on the man a significant risk of becoming infected. The cumulative results of 13 studies collected in a 1994 textbook on AIDS indicates

that 20 percent of male partners of women with HIV became HIV-positive themselves, with a majority of the studies finding a statistically significant risk of infection. . . . Second, an infected woman risks infecting her child during gestation and childbirth, i.e., perinatal transmission. Petitioner concedes that women infected with HIV face about a 25 percent risk of transmitting the virus to their children. . . . Petitioner points to evidence in the record suggesting that antiretroviral therapy can lower the risk of perinatal transmission to about 8 percent. . . . We need not resolve this dispute in order to decide this case, however. It cannot be said as a matter of law that an 8 percent risk of transmitting a dread and fatal disease to one's child does not represent a substantial limitation on reproduction. . . . In the end, the disability definition does not turn on personal choice. When significant limitations result from the impairment, the definition is met even if the difficulties are not insurmountable. For the statistical and other reasons we have cited, of course, the limitations on reproduction may be insurmountable here. Testimony from the respondent that her HIV infection controlled her decision not to have a child is unchallenged.

The decision was hailed by AIDS activists as a major victory. The *Washington Post* quoted Daniel Zingale, Executive Director, AIDS Action, as saying the Court decision was "the most important legal victory for people with HIV in the history of the epidemic."[11] The *Washington Post* article also stated that many felt the decision might encourage more Americans to find out their HIV status because they need not fear discrimination in employment or public accomodation in light of *Bragdon v. Abbott*.

Runnenbaum v. Nationsbank of Maryland, WL 465301 (1997)

The U.S. Court of Appeals for the Fourth Circuit upheld a grant of summary judgment against William Runnenbaum, an HIV-positive gay man, in an employment discrimination suit, finding he was not protected by the Americans with Disabilities Act (ADA) and that he failed to meet his prima facie case. The court was split six to five. The lower court had ruled that even though Runnenbaum met the disability criteria, he was unable to prove that his disability was the cause for his termination from his job. The Circuit Court found that Runnenbaum did not meet the act's criteria for disability, which are "(a) a physical or mental impairment that substantially limits one or more of the major life activities of such individual; (b) a record of such an impairment; or (c) being regarded as having such an impairment." Judge Karen J. Williams found that "under these definitions, asymptomatic HIV infection is simply not an impairment; without symptoms, there are no diminishing effects on the individual." In the dissenting opinion, however, Judge Michael wrote: "I believe the majority means to create a per se rule excluding those with asymptomatic HIV from the protections of the ADA. It essentially admits as much, noting that its definition of disability 'suggests that asymptomatic HIV infection will never qualify' as a disability. [The decision] moves this circuit even further from the mainstream of ADA interpretation. More importantly, it moves us completely away from the interpretation that Congress clearly intended."

Hernandez v. Prudential Insurance Company, WL 619224 (1997)

This U.S. District Court decision found that an asymptomatic HIV-positive man, Steve Hernandez, did qualify as disabled under the Americans with Disabilities Act and therefore could sue his former employer under the act. Prudential had sought summary judgment on the grounds that Hernandez had neither shown he was disabled nor informed the proper supervisors of his HIV status. After learning he was HIV positive, Hernandez had told a supervisor of his status and had requested less stressful assignments and time off for medical appointments. After an unfavorable employee evaluation, he resigned and subsequently sued Prudential for making his work situation unbearable.

The important finding of the court was that Hernandez did meet ADA disability criteria by proving he was HIV positive, a condition that although not a disability per se was a "fatal disease" from which "no one has ever recovered." Therefore, his HIV infection substantially impaired a major life activity, and the court held that the issue of whether the working conditions at Prudential had forced Hernandez to resign could be decided at a trial.

Gonzales v. Garner Food Services, Inc., 89 F.3d 1523, 11th Cir. (August 2, 1996)

The 11th District Court ruled that an HIV-positive former employee could not sue his former employer because a lifetime cap on AIDS-related benefits in his medical policy was modified retroactively under the ADA.

Timothy Bourgeois worked at a Hardee's restaurant until 1991, when the restaurant's parent corporation, Garner Food Services (GFS), discovered he had AIDS and fired him to avoid paying future medical claims. Following his termination, Bourgeois exercised his right under COBRA to continue to subscribe to the company's medical plan, which provided coverage up to a $1 million lifetime limit. At least in part because of Bourgeois's continued participation, GFS (later GFF) amended the plan to impose a $40,000 lifetime cap on AIDS-related claims.

The ADA, which became effective in July 1992, prohibits employers from discriminating against a "qualified individual with a disability [QID]." The ADA defines a QID as "an individual with a disability who, with or without reasonable accommodation, can perform the essential functions of the employment position that such individual holds or desires." Covered disabilities include AIDS.

Before he died in September 1992, Bourgeois exhausted the benefits available under the AIDS cap and was denied $90,000 in excess claims. Bourgeois's representative sued, claiming the denial constituted a continuing violation of the ADA. The 11th Circuit dismissed the case without deciding the continuing violation issue, ruling that "Bourgeois does not satisfy the QID requirement under the plain language of the ADA, because he neither held nor desired to hold a position with GFF at or subsequent to the time the alleged discriminatory conduct was committed. Rather, Bourgeois was a participant in the health benefit plan only by virtue of his status as a former employee."

The dissenting opinion was written by Judge Anderson, who observed that the stated purpose of the ADA is "to provide a clear and comprehensive national mandate for the elimination of discrimination against individuals with disabilities" (42 U.S.C. sec. 12101[b][1]) and that the statute was clearly a remedial one enacted in the context of a long line of court rulings "that remedial statutes are to be construed liberally." Judge Anderson wrote, "It would be counterintuitive, and quite surprising, to suppose (as the majority nevertheless does) that Congress intended to protect current employees' fringe benefits but intended to then abruptly terminate that protection upon retirement or termination, at precisely the time that those benefits are designed to materialize."

Poff v. Caro, 542 A.2d 900, N.J. Super L. (1988)

Three homosexuals filed a complaint with the Department of Human Rights when a landlord would not rent an apartment to them because he feared the potential tenants would be infected with HIV and would infect his family. The court found that persons at risk of HIV infection are part of the protected class under laws protecting the handicapped from discrimination.

Biting

Thomas v. Atascadero Unified School District, 662 F.Supp. 376, C.D. Cal. (1987)

Ryan Thomas was a kindergartner who had received an HIV-infected blood transfusion following his premature birth. After a lengthy administrative procedure, he was admitted to class with other children whose parents had agreed to allow them to be his classmates. Ryan subsequently bit another child and was suspended. The school board voted to bar him from school and give him a tutor. The court ruled that Ryan did not pose a risk to his classmates, as biting was not a scientifically established mode of transmission of the virus that causes AIDS. Ryan was allowed to attend school under CDC guidelines, and the court found he could be disciplined or suspended for other conventional reasons in the future.

Employment and Workplace Issues

Raytheon Company v. Fair Employment and Housing Commission, Estate of Chadbourne, Cal. Sup. Ct., Santa Barbara County, 261 Cal. Rptr. 197, Cal.App.2d Dist. (1989)

The deceased party, Chadbourne, had been a quality control analyst for Raytheon, which agreed he had been a satisfactory employee. Chadbourne worked closely with other employees and shared an office with five people. He developed *Pneumocystis carinii* pneumonia (PCP) and was diagnosed with AIDS. His physician informed Raytheon that Chadbourne would be able to return to work when he had recovered, but the company refused to allow him to return. Chadbourne's estate sued for back pay, but Raytheon argued that it had acted to protect other employees. After a lengthy proceeding, the court found that Chadbourne had incurred a handicap under the law and was otherwise qualified to work, that Raytheon's beliefs about HIV transmission were ill founded, and that the company had discriminated against Chadbourne.

Chalk v. U.S. District Court of California, Orange County Superintendent of Schools, 840 F.2d 701, 9th Cir. (1988)

Chalk was a teacher of hearing-impaired students who was transferred from his classroom to an administrative position when he was diagnosed with HIV. His pay remained the same. Chalk argued that his medical condition allowed him to continue in the classroom and that he was otherwise qualified to work. The court ruled in his favor, finding that a person with a contagious disease can be otherwise qualified to work if, with some reasonable accommodation, the person can perform his or her job without exposing others to risk. To reach that decision, a court must review the nature, duration, and severity of the risk of transmission of the disease, as well as the probability that it would be transmitted and cause harm. Such a review must be based on up-to-date medical judgments and must consider the opinions of public officials. The court found that HIV infection did not constitute a threat to the students and that Chalk would be irreparably harmed psychologically by being taken out of the classroom—a harm that could not be compensated.

T. v. A Financial Services Co., N.Y. Sup. Ct. (1988)

T. worked in the travel department of a large investment banking firm when he was diagnosed with AIDS and Kaposi's sarcoma (KS). T. had missed work because of medical appointments, and a supervisor asked him whether he had AIDS. T. gave a truthful answer. Because of his KS lesions, T. suffered frequent cuts on his face. On one such occasion, he was sent home from work; he was later placed on disability for a month because of a second incident. When he returned to the office, he was told he was allowed to touch only his own computer and telephone and that he would be sent home if further cuts occurred. The court found these procedures constituted unlawful discrimination and that any such restrictions would have to apply to all employees. The court ordered that T. was to report to the company's health station in the event of a cut and required that all company employees take an AIDS education course.

Doe v. Westchester County Medical Center, New York State Department of Health and Human Services (December 9, 1988)

Pharmacist John Doe was hired by the Westchester County Medical Center in 1986 and reported for a preemployment physical. A nurse told the physician that Doe had been a patient at the hospital more than a year earlier and that he was HIV positive. The medical center then refused to give Doe the position. The Office of Civil Rights of the Department of Health and Human Services ruled that the employer's position violated Section 504 of the 1973 Rehabilitation Act. That ruling followed 1991 news reports of and public debate over a Florida incident in which five patients had tested HIV positive after being treated by an infected dentist, which the Westchester County Medical Center had used as its rationale for refusing to hire John Doe more than five years earlier.

Iacono v. Town of Huntington Security Division et al.

Iacono was a security guard at a commuter rail station; he was on sick leave from February to July 1987 and was diagnosed with AIDS in March during the leave. In May, when his physician certified that he was ready to return to work, Iacono told a supervisor that he was able to return and also that he had AIDS. He was advised not to share that information, not to worry about his job, and to see the town doctor before returning to work. Iacono had to wait seven weeks to see the doctor, and he then returned to work. He was reassigned to a work location with no heat or sanitary facilities, his publicly owned vehicle was taken away, he was told to purchase his own gas, and he was given his own radio. In January 1988, Iacono was suspended without pay, and in May of that year he was fired. The state agency found Iacono had been discriminated against on the basis of his handicap.

Paul F. Cronan v. New England Telephone Company, 41 FEP 1273, Mass. Sup. Ct. (1986)

In May 1985, Paul Cronan had worked for the New England Telephone Company for 12 years when he was diagnosed with symptoms related to HIV infection and was placed under a doctor's care. After being asked repeatedly, he told a supervisor the nature of his illness because he feared losing his job. A promise of confidentiality was subsequently broken when his diagnosis was disclosed to management and other employees. After having been advised of a negative reaction by his coworkers, Cronan did not return to work and was placed on indefinite disability. A few months later, he was diagnosed with AIDS. The court found grounds for a claim of invasion of privacy and ruled that Cronan had a handicap under the terms of the law.

As part of the settlement, the telephone company donated $30,000 to AIDS education and prepared an educational brochure for workers. Cronan returned to work in October 1986, and some of his coworkers staged a walkout in protest.

HIV and Health Care Professionals

Estate of Behringer v. Princeton Medical Center, No. L88-2550, N.J. Sup. Ct. (April 25, 1991)

In the wake of publicity surrounding a Florida dentist's possible transmission of HIV to five of his patients, *Behringer* attracted attention because of its departure from the federal government's standard of significant risk in determining a disabled person's employability. A New Jersey judge ruled it was appropriate for an HIV-positive surgeon to be barred from practice at the Princeton Medical Center, which the surgeon had sued after his serostatus had become widely known there. The judge also stated that surgeons were required to disclose any risk factor a patient might want to know prior to an invasive procedure, ignoring the fact that the risk of HIV is not quantifiable in such a situation. The ruling suggested that the routes of HIV transmission are not firmly established, threatened other antidiscrimination rulings, and seemed to suggest that HIV-positive surgeons could be deprived of their livelihood on apparently slim justification.

HIV-Positive Children and Their Rights

Ray v. School District of DeSoto County, 666 F.Supp. 1524, M.D. Fla. (1987)

Three hemophiliac Ray brothers contracted HIV from blood products and were denied access to the public school because of their HIV status. The court ruled that the boys would suffer irreparable harm by being denied a classroom education and that they presented little or no threat to the public; they were already suffering emotionally because of their exclusion. As in the *White* case, the court ordered that the boys be allowed into the school, instructed that CDC guidelines should be carefully followed, and prohibited the boys' participation in sports. The boys and their parents were to be tested for HIV every six months, with the results reported to the court. In addition, the court ordered that the boys had to observe a high standard of hygiene, cover all sores and lesions, and avoid any school incident in which HIV transmission was possible. The court further ordered that the boys were to receive comprehensive sex education and suggested that this instruction be extended to the entire school system. The school board was also ordered to provide HIV/AIDS education for parents.

After the ruling, the boys' parents and the school district reached a settlement that called for the Rays to be paid more than $1 million over a period of several years. Subsequently, some members of the local community formed the Citizens against AIDS in Schools Committee and organized a successful boycott of the Ray brothers' school. The mayor removed his son from the school, the Rays received death threats, and on August 28, 1987, the Ray's home was destroyed by fire (arson).

Bogard v. White, Clinton Cir. Ct., Indiana, No. 86-144; ACLU Amicus Curiae Brief (April 9, 1986); Court's Finding of Fact and Order (April 10, 1986); Findings of Special Education Appeals Board (February 14, 1986)

Ryan White was a hemophiliac who entered seventh grade at Western Middle School in Kokomo, Indiana, in August 1984. In December of that year, he was hospitalized with pneumonia and diagnosed as HIV positive. He was too ill to keep up with his schoolwork and prepared to repeat a grade in fall 1985. The school superintendent refused to allow Ryan to come to school; instead, he was connected to his class by a speaker phone.

Seven months later, a Special Education Appeals Board ordered that Ryan be admitted to school, subject to recent state guidelines on the presence of HIV-infected children in school. Hours after his return, Ryan was ordered out of class when a state court granted other students' parents an injunction staying the decision of the appeals board. The injunction was subsequently dissolved, and Ryan returned to school. His case had attracted national publicity and the interest of celebrities and activists. After the final court decision, when the Whites faced continued hostility from people in Kokomo, prominent supporters helped them move to Cicero, Indiana.

HIV Status and the Right to a Fair Trial

Wiggins v. Maryland,
315 Md. 232, 554 A.2d 356 (1989)

Wiggins was tried and convicted of murder; he was thought to be HIV positive because of the number of participants in his trial who were drug users, homosexuals, or both. Because of his suspected serostatus, during his trial court personnel wore rubber gloves, bound him, and remained a certain distance from him. Wiggins argued on appeal that those measures had deprived him of a fair trial. The Maryland Court of Appeals agreed and granted him a new trial.

Housing

Baxter v. City of Belleville, Illinois,
720 F.Supp. 720, S.D. Ill. (1989)

Baxter used the 1988 Fair Housing Act amendments to protect people with disabilities, including HIV-infected people. The Belleville city administration had stopped Charles Baxter from opening a nonprofit residence for PWAs in need of housing. The American Civil Liberties Union argued that this act violated federal law. The court found that the discrimination was based almost solely on misapprehensions about HIV transmission, ruled that the city could not prevent Baxter from obtaining the special permit needed for the residence, and agreed to allow the house to be opened.

Parental Rights

CSCYF/DFS v. Bryant, WL 436439 (1996)

Delaware Family Court Judge Chapman denied a petition by the Division of Family Services (DFS) to terminate the parental rights of an HIV-positive mother regarding her HIV-positive son. Joyce Bryant had given birth to her son Ra'Shien in 1991 while serving a sentence for first-degree robbery and second-degree kidnapping. Over the next five years, Bryant had numerous problems meeting the terms of her probation and had experienced a drug problem, depression, and multiple suicide attempts. The DFS had placed Ra'Shien in two foster homes in which the foster parents wanted to adopt him, but Bryant refused to give up her parental rights even though her contact with Ra'Shien was limited to supervised visits. The court found the DFS had not met the necessary burden of proof to terminate Bryant's parental rights and that some of the charges against her were no longer relevant. The decision suggests that the serostatus of both mother and child does not constitute justification to terminate parental rights.

Rape and Attempted Murder

Smallwood v. State of Maryland, WL 42878 (1996)

Timothy Smallwood was diagnosed HIV positive in 1991, while incarcerated, and he told prison officials he would practice safe sex. In 1993, he and a friend robbed a woman at gunpoint; Smallwood then sexually assaulted the woman, inflicting "slight penetration" without a condom. In a bench trial, he was convicted of armed robbery and rape, and, because of his HIV status, received concurrent sentences for attempted murder, assault with intent to murder, and reckless endangerment.

Although he lost his appeal in a lower court, the Maryland Court of Appeals—the highest in Maryland—reversed the attempted murder, assault with intent to murder, and reckless endangerment convictions. The court ruled that by itself, a rapist's knowledge of his HIV-positive status is insufficient to sustain an attempted murder conviction.

Sentencing and the Impact of Seropositive Status

Montanez-Anaya v. U.S., WL 351634, 1st Cir. Ct. (1997), and U.S. v. Smith, WL 346045, 4 Cir. Ct. (1997)

Although the dispositions in these cases were unpublished at the time of this writing, the courts' decisions are consistent with other findings involving sentencing guidelines for HIV-positive defendants. Both federal appeals courts found that under federal sentencing guidelines, defendants with HIV/AIDS are not normally entitled to downward departures (or shorter periods of incarceration) because of their diagnoses, emphasizing that such a departure would be appropriate only in cases in which a defendant's health was so completely compromised by AIDS that he or she could not possibly represent any danger to society.

Sexual Acts by HIV-Positive Individuals Who Do Not Divulge Their Status

People v. Jensen, 564 N.W. 192 (1997)

The Michigan Court of Appeals affirmed the conviction of a legally incapacitated woman, Brenda Jensen, under a statute criminalizing sex acts by HIV-positive individuals who do not inform their partners of their serostatus, and it upheld her 32-month prison sentence. Jensen, who lived in a group home, had informed her legal guardian that she had engaged in unprotected sex. The guardian immediately contacted the police, who arrested Jensen.

The appeal was based on three issues: that testimony that might have cleared Jensen was denied at the original trial; that the charges were based on results of Jensen's blood test, which should not have been admitted as evidence; and that the sentence was unduly harsh. Both the lower court and the appeals court rejected the admissibility of a statement by Jensen's roommate, who said Jensen had told her she feared the man with whom she had engaged in sex would kill her and that he would not leave the room until they had sex. The court ruled that Jensen's blood test was inadmissible but that substantial evidence revealed that Jensen knew her HIV status. Further, the court found that her sentence was fair.

Social Security Appeals

[Author's comment: HIV-positive individuals—and many others who face grave conditions such as cancer—frequently go through a maze of applications, interviews, and hearings to secure adequate social services. Disabled individuals often wait months for a social security determination and must then appeal if benefits are denied. The following case is far too typical.]

Pratts v. Chatter, WL 455685 (1996)

In May 1996, the U.S. Court of Appeals for the 2nd District reversed a district court decision that found that the Social Security Administration had erred in determining whether Edwind F. Pratts, who was HIV positive, qualified for social security disability. Pratt, who had tested positive in 1988 and was taking

AZT, began to experience a host of medical problems, including weight loss, dizziness, headaches, diarrhea, rashes, anemia, and positional vertigo. The Social Security Administration found he did not meet the criteria for disability because he might still be able to perform light work.

The appeals court ruled that the lower court had made its decision based on an incomplete record, because much of the expert testimony had been eliminated from the record by a clerical error. Additionally, the judge's decision clearly contradicted entries in Pratts's medical records and misplaced the burden of proof, which should have been with the Social Security Administration, to prove Pratts could indeed perform light work.

Testing and Confidentiality

James v. State of Florida, WL 330537 (1997)

The District Court of Appeals for the 4th District struck down an order that Lakisha James be tested for HIV at the request of a person he had attacked. James had stabbed the victim in the neck, but there was no allegation that James had bled on the victim. The court ruled that a victim's right to demand the test could be applied only in cases that involved "transmission of body fluids from one person to another." No exchange of body fluids had taken place in this case, so the victim could not require that the defendant be tested for HIV.

United States of America v. David James Ward, Appell C03.273 (1997), U.S. Ct. of App. for the 3rd Circuit, Nos. 96-5789, 97-5082 (November 13, 1997)

This case explored the issue of whether someone suspected of sexual assault can be ordered to take an HIV test. Ward had pleaded guilty to kidnapping and repeatedly sexually assaulting a woman in New Jersey over a three-day period in December 1995. Ward had a prior history of similar crimes and was sentenced to sixty years in prison. He appealed his conviction on two grounds: that his Fourth Amendment protection against unreasonable search and seizure had been violated by the requirement that he be tested for HIV and that his prior conviction should not have been a factor in upgrading his sentence. The appeals court ruled against the second claim but remanded the issue of search and seizure back to the lower court.

The lower court had ruled that the court had "inherent authority" to order such a test based on its commitment to shield the criminal justice system from "abuses and injustice" and to "protect witnesses." The appeals court ruled that inherent authority could not be held as precedent when appropriate statutory law could be applied. It cited the 1994 Violence against Women Act, in which the U.S. Congress gave the district courts the authority to order that a criminal defendant charged with sex crimes in which there was a risk of HIV transmission be subjected to a confidential HIV test in which the results would be made available only to the alleged victim, her health care providers, and, if the court so ordered, the defendant himself. The appeals court remanded the case back to the lower court to make a decision based on fair application of the relevant law within twenty days.

ACT UP Triangle v. Commission for Health Services, 472 S.E.2d 605 (July 16, 1996)

In this case, the North Carolina Court of Appeals denied an ACT UP challenge of the State Health Department's implementation of confidential testing rather than anonymous testing for HIV. In April 1994, the North Carolina chapter of ACT UP had filed a petition to change a regulation proposed by the state's Commission for Health Services to eliminate anonymous HIV testing by local health departments by September 1994. ACT UP sought to extend the anonymous testing policy indefinitely and to repeal the provision. The commission rejected ACT UP's proposal later in April.

In June, ACT UP won an injunction in Wake County Superior Court, which reversed the commission's decision on the grounds that the provision on confidential testing was temporary and would expire in June 1995 unless replaced by a permanent rule. The commission repealed the temporary regulation in February 1995, thereby eliminating anonymous testing at local health departments. The commission stated further that ACT UP's petition was denied, and ACT UP went back to court to amend its original complaint to include this latest action by the commission. The court granted ACT UP's petition but denied the relief sought, finding in favor of the commission.

The Court of Appeals ruled that the Superior Court had no jurisdiction to review the commission's rule-making authority because North Carolina law does not provide for judicial review of such authority. Furthermore, the Court of Appeals found the court had erred in allowing the amended complaint, thereby effectively putting the matter to rest.

Doe v. Lockwood, WL 367046 (June 27, 1996)

Federal and state claims pertaining to the public disclosure of a man's HIV status were dismissed by the U.S. Court of Appeals for the 6th Circuit. The man and his fiancée had tested HIV positive in 1993. The test counselor notified the local Health Department that John Doe intended to "infect unknowing female sexual partners." In September of that year, John Doe began serving a six-month prison term for receiving stolen property. To obtain medical leave so his HIV-related health condition could be treated outside of prison, Doe was forced to divulge his HIV status in open court.

In December 1993, the local paper published a series of articles describing the local deputy health commissioner's concern about his inability to divulge John Doe's name because of the law. When a woman who had engaged in relations with John Doe became the subject of a domestic dispute that resulted in a police report, however, the newspaper published his name—which had been mentioned in the report—in a headline that read "AIDS Carrier Identified." John Doe and his fiancée filed suit, arguing that their procedural and substantive due process rights had been violated. The court ruled against them, stating that the plaintiffs had failed to prove that John Doe's HIV status was not a matter of public record. The court argued that although Doe had been forced to divulge his HIV status to receive proper medical treatment, he could have requested that his medical records be sealed and be kept confidential, which he did not.

Notes

1. White House. 1997. *The National AIDS Strategy*, p. 23. Washington, D.C.: The White House.

2. Catherine Hanssens. 1998. "From Unsafe to Illegal: Who's Responsible for New Infections? Criminalization Says It's the PWA. Prevention Says Both Partners. Right Now, Criminalization Is Winning." *Poz*, May: 62.

3. Ibid.

4. Ibid., p. 73.

5. Ibid., p. 63.

6. Eric Lerner. 1993. "HIV Criminal Prosecutions Becoming More Com-

mon." *Baltimore Alternative*, January.

7. Ibid.

8. Ibid.

9. Hanssens, "From Unsafe to Illegal," pp. 60–63, 72–73.

10. Kathleen C. Buckley, December 5, 1997, private communication.

11. Joan Biskupic and Amy Goldstein. 1998. "HIV Law Covers HIV, Justices Rule." *Washington Post*, June 26, A17.

Government Agencies, Organizations, and Hot Lines

7

Federal Agencies

The following is a list of addresses and telephone numbers for the many U.S. government organizations that offer information on a variety of AIDS-related topics.

Centers for Disease Control and Prevention (CDC)
1600 Clifton Road, NE, 26 Executive Park
Atlanta, GA 30333
Tel: (404) 639-3311; AIDS Clinical Trials Information Service: (800) TRIALS-A; CDC National AIDS Hot Line: (800) 342-AIDS; CDC Spanish AIDS Hot Line: (800) 342-SIDA; CDC Business and Labor Resource Service: (800) 458-5231; Deaf Access/TDD: 1-800-243-7012

The goals of the Centers for Disease Control (CDC) include preventing HIV infection, reducing associated mortality and morbidity, and tracking statistics associated with the HIV/AIDS epidemic. The CDC sponsors the National AIDS Information Clearinghouse, described in the next section, and oversees the CDC National AIDS Hot Line, which provides information and referrals; the Business Responds to AIDS Program, which pro-

235

vides a workplace education program and referrals for businesses; the AIDS Clinical Trials Information Service, which provides information on federally and privately funded clinical trials; the HIV/AIDS Treatment Information Service, which provides information on federally approved HIV/AIDS treatments and guidelines for their correct use to health care professionals and patients; and the HIV Prevention Marketing Initiative, a large-scale program designed to minimize behaviors that contribute to the spread of HIV/AIDS.

Department of Health and Human Services (DHHS)
Office of the Secretary
200 Independence Avenue, NW, Room 615-F
Washington, DC 20201
Tel: (202) 245-6296

Publications: *Guidelines for the Use of Antiretroviral Agents in HIV-Infected Adults and Adolescents; Guidelines for the Use of Antiretroviral Agents in Pediatric HIV Infection; Report of the NIH Panel to Define Principles of Therapy of HIV Infection.*

Food and Drug Administration (FDA)
and **FDA Center for Drug Research**
5600 Fishers Lane
Rockville, MD 20857
Tel: (301) 443-2410

The Food and Drug Administration (FDA) is the government body that approves all medications and food additives for use by the public.

Health Resources and Services Administration (HRSA)
HRSA HIV/AIDS Bureau
5600 Fishers Lane
Parklawn Building, Room 7-46
Rockville, MD 20857
Tel: (301) 443-4588

The Health Resources and Services Administration (HRSA) administers the Ryan White CARE Act, which entails providing support services for people living with AIDS, education and training of HIV/AIDS health professionals, support for case management, assistance in purchasing medications, outreach education, counseling, testing, hospice care, and other services for low-income and medically underserved populations.

National Institutes of Health (NIH)
National Institutes of Allergy and
Infectious Diseases (NIAID)
Building 31, Room 7A-50
Bethesda, MD 20892
Tel: (301) 496-5157 (main information number); AIDS Clinical Trials: (800) 243-7644 M–F 12–3 P.M. EST

The National Institutes of Health (NIH) and the National Institutes of Allergies and Infectious Diseases (NIAID) conduct AIDS clinical trials at the NIH and provide the public with information about HIV/AIDS, affected populations, vaccine research, and the clinical trials.

Publications: *AIDS Clinical Trials Information Service; Clinical Trials for AIDS Therapies; Evidence HIV Causes AIDS; HIV/AIDS Vaccines and HIV Infection and AIDS*; and many other well-researched and lucid fact sheets on AIDS and specific populations.

Also under the NIH:
The **National Library of Medicine (NLM)** provides numerous AIDS informational resources, including three major on-line AIDS databases (AIDSLINE, AIDSDRUGS, and, AIDSTRIALS), all of which are part of the NLM's MEDLINE database. To obtain a free information packet, call 1-800-638-8480 or write: Office of Communications, Building 31, Room 7A-32, Bethesda, MD 20892.

Substance Abuse and Mental Health
Services Administration (SAMHSA)
SAMHSA Office on AIDS
5600 Fishers Lane, Room 12C-10
Rockville, MD 20857
Tel: (301) 443-5305

The Substance Abuse and Mental Health Services Administration (SAMHSA) is concerned primarily with improving the quality and availability of substance abuse prevention programs through early intervention, treatment, and rehabilitation services. SAMHSA also provides national leadership on AIDS policy and services.

U.S. Conference of Mayors (USCM)
USCM HIV/AIDS Program
1620 I Street, NW, 4th floor
Washington, DC 20006
Tel: (202) 293-7330

The U.S. Conference of Mayors (USCM) provides grants for HIV prevention activities, offers technical assistance to local organizations and health departments, and explores the impact of HIV at the municipal level.

National Nonprofit Organizations

Many excellent organizations nationwide provide HIV/AIDS-related services that range from counseling to lobbying. The criterion for inclusion in the following list is that the organization provides its service on a national level. Hence, even though the Gay Men's Health Crisis, for example, has established a national presence through its advocacy and its newsletter, its clientele lives in the New York metropolitan area and is not included here. Therefore, the organization is not included here, although its contact information is included in the section on local organizations and in the compilation of references.

AIDS Action Council
1875 Connecticut Avenue, NW
Washington, DC 20009
Tel: (202) 986-1300 (ext. 47); Fax: (202) 986-1345

The AIDS Action Council is a lobbying organization that represents other AIDS service organizations and provides information on federal legislation and policy.

Publications: *Fact Sheets/Question and Answer Sheets: Americans with Disabilities Act; Needle Exchange Programs (Questions and Answers); Why the Ryan White CARE Act Public Health Program Must Continue after Health Care Reform.* Many brochures are free to members; samples sent upon request. Free conference report of a working group convened by AIDS Action. Several booklets are also available; please contact the agency for a complete list.

AIDS Research Information Center (ARIC)
20 South Ellwood Avenue, Suite 2
Baltimore, MD 21224-2241
Tel/Fax: (410) 342-ARIC (2742)

The AIDS Research Information Center (ARIC) provides information on HIV/AIDS medications in layperson's language to anyone who is HIV positive or who is caring for someone who is. ARIC's motto is "Patient Empowerment through Information."

This small organization, which grew out of ACT UP Baltimore's Treatment and Data Committee, has achieved national stature through its Internet presence and its comprehensive *AIDS Medical Glossary.*

AIDS Treatment Data Network
611 Broadway, Suite 613
New York, NY 10012
Tel: (212) 260-8868; (800) 734-7104; Fax: (212) 260-8869

The AIDS Treatment Data Network is a national clearinghouse for accurate, accessible information on AIDS and HIV issues, including medical and social issues.

Publications: *Treatment Review* (newsletter); *Simple Facts Information Sheets,* which provide information on AIDS-related drugs and opportunistic infections written in clear English; *AIDS/HIV Experimental Treatment Directory,* a directory of trials in New York, New Jersey, Connecticut, Philadelphia, and Washington, D.C. These and other materials are also available in Spanish.

American Civil Liberties Union (ACLU)
ACLU AIDS Project
125 Broad Street, 18th floor
New York, NY 10004

The ACLU AIDS Project undertakes impact litigation and monitors legislation on issues that affect the legal rights of HIV-positive people on the state and national levels.

Publications: William B. Rubenstein et al., *The Rights of People Who Are HIV Positive: The Authoritative ACLU Guide to the Rights of People Living with HIV Disease and AIDS.*

American Foundation for AIDS Research (AmFAR)
733 Third Avenue, 12th floor
New York, NY 10017
Tel: (212) 682-7440 or (800) 764-9346; Fax: 682 9812

As the largest private-sector organization in the United States involved in AIDS research and education, the American Foundation for AIDS Research (AmFar) funds biomedical research on AIDS, conducts education programs, and supports innovative projects on HIV/AIDS.

Publications: *AIDS/HIV Treatment Directory,* which describes currently available treatments for AIDS and the trials in which they are being used (updated quarterly); TxLINK, a searchable data-base version of the *AIDS/HIV Treatment Directory* available on IBM-compatible diskette; *AIDS Clinical Trial Handbook,* which answers questions about participation in clinical trials in nontechnical language (available in English and Spanish); *AIDS Targeted Information* (ATIN), a publication sponsored by AmFar that is published monthly and provides abstracts of and critical commentary on the latest scientific and medical literature, highlights significant scientific reports, and is a fairly comprehensive digest of AIDS publications. For additional publications, please contact the agency.

American Red Cross
1750 K Street, NW, Suite 700
Washington, DC 20006
Tel: (202) 973-6025
American Red Cross's AIDS Education Office
1730 D Street, NW
Washington, DC 20006
Tel: (202) 737-8300

The American Red Cross, known for administering blood centers across the United States, provides a certification program on HIV instruction in both English and Spanish, as well as extensive support materials.

Publications: Numerous print and nonprint HIV educational publications are available in English. *Reasons to Care: The Many Faces of HIV* (video) uses a documentary style to show people living with HIV infection. The *Basic HIV/AIDS Program* informational brochure describes course components and resource materials for this modular program. The *American Red Cross Basic HIV Facts Book* provides basic information about HIV and AIDS in a question-and-answer format suitable for laypersons and health professionals; topics include HIV transmission and prevention, testing, the U.S. blood supply, the social impact of HIV infection, first aid, CPR, aquatics, and children with HIV. Contact your local Red Cross office for pricing information.

In addition to providing basic HIV/AIDS educational materials in English, the Red Cross also offers *The American Red Cross Hispanic HIV/AIDS Program,* which offers a wealth of materials in Spanish that were produced in concert with Hispanic organizations and written in Spanish by Spanish speakers. Program support materials include *Mi Hermano*—an award-winning, 31-minute video that shows a Hispanic family dealing with the AIDS-related death of its eldest son—as well as posters, illustrated pamphlets, a comic book, a newsletter, and other publications. Contact the Red Cross for complete information.

American Social Health Association (ASHA)
P.O. Box 13827
Research Triangle Park, NC 27709
Tel: (800) 227-8922

The American Social Health Association (ASHA) operates the CDC National AIDS Hot Line, as well as its Sexually Transmitted Diseases and National Herpes Hot Lines. ASHA provides both printed materials and referrals and offers *Classroom Calls* to be used in classrooms to enhance discussions of HIV/AIDS.

Carl Vogel Foundation
2025 I Street NW, Suite 917
Washington, DC 20006
Tel: (202) 289-4898

The Carl Vogel Foundation is one of the nation's oldest and most respected buyer's clubs. For anyone living with HIV who wants to investigate, try, or purchase underground therapies, this is an excellent place to start. The foundation also provides nutritional counseling and services; treatment information; complementary therapies, including acupuncture, massage, and Chinese herbal formulas; an on-site resource library; educational workshops; and town meetings with researchers and physicians.

Publications: *HIV Update* (newsletter).

Community Research Initiative on AIDS (CRIA)
275 7th Avenue, 20th floor
New York, NY 10001-6708
Tel: (212) 924-3934; Fax: (212) 924-3936

Founded in 1991, the Community Research Initiative on AIDS (CRIA) is a community-based nonprofit organization whose stated mission is to conduct rapid and cost-effective research, with the highest scientific standards, on promising AIDS treatments in time to help those who are already infected. CRIA conducts its own clinical trials of promising medications; contact the organization for a list of current trials.

Publications: *CRIA Update* (newsletter).

Human Rights Campaign Fund
1012 14th Street, NW, Suite 607
Washington, DC 20005
Tel: (202) 628-4160; Fax: (202) 347-5323

The Human Rights Campaign Fund is a lobbying organization that specifically targets concerns of the gay and lesbian community—including AIDS issues—such as discrimination and funding for HIV treatment.

Mothers' Voices
165 West 46th Street, Suite 701
New York, NY 10036
(212) 730-27777

Mothers' Voices is a national organization with chapters across the United States that was founded by mothers who have lost an HIV-positive child. The group provides education and advocacy on HIV/AIDS issues.

NAMES Project Foundation
310 Townsend Street, Suite 310
San Francisco, CA 94107
(415) 882-5500

The Names Project memorializes thousands of people who have died of AIDS through its Memorial Quilt. Started in San Francisco by Cleve Jones in 1987, the foundation has numerous chapters throughout the United States.
Publications: *Common Threads* (video).

National AIDS Information Clearinghouse
P.O. Box 6003
Rockville, MD 20849-6003
Tel: 800-458-5231; in Maryland: (301) 763-5111 (9 A.M.–7 P.M. EST M–F); TTD/Deaf Access: (800) 243-7012; International: (301) 217-0023

The National AIDS Information Clearinghouse is a resource for U.S. government documents on HIV/AIDS issues.

Publications: Publications include *The White House National AIDS Strategy Report, 1997* (#D422); *Implementation of Advisory Council Recommendations* (#D925); *HIV and AIDS Trends, The Changing Landscape of the Epidemic: A Closer Look* (#D028); and the *Surgeon General's Report to the American Public on HIV Infection and AIDS,*

1993 (#D323), among others. Contact the clearinghouse for a complete list of publications. The University of California at San Francisco's Center for AIDS Prevention Studies has developed HIV Prevention Fact Sheets that summarize specific topics important for AIDS prevention that are available in English and Spanish; to order print copies, call the clearinghouse at 1-800-458-5231. For information on all publications, call the clearinghouse or use the Internet order form.

National AIDS Treatment Advocacy Project (NATAP)
580 Broadway, Suite 402
New York, NY 10012
(212) 219-0106; (888) 26-NATAP

The National AIDS Treatment Advocacy Program (NATAP) provides comprehensive, up-to-date information about AIDS treatments.

Publications: *NATAP Reports* (newsletter); *NATAP's New Protease Inhibitor User's Guide.*

National Alliance of State and Territorial AIDS Directors
444 North Capitol Street, NW, Suite 339
Washington, DC 20001
(202) 434-8090

The National Alliance of State and Territorial AIDS Directors administers HIV/AIDS health care, prevention, and support programs funded by the states and the federal government and counsels federal policymakers on AIDS issues with the goal of creating a comprehensive national AIDS agenda.

Publications: *State AIDS Drug Assistance Programs: A National Status Report on Access.*

National Association of People with AIDS (NAPWA)
1413 K Street, NW, 7th floor
Washington, DC 20005
Tel: (202) 898-0414; Fax: (202) 898-0435; NAPWA-Link computer BBS: (703) 998-3144 (8-N-1)

The National Association of People with AIDS (NAPWA) is the first national organization founded and directed primarily by people living with HIV disease. NAPWA, founded in 1983, serves as a national clearinghouse of information and technical assistance for HIV-positive individuals and AIDS service organizations. Its focus is on information, training, and advocacy. NAPWA also operates a speaker's bureau.

National Council of Churches/AIDS Task Force
475 Riverside Drive, Room 572
New York, NY 10115
Tel: (212) 870-2421

The National Council of Churches is an organization of churches that addresses AIDS issues from a Christian perspective.

National Council of LaRaza AIDS Center
1111 19th Street, NW, Suite 1000
Washington, DC 20036
Tel: (202) 785-1670

The National Council of LaRaza AIDS Center provides technical assistance and training to Hispanic organizations to help reduce the spread of HIV/AIDS in that community.

National Gay and Lesbian Task Force
and Policy Institute (NGLTF)
2320 17th Street, NW
Washington, DC 20009-2702
Tel: (202) 332-6483

The National Gay and Lesbian Task Force and Policy Institute (NGLTF) works with a variety of governmental and nongovernmental organizations to lobby and educate people on issues of concern to the gay and lesbian community, including the rights of HIV/AIDS patients.

National Hemophilia Foundation (NHF)
116 West 32nd Street, 11th floor
New York, NY 10001
Tel: (212) 328-3700

The National Hemophilia Foundation (NHF) is a national advocacy organization and information resource for people living with hemophilia. The NHF has an on-site information library on AIDS-related issues that emphasizes the needs of hemophiliacs living with AIDS.

Publications: *Living with HIV for Children; Living with HIV for Adolescents; Living with HIV for Adults; HIV Treatment Information.*

National Minority AIDS Council (NMAC)
1931 13th Street, NW
Washington, DC 20009
Tel: (202) 483-6622

The National Minority AIDS Council (NMAC) is a membership organization that sponsors regional conferences that focus on financial planning and fundraising, technical assistance, volunteer training, and community outreach for AIDS service organizations that have minority clientele.

National Native American AIDS Prevention Center (NNAAPC)
3515 Grand Avenue, Suite 100
Oakland, CA 94610
Tel: (510) 444-2051

The National Native American AIDS Prevention Center (NNAAPC) provides outreach, training, technical assistance, a national hot line, and information on HIV/AIDS for Native American communities.

Publications: *Seasons* (quarterly newsletter); *HIV Prevention for Gay/Bisexual/Two-Spirit Native American Men: A Report of the National Leadership Development Workgroup for Gay/Bisexual/Two-Spirit Native American Men.*

National Women's Health Network
514 10th Street, NW, Suite 400
Washington, DC 20004
Tel: (202) 347-1140

The National Women's Health Network is an advocacy group for women with HIV/AIDS.

Publications: *Living with HIV and AIDS; Basic Facts on HIV and AIDS.*

Parents and Friends of Lesbians and Gays (PFLAG)
P.O. Box 27605
Washington, DC 20038-4605
Tel: (202) 638-4200

Publications: *Family AIDS Support Notebook* provides basic information for families of people with HIV/AIDS.

Pharmaceutical Research and Manufacturer's Association
1100 Fifteenth Street, NW
Washington, DC 20005
Tel: (202) 835-3400

The Pharmaceutical Research and Manufacturer's Association is a professional organization of the pharmaceutical industry that is also an outstanding source of information on drugs in development to fight AIDS/HIV.

Publications: *AIDS Medicines in Development*, free annual report on new AIDS drugs and vaccines in development.

Project Inform (PI) and
Treatment Action Network
1965 Market Street, Suite 220
San Francisco, CA 94103
PI Tel: (415) 558-9051; AIDS/HIV Information Hot Line: (800) 822-7422; Treatment Action Network Tel: (415) 558-8669; (415) 626-7231; Fax: (415) 558-0684

Project Inform (PI) is one of the first and most comprehensive information resources on HIV/AIDS. PI provides extensive fact sheets and current medical information on many aspects of HIV/AIDS medications. Treatment Action Network is PI's treatment activist arm.

Publications: *PI Perspectives* (newsletter).

Test Positive Aware Network
1258 West Belmont Avenue
Chicago, IL 60657-3292
Tel: (773) 404-8726; Fax: (773) 404-1040

Test Positive Aware Network is a nonprofit organization that provides information and support to all those concerned about HIV/AIDS-related issues.

Publications: *Positively Aware* (newsletter).

Treatment Action Group
200 East 10th Street, Suite 601
New York, NY 10003
Tel: (212) 260-0300; Fax: (212) 260-8561

Treatment Action Group, a nonprofit organization, grew out of ACT UP New York. The agency provides information and advocacy on treatments for AIDS/HIV.

Publications: *TAGline* (newsletter in English and Spanish).

Visual AIDS
526 West 26th Street, Room 510
New York, NY 10001
Tel: (212) 627-9855

Visual AIDS is a volunteer organization that seeks to increase AIDS awareness through image and video and by sponsoring programs and events, such as the Ribbon Project, Day without Art, Electric Blanket, and the Archive Project for artists with HIV/AIDS. The organization provides various support services for artists living with AIDS.

Women Organized to Respond to
Life-Threatening Diseases (WORLD)
P.O. Box 11535
Oakland, CA 94611
Tel: (510) 658-6930

Women Organized to Respond to Life-Threatening Diseases (WORLD) is an information resource and advocacy organization for HIV-positive women.

Publications: *WORLD/MUNDO* (newsletter).

PWA Organizations in Canada and the United States by Province and State

The following is a list of organizations for people living with HIV/AIDS from *AIDS Treatment News*, (800) TREAT-1-2 or (415) 255-0588. The list includes activist and support organizations. To learn about local ACT UP affiliates, call the ACT UP Network, (215) 731-1844. To learn about other PWA organizations, call the National Association of People with AIDS (NAPWA), (202) 898-0414.

There are over 10,000 AIDS organizations in the United States alone; only a few can be included in this specialized list. To learn about services and organizations in your area, call the National AIDS Hot Line, (800) 342-AIDS, 24 hours a day; for the same information in Spanish, call (800) 344-SIDA, 8 A.M.–2 A.M. EST, 7 days a week.

Canada

British Columbia: *Vancouver*—Pacific AIDS Resource Center (604) 681-2122; *Victoria*—PWA Society (604) 383-7494
Nova Scotia: *Halifax*—PWA Coalition Nova Scotia (902) 429-7922
Ontario: *Ottawa*—Canadian AIDS Society (613) 230-3580; *Toronto*—AIDS Action Now! (416) 928-2206; Community AIDS Treatment Information Exchange (800) 263-1638 (Canada and northern United States) or (416) 944-1916; Toronto PWA Foundation (416) 506-1400
Quebec: *Montreal*—CPAVIH (514) 282-6673

United States

Alabama: *Birmingham*—Alabama Task Force on AIDS (205) 781-6448

Arizona: *Phoenix*—Arizona Human Rights Fund (602) 530-1660; Being Alive (602) 955-4673; Body Positive (602) 955-4673; *Tucson*—PACT for Life (602) 770-1710

California: *Long Beach*—Being Alive Long Beach (310) 434-9022; *Los Angeles*—ACT UP Los Angeles (213) 669-7301; APLA Grassroots Hot Line (213) 993-1680; Being Alive (213) 667-3262; Mothers' Voices (310) 397-5812; Woman Alive (213) 965-1564; *Oakland*—ACT UP East Bay (510) 568-1680; Women Organized to Respond to Life-Threatening Diseases (510) 658-6930; *Orange County*—Being Alive Orange County (714) 362-5483; *Redondo Beach*—Being Alive South Bay (310) 792-0377; *San Diego*—Being Alive San Diego (619) 291-1400; *San Francisco*—ACT UP Golden Gate (415) 252-9200; AIDS Vaccine Advocacy Coalition (415) 248-1330; Bay Area Young Positives (415) 487-1616; Black Coalition on AIDS (415) 346-2364; Project Inform (800) 822-7422; (Project Inform Treatment Action Network (415) 558-8669); Women's AIDS Network (415) 621-4160; *Santa Barbara*—ACT UP Santa Barbara (805) 569-3299; *West Hollywood*—Being Alive (310) 358-2281

Colorado: *Denver*—PWA Coalition Colorado (303) 329-9379

District of Columbia: *Washington*—ACT UP Washington (202) 547-6780; AIDS Cure Party (202) 547-6780; HIV Community Coalition of Metropolitan Washington, D.C. (800) 558-AIDS or

(202) 543-6777; National Association of People with AIDS (202) 898-0414

Florida: *Clearwater*—AIDS Community Project of Tampa Bay (813) 449-2437; *Fort Lauderdale*—ACT UP Fort Lauderdale (954) 764-7670; PWA Coalition Broward (954) 565-9119; *Jacksonville*—PWA Coalition (904) 387-2992; *Miami*—Body Positive (305) 576-1111; Mothers' Voices (305) 371-4608; PWA Coalition (305) 573-6010; Palm Beach—PWA Coalition (407) 655-3322

Georgia: *Atlanta*—ACT UP Atlanta (404) 874-6782; AIDS Survival Project (404) 874-7926; Mothers' Voices (800) 342-6705; Women's Information Service and Exchange (800) 326-3861 or (404) 817-3441; *Macon*—Rainbow Center (800) 374-2437

Hawaii: *Honolulu*—Life Foundation (808) 521-2437; PWA Coalition Hawaii (808) 942-7922; *Kapaa, Kauai*—Malama Pono, the HIV Service Agency of Kauai (808) 822-0878

Illinois: *Champaign*—Gay Community AIDS Project (217) 351-2437; *Chicago*—Chicago Women's AIDS Project (773) 271-2242; Mothers' Voices (800) 342-6705; Test Positive Aware Network (312) 404-8726; *Peoria*—Friends of PWAs (309) 671-2144

Indiana: *Bloomington*—Project FIND (812) 337-2221; *Indianapolis*—ICAAN (317) 920-3190

Iowa: *Davenport*—AIDS Project Quad Cities (319) 328-5464; *Waterloo*—Cedar AIDS Support System (319) 292-2437

Kentucky: *Lexington*—AIDS Volunteers (606) 278-6274; *Louisville*—KIPWAC (800) 676-5490

Louisiana: *New Orleans*—PWA Coalition (504) 524-3488

Maryland: *Baltimore*—AIDS Action Baltimore (410) 837-2437; PWA/HIV Coalition (410) 625-1677

Massachusetts: *Boston*—ACT UP Boston (617) 492-2887; Committee of Ten Thousand (800) 488-2688; Living Center (617) 236-1012; Multi-Cultural AIDS Coalition (617) 442-1622; Search for a Cure (617) 536-2474; *Mashpee*—Upper Cape PWA Coalition (508) 540-0116; *Provincetown*—ACT UP Provincetown (508) 487-3049; Provincetown Positive (508) 487-3998

Michigan: *Detroit*—Friends Alliance (313) 831-4400; *Grand Rapids*—AIDS Resource Center (616) 459-9177

Minnesota: *Minneapolis*—Aliveness Project (612) 822-7946; WOMAN (612) 373-2461

Missouri: *St. Louis*—ACT UP Treatment Issues Group (314) 918-0820

New Jersey: *Audubon*—AIDS Coalition of Southern New Jersey (609) 573-7900; *New Brunswick*—New Jersey Women and AIDS Network (908) 846-4462

New Mexico: *Santa Fe*—Northern New Mexico PWA Coalition (505) 820-2540

New York: *Albany*—ACT UP Albany (518) 861-6337; *Long Island*—PWA Coalition (516) 225-5700; *New York City*—ACT UP New York (212) 642-5499; AIDS Treatment and Data Network (800) 734-7104 or (212) 260-8868; Housing Works (212) 966-0466; Lesbian AIDS Project (212) 337-3532; Mothers' Voices (800) 342-6705; National AIDS Treatment Advocacy Project (212) 219-0106; New York AIDS Coalition (212) 629-3075; PWA Coalition of New York (800) 828-3280 or (212) 647-1415; Stand Up Harlem (212) 926-4541; Treatment Action Group (212) 260-0300; Treatment and Data Committee of New York (212) 929-4952

North Carolina: *Research Triangle Park*—ACT UP Triangle (919) 990-1197

Ohio: *Cleveland*—ACT UP Cleveland (216) 556-0438; *Columbus*—Ohio AIDS Coalition (614) 444-1683

Oklahoma: *Bethany*—Other Options (800) 448-2497 or (405) 495-2732

Oregon: *Milwaukee*—CCARE (503) 653-8738; *Portland*—Advocacy Council of Oregon and Southwest Washington (503) 284-6807

Pennsylvania: *Philadelphia*—ACT UP Philadelphia (215) 731-1844; AIDS Law Project of Pennsylvania (215) 587-9377; Critical Path AIDS Project (215) 545-2212; Project TEACH (215) 985-4448;

We the People (215) 545-6868; Women with Immune System Disorders Organizing and Meeting (215) 732-6560; *Pittsburgh*—Cry Out!/ACT UP (412) 683-9741

South Dakota: *Sioux Falls*—ACT UP South Dakota (605) 332-3966

Tennessee: *Memphis*—Friends for Life HIV Resources (901) 272-0855; *Nashville*—Nashville Cares HEART Line (800) 845-4266

Texas: *Austin*—AIDS Services of Austin (512) 451-2273; Texas AIDS Network (512) 447-8887; *Galveston*—AIDS Coalition of Coastal Texas (409) 763-2437; *Houston*—PWA Coalition (713) 522-5428

Utah: *Salt Lake City*—PWA Coalition Utah (801) 484-2205

Vermont: *Brattleboro*—Vermont PWA Coalition (802) 229-5754

Washington: *Seattle*—Health Information Network (206) 784-5655; People of Color against AIDS Network (206) 322-7061; Seattle Treatment Education Project (206) 329-4857

West Virginia: *Morgantown*—Mountain State AIDS Network (304) 292-9000

Wisconsin: *Madison*—AIDS Network (608) 252-6540

Wyoming: *Casper*—Wyoming AIDS Project (307) 237-7833

State AIDS Hot Lines

[Note: All numbers are subject to change.] These hot lines are usually staffed with someone knowledgeable about HIV/AIDS who can provide referrals to various AIDS services in the city or state. Every state has a hot line, and nearly all have statewide toll-free numbers; a few also have numbers accessible for the hearing impaired. The majority of the hot lines are run by state health departments, although a few are privately operated. Typically, they are open Monday through Friday from 9 A.M. to 5 P.M.; some are also open evenings and Saturdays.

Alabama: (800) 228-0469

Alaska: (800) 478-AIDS; Nationwide: (907) 276-4880

Arizona: (800) 342-2437

Arkansas: (800) 364-AIDS

California: Northern California: (800) 367-2437; Nationwide: (415) 863-2437; TTY/TDD: (415) 864-6606. Southern California: (800) 922-2437; Spanish: (800) 400-SIDA; TTY/TDD: (800) 553-2437; Los Angeles: (213) 876-2437

Colorado: (800) 252-AIDS; Denver only: (303) 782-5186; TTY/TDD: (303) 691-7719

Connecticut: (800) 203-1234

Delaware: (800) 422-0429

District of Columbia: (202) 332-AIDS; TTY/TDD: (202) 797-3575; within metro D.C. and Virginia: (800) 322-7432

Florida: (800) 352-AIDS; Haitian Creole: (800) 243-7101; Spanish: (800) 545-SIDA

Georgia: (800) 551-2728; Nationwide: (404) 876-9944; Atlanta: (404) 876-9944; TTY/TDD: (404) 876-9950

Hawaii: (808) 321-1555; Nationwide: (808) 922-1313

Idaho: (800) 342-AIDS

Illinois: (800) 243-AIDS; TTY/TDD: (800) 782-0423

Indiana: (800) 848-AIDS; TTY/TDD: (800) 972-1846

Iowa: (800) 445-AIDS

Kansas: (800) 232-0040

Kentucky: (800) 840-2865

Louisiana: (800) 992-4379

Maine: (800) 851-AIDS

Maryland: (800) 638-6252; Baltimore: (410) 945-AIDS; metro D.C. and Virginia: (800) 322-7432; Hispanic AIDS Hot Line: (301) 949-0945; Baltimore only TTY area: (410) 333-2437

Massachusetts: (800) 235-2331; Nationwide: (617) 536-7733; TTY/TDD: (617) 437-1672

Michigan: (800) 872-AIDS; Spanish: (800) 826-SIDA; TTY/TDD: (800) 332-0849; Teens: (800) 750-TEEN; Health Care Workers: (800) 522-0399

Minnesota: (800) 248-AIDS; Nationwide: (612) 870-0700

Mississippi: (800) 826-2961

Missouri: (800) 533-AIDS

Montana: (800) 233-6668; Eastern Montana: (800) 675-2437; Western Montana: (800) 663-9002

Nebraska: (800) 782-AIDS

Nevada: (800) 842-AIDS

New Hampshire: (800) 752-AIDS

New Jersey: (800) 624-2377; TTY/TDD: (201) 926-8008

New Mexico: (800) 545-AIDS

New York: New York: (718) 638-2074; New York (counseling): (800) 872-2777 (M–F 2 P.M.–8 P.M., Sat/Sun 10 A.M.–6 P.M.); Taped Information, 24 hrs.: (800) 541-2437 (counselors: M–F 8 A.M.–8 P.M., Sat/Sun 10 A.M.–6 P.M.); Treatment Information: (800) 633-7444; Spanish: (800) 233-7432; GMHC AIDS Hot Line: (212) 807-6655 (M–F 10 A.M.–9 P.M., Sat 12–3 P.M.); GMHC TDD: (212) 645-7470; People with AIDS Coalition: (212) 647-1420 (staffed by HIV-positive people); Mothers of PWAs (outside New York): (800) 828-3280 (M, W+F 2–6 P.M.); Long Island People with AIDS: (516) 225-5700; Long Island AIDS Hot Line: (516) 385-AIDS (M–F 9 A.M.–9 P.M., tape after hours); Albany: (800) 233-SIDA

North Carolina: (800) 342-AIDS

North Dakota: (800) 472-2180; Nationwide: (701) 224-2376

Ohio: (800) 332-AIDS; TTY/TDD: (800) 332-3889

Oklahoma: (800) 535-AIDS; TTY/TDD: (800) 535-AIDS

Oregon: (503) 223-AIDS; Area Codes 503, 206, and 208: (800) 777-2437

Pennsylvania: (800) 662-6080; Critical Path AIDS Project: (215) 545-2212

Puerto Rico: (800) 981-5721; Linea de Infor SIDA y Enfermedades de Transmision Sexual Nationwide: (809) 765-1010

Rhode Island: (800) 726-3010

South Carolina: (800) 322-AIDS

South Dakota: (800) 592-1861

Tennessee: (800) 525-AIDS

Texas: (800) 299-AIDS; TTY/TDD: (800) 252-8012

Utah: (800) 366-AIDS; Nationwide: (800) 487-2100

Vermont: (800) 882-AIDS

Virgin Islands: (809) 773-AIDS

Virginia: (800) 533-4148; Hispanic: (800) 322-7432; Spanish: (800) 322-SIDA

Washington: (800) 272-AIDS

West Virginia: (800) 642-8244

Wisconsin: (414) 273-AIDS

Wyoming: (800) 327-3577

Patient Assistance Programs

The following is a list of contacts with patient assistance programs designed by various pharmaceutical companies to provide patients and their health care providers with correct information about prescription drug use and to provide access to medications to patients who cannot afford them or who need access to an experimental medication not yet approved by the FDA.

Abbott: (800) 659-9050 for ritonavir (Norvir); (800) 688-9118 for clarithromycin (Biaxin) (providers only)

Adria: (800) 795-9759 for rifabutin (Mycobutin)

Agouron: (800) 621-7111 for nelfinavir (Viracept); also (619) 622-3009

Alza: (800) 321-3130 for testosterone patch (Testoderm)

Amgen: (800) 272-9376 for filgrastim (G-CSF/Neupogen) and erythropoietin (Epogen)

Astra: (800) 388-4148 for foscarnet (Foscavir)

Bio-Pharm: (800) 787-8268 (AmBiosome)

Bio-Technology General: (800) 741-2698 for oxandrolone (Oxandrin)

Bristol-Myers Squibb: (800) 272-4878 for stavudine (d4T/Zerit), didanosine (ddI/Videx), megestrol acetate (Megace)

Celgene: (800) 801-8328 (thalidomide—for wasting)

Chiron Vision: (800) 843-1137 for ganciclovir implants (Vitrasert)

CIBA: [merged with Sandoz to form Novartis] (800) 257-3273 for clofazimine (Lamprene)

Eli Lilly: (317) 276-2950 for vancomycin (Vancocin)

Fujisawa: (800) 888-7704 (ext. 8604, 8607) for aerosolized pentamidine (Nebupent)

Gilead: (800) 445-3235 (Cidofovir gel for herpes)

Glaxo Wellcome: (800) 501-4672 (Abacavir—for dementia); (800) 722-9294 (ext 54418) for acyclovir (Zovirax), atovaquone (Mepron), AZT (zidovudine/Retrovir), pyrimethamine (Daraprim), TMP/SMX (Septra), lamivudine (3TC/Epivir), abacavir (1592U89), 141W94 (VX-478)

Hoffmann-La Roche: (800) 282-7780 for saquinavir (Invirase);

(800) 285-4484 for zalcitibine (ddC/HIVID); (800) 526-6367 for TMP/SMX (Bactrim); (800) 443-6676 for interferon-alpha (Rolferon)

Immune Response Corp.: (800) 684-8624 for HIV-1 Immunogen (REMUNE); occasional open label access. Also (760) 431-7080

Immunex: (800) 334-6273 for sargramostim (GM-CSF/Leukine)

Janssen: (800) 544-2987 for itraconazole (Sporanox) and keto-conazole (Nizoral)

Lederle: (800) 533-2273 for ethambutol (Myambutol)

Merck: (800) 850-3430 for indinavir (Crixivan)

Miles: (800) 468-0894 (ext 5170) for ciprofloxacin (Cipro)

Ortho Biotech: (800) 553-3851 for erythropoeitin (Procrit)

Parexel International Corp: (800) 595-5494 (Viramune or Nivara-pine for children only)

Parke-Davis: (800) 223-0432 for paromomycin (Humatin)

Pfizer: (800) 646-4455 for fluconazole (Diflucan); (800) 742-3029 for azithromycin (Zithromax); (800) 221-3033 for more informa-tion; also (606) 255-7442; (212) 573-3954

Pharmacia/Upjohn: (800) 711-0807 for delavirdine (Rescriptor) Roche Molecular Diagnostic Systems: (800) 526-6367 for informa-tion on Amplicor viral load tests

Roxane Labs: (800) 274-8651 for dronabinol (Marinol) and vari-ous narcotics

Sandoz [merged with Ciba to form Novartis]: (800) 447-6376 for octreotide (Sandostatin)

Schering-Plough: (800) 521-7157 for interferon alpha (Intron-A)

Sequus: (800) 375-1658 for liposomal doxorubicin (Doxil)

Smith Kline Beechame: (800) 877-7074 (ext 6454) for Albendazole for microsporidiosis

Syntex: (800) 444-4200 for ganciclovir (Cytovene IV); (800) 596-4630 for oral ganciclovir (Cytovene oral)

UniMed Pharmaceuticals: (800) 864-6330 (ext 3032) for NTZ-cryptosporidiosis

Univax: (800) 789-2099 for IV gamma-globulin immunoglobulin gamma (IVIG/WinRho)

U.S. Bioscience: (800) 887-2467 for trimetrexate (Neutrexin)

Vertex: (617) 577-6000 for VX-478 (new protease inhibitor) [Note: this drug is under development with Glaxo Wellcome and Kissei; we are expecting expanded access or p.a. program shortly.]

Vestar: (800) 247-3303 for liposomal daunorubicin (Daunoxome)

Reference Materials

8

I n the years since 1981, much has been written about the scientific and medical aspects and history of the HIV/AIDS epidemic, as well about the social, political, and economic impact of the epidemic on the United States. Primary sources for many books and bibliographies have been the wealth of national and international scientific, medical, and public health professional journals that have reported major developments on the subject, along with newsletters of U.S. service and advocacy organizations. Yet, the nature of HIV/AIDS is such that developments of all kinds occur regularly, outdating even the most recent publications. Further, many of the frequently used primary sources are not readily available to the general reader or are overwhelming in their number or content.

The following selected bibliography has been assembled with these considerations in mind. The topic areas cover a wide variety of subject matter, and the entries have been chosen with an interest in the quality and accuracy of the information conveyed, as well as a concern for the accessibility of the resources and their ability to serve as paths to other sources of current information. The resources will help readers interested in either general or specific knowledge about HIV/AIDS. In addition, many of the organizations listed in Chapter 7 make available publications that are not listed here.

Print Materials

Reference Books

Anderson, Gary, ed. *Courage to Care: Responding to the Crisis of Children with AIDS.* Washington, D.C.: Child Welfare League of America, 1990. 416p. ISBN 0-87868-401-8.

The Public Health Service estimated that the number of CDC-defined AIDS cases would reach 270,000 by the end of 1991; of those, 3,000 would be pediatric cases. This volume of more than two dozen essays from practitioners, social workers, and others involved in the lives and care of children with HIV/AIDS is published by one of the foremost child welfare organizations in the United States.

Andrulis, Dennis P. *Crisis at the Front Line: The Effect of AIDS on Public Hospitals.* New York: Priority Press Publications, 1989. 93p. ISBN 0-87078-266-5.

Andrulis argues that the HIV/AIDS crisis has not brought on a crisis in the health care delivery system but instead has exposed major flaws in the existing system.

Bartlett, John G., M.D. *Medical Management of HIV Infection.* Baltimore: Johns Hopkins University School of Medicine, 1997. 296p. ISBN 0-924402809-0.

Bartlett is one of the leading HIV treatment specialists in the United States. This book represents the state of the art in primary HIV care and is an essential reference for both medical professionals and HIV patients.

Bell, Stacey J., and R. Armour Forse. *Positive Nutrition for HIV Infection and AIDS.* Minneapolis: Chronimed, 1996. ISBN 616-9792-B.

Proper nutrition is a vital consideration for people living with HIV, who have unique dietary requirements. Written as a self-help manual, this book seeks to educate and empower people with AIDS (PWAs) and their caregivers to adopt proper nutrition to enhance the well-being of PWAs.

Berer, Marge, and Sundana Ray. *Women and AIDS.* London: Pandora Press, 1993. ISBN 0-04-440-876-5.

This international resource book is designed to help HIV-positive women confront the many issues they face, including those that involve reproductive health, sexual relationships, and the unique health consequences of HIV infection in women. Particularly valuable are the many different perspectives presented, which represent the international impact HIV has had on women.

Clum, Nathan. *Take Control: Living with HIV and AIDS.* Los Angeles: AIDS Project Los Angeles, 1996. ISBN 362-1969-C.

This book represents an easy-to-follow guide of how to live with HIV and remain healthy.

Crockett, Paul Hampton. *HIV Law: A Survival Guide to the Legal System for People Living with HIV.* New York: Three Rivers Press, 1997. ISBN 344-7304-C.

This useful source of legal information covers practical issues for a person living with HIV, such as how to maneuver through the Social Security System and how to address issues that involve health and life insurance. The book gives solid advice on living wills, wills, and estate planning. Appendixes feature a glossary and a source guide.

Ferri, Janice, and Jill Schwendeman. *There Is Hope: Learning to Live with HIV.* 3d ed. Mount Prospect, Ill.: HIV Coalition, 1997. ISBN 362-1969-T.

This book is designed to help those recently diagnosed with HIV to deal with their condition in a focused and practical manner. The book's reader-friendly tone helps encourage patients to monitor their lifestyle and health with the goal of becoming long-term survivors. Appendixes feature listings of resources by region, health care monitoring worksheets, and other valuable information.

Foundation Center. *AIDS Funding.* Washington, D.C.: Foundation Center, 1991. 175p. ISBN 0-87954-243-8.

This guide to giving by foundations and charitable organizations contains profiles of donors and the grants they have given for

HIV/AIDS-related issues, including research, education, services, and other areas.

Frumkin, Lyn R., and John Mi Leonard. *Questions and Answers on AIDS.* 3d ed. Oradell, N.J.: Medical Economics Books, 1997. ISBN 616-9792-F.

This easy-to-read book features 144 questions about HIV and AIDS, covering issues such as transmission, treatment, and public policy. It includes an appendix of Internet sites, a bibliography, and a list of support organizations.

Goudsmit, Jaap. *Viral Sex: The Nature of AIDS.* New York: Oxford University Press, 1997. ISBN 614-5993-G.

This book invokes a provocative discussion of the way HIV may have evolved through a history of the attempt by science to understand the virus. Much of the research focuses on the theory that the disease may have evolved from a simian virus that became manifested in humans as they invaded the monkeys' native African rainforests.

Hardy, Lee. *ARIC's Encyclopedic AIDS Medical Glossary.* 2d ed. Baltimore: AIDS Research Information Center, 1997.

This comprehensive glossary from a leading Internet AIDS medical information provider features over 3,000 definitions of HIV-related medical terms. In addition, extensive appendixes cover everything from the latest advances in vaccine development to drug guides and the doctor-patient relationship. The book is an excellent resource for both HIV patients and the professionals who provide services for those patients.

Houts, Peter S., ed. *American College of Physicians Home Care Guide for HIV and AIDS.* Philadelphia: American College of Physicians, 1998. ISBN 362-1969-H.

This straightforward guide, geared to the layperson, is designed to help caregivers care for PWAs at home. Issues discussed include the medical, social, and psychological needs of the patient. The book follows a step-by-step format.

Janeway, Charles A. Jr., and Paul Travers. *Immuno Biology: The Immune System in Health and Disease.* London and New York: Current Biology and Garland Publishing, 1994. ISBN 0-8153-1691-7.

This textbook is an excellent basic introduction to the immune system and its complexities. The book is intended for undergraduate medical students but is accessible to college-educated readers with little science background. The clear color graphics help to make the topics presented understandable.

Johnson, Earvin "Magic." *What You Can Do to Avoid AIDS.* New York: Time Books, 1992. 192p. ISBN 0-8129-2063-5.

This book, written by a former National Basketball Association star who announced he had HIV in late 1991, is aimed at adolescents. The book contains factual information on HIV/AIDS and explicit advice on safer sexual practices; it is also available on cassette.

Kinsella, James. *Covering the Plague: AIDS and the American Media.* New Brunswick, N.J.: Rutgers University Press, 1990. 299p. ISBN 0-8135-1481-9.

For many observers, the HIV/AIDS epidemic has taken shape in the public's mind largely through the media coverage it has received. With each characterization of HIV as the disease of a particular group, it has taken longer for the public to recognize the urgent need for education and prevention. This book analyzes the media's role in the epidemic.

Mandell, Gerald L., and Donna Mildivan, eds. *Atlas of Infectious Disease.* Volume 1: *AIDS.* Philadelphia: Current Medicine, 1997. ISBN 0-443-07946-3.

This is a visual reference book on AIDS and its associated opportunistic infections, with extensive full-color graphics and photographs. The book is targeted toward medical professionals as a diagnostic tool. Many technical terms are used, but the exposition is clear and well illustrated. The layperson should be forewarned that many of the photographs of opportunistic infections, particularly skin infections and sexually transmitted diseases (STDs), are very explicit.

McMillan, Lisa, Jill Jarvie, and Janet Brauer. *Positive Cooking: Cooking for People Living with HIV.* Garden City Park, N.Y.: Avery, 1997. ISBN 616-9792-M.

This book features 200 recipes designed to meet the basic nutritional needs of people living with HIV. Reference information is given on vitamin and mineral supplements, caloric intake, weight maintenance, and safe food preparation. Symptom-specific weekly meal plans are included designed to address issues critical to those living with HIV, such as weight gain, fatigue, and nausea.

Nussbaum, Bruce. *Good Intentions: How Big Business and the Medical Establishment Are Corrupting the Fight against AIDS.* New York: Atlantic Monthly Press, 1990. 352p. ISBN 0-87113-385-7.

The interaction between pharmaceutical manufacturers, such as AZT's Burroughs Wellcome, and the medical/scientific research establishment has been a source of controversy, especially because Burroughs has charged tens of thousands of dollars annually to PWAs taking AZT. This book examines how big business and medical establishment interact.

Petrow, Steven, ed. *The HIV Drug Book.* New York: Pocket Books, 1997. 688p. ISBN: 0-6171-53518-8.

This book, developed by Project Inform, is a comprehensive illustrated guide to virtually every HIV/AIDS-specific treatment in existence. Written in clear language, the book is an essential resource for both medical professionals and patients.

Powell, Josh. *AIDS and HIV-Related Diseases: An Educational Guide for Professionals and the Public.* New York: Insight Books, 1996. ISBN: 616-9792-P.

This book describes HIV and its methods of transmission and explores the history and progression of the disease, testing issues, treatment options, demographics, and AIDS education.

Rotello, Gabriel. *Sexual Ecology: AIDS and the Destiny of Gay Men.* New York: Dutton, 1997. ISBN 362-1969-R.

Rotello argues in favor of monogamy as a means of containing the spread of AIDS in the gay community and as a survival and assimilation strategy. The book analyzes why gays have been particularly stricken by HIV/AIDS.

Rubenstein, William, Ruth Eisenberg, and Lawrence Gostin. *The Rights of People Who Are HIV Positive.* Carbondale: Southern Illinois University Press, 1996. ISBN 344-7304-R.

This handbook, developed by the ACLU, focuses on the basic

legal rights of HIV-positive individuals. The book is structured in a simple question-answer format, which makes it readily accessible to both laypersons and professionals.

Shilts, Randy. *And the Band Played On: Politics, People, and the AIDS Epidemic.* New York: St. Martin's Press, 1987. 653p. ISBN 0-312-00994-1.

Widely viewed as the definitive documentary study of how AIDS developed into a major health and social issue in the United States, Shilts's carefully crafted and very readable book tells his version of the beginning of the infection from its pre-1980 identification as a gay disease to the mid-1980s, when it became a political and social issue as well as a health problem. Shilts brings to life the players, politics, and suffering of the early years.

Newsletters and Pamphlets

Many AIDS treatment information newsletters are in print in the United States, and this list is only a sample. The newsletters included here have been chosen for two basic reasons: First, the information they provide is medically accurate, and second, subscriptions are either very inexpensive or free to people with HIV/AIDS.

AIDS treatment newsletters represent an important resource for HIV-positive persons, one too few PWAs use. This is unfortunate, because the newsletters are perhaps the best source of up-to-date, accurate information on AIDS treatments currently available.

Through such newsletters, HIV-positive persons can obtain life-saving information of which even their doctors may not be fully aware. HIV-positive individuals who remain informed enough to know when and if they are getting proper, effective medical care generally live the longest and enjoy the greatest quality of life, which makes AIDS treatment newsletters a vital defense strategy for those with HIV. The vast majority of these newsletters are free to persons with HIV/AIDS, so there is no barrier to receiving them. Treatment advocates urge all people living with HIV infection, regardless of their state of health or medical condition, to read these and other newsletters devoted to treatment issues.

Many of these newsletters are also available through various World Wide Web archive sites. Two good sources of AIDS newsletters are the excellent AEGIS Website and the Critical Path AIDS Project, both of which keep their large collections fairly current.

This list was originally written by Lee Hardy of the AIDS Research Information Center and has been updated many times since it first appeared in the *Baltimore Alternative* in October 1991.

AIDS/HIV Treatment Directory
American Foundation for AIDS Research (AmFAR)
733 Third Avenue, 12th floor
New York, NY 10017-3204
(212) 682-7440 (ext 106)

This quarterly publication contains good basic information on treatments for HIV and opportunistic infections, lists of compassionate use programs, and an extensive glossary and list of publications. Subscriptions $44/year; free to PWAs from the National AIDS Information Clearinghouse at (800) 458-5231.

AIDS Medicines in Development
Pharmaceutical Research and Manufacturers Association
1100 15th Street, NW
Washington, DC 20005
Tel: (202) 835-3400; Fax: (202) 785-4834

This publication is not exactly a newsletter but instead is an industry overview of drugs and therapies for HIV infection and a source of basic statistics and other information on AIDS drugs in current development. The resource is concise but not always complete; it seems to move more toward cheerleading and include less real news each year. Free to everyone. Published annually.

AIDS Treatment News
ATN Publications
P.O. Box 411256
San Francisco, CA 94141
Tel: (800) 873-2812 or (415) 255-0588; Fax: (415) 255-4659; E-mail: aidsnews@igc.apc.org

This newsletter is a solid source of AIDS treatment and policy information. A year's subscription is $100 for individuals or $60 for six months; institutional rates are $230/year, with nonprofit group rates of $115/year. Special discounted prices of $45/year or $24 for six months are available for people with financial difficulties; however, as with many of these newsletters, no one is denied a subscription because of a lack of ability to pay. Published every two weeks.

AIDS Treatment Update
NAM Charitable Foundation, Unit 52
The Eurolink Centre, 49 Effra Road
Great Britain SW2 1BZ
Tel: 011-71-737-1846; E-mail: eking@nam.org.uk

Subscriptions to individuals within the United Kingdom are free, and those to institutions are 18 £/year. Overseas (outside the European Community): an additional 15 £/year. Published monthly.

Alive and Kicking
We the People Living with AIDS/HIV of the Delaware Valley
425 South Broad Street
Philadelphia, PA 19147-1126
Tel: (215) 545-6868; E-mail: drfair@critpath.org

This is perhaps the best local/national AIDS news collection service in the United States and is one of the best newsletters on both medical and social AIDS issues published anywhere. Subscriptions appear to be free to everyone. Published monthly.

A&U—America's AIDS Magazine
25 Monroe Street, Suite 205
Albany, NY 12210
Tel: (518) 426-9010; E-mail: mailbox@aumag.org

This general interest monthly AIDS publication features celebrity interviews and reviews of AIDS-related art, films, books, and poetry. Cover price: $3.95 U.S., $4.95 Canada. Subscriptions start at $9.95, although the magazine is frequently distributed at no cost through AIDS service organizations.

Being Alive
PWHIV/AIDS Action Coalition
3626 Sunset Boulevard
Los Angeles, CA 90026
Tel: (213) 667-3262; E-mail: BngAlive@aol.com

This newsletter stands out because it has sections in Spanish and covers a wide range of topics of interest to PWA/HIVs. Subscriptions are $20/year and $12/six months; free subscriptions are available to those who cannot pay. Published monthly.

The Body Positive
Body Positive, Inc.
2095 Broadway, Suite 306
New York, NY 10023
Tel: (212) 721-1346 or (212) 721-1618

This publication is oriented largely toward social issues but includes some HIV/AIDS treatment information, as well as indepth coverage of problems with HIV in prisons. Contribution of $35 or more are requested, although PWA/HIVs unable to pay receive free subscriptions. Published 11 times a year.

Bulletin of Experimental Treatment for AIDS (BETA)
San Francisco AIDS Foundation, BETA Subscription Department
P.O. Box 426182
San Francisco, CA 94142
Tel: (415) 487-3000; Northern California: (800) FOR-AIDS; Fax: (415) 487-3089 or (415) 487-3009

This quarterly publication explores the latest treatment advances against HIV and its related opportunistic infections. Subscriptions are free for residents of San Francisco, $45 for nonresidents, $90 for organizations. English or Spanish edition (one only)—individuals: $75/year, organizations: $165/year; both English and Spanish editions—individuals: $120/year, organizations: $295/year; outside United States and Canada—add $20 per edition.

Canadian AIDS News
Canadian Public Health Association
AIDS Education and Awareness Program
400-1565 Carling Avenue
Ottawa, ON, Canada KIZ 8RI
Tel: (613) 725-3769

This newsletter focuses on AIDS education in Canada. Subscriptions are free.

Children with AIDS
1800 Columbus Avenue
Roxbury, MA 02119
Tel: (617) 442-7442

This publication is a good source of medical/treatment information on the very different process of AIDS in children; also addresses some social issues. Published bimonthly. Subscriptions: $25.

The Common Factor
Committee of Ten Thousand
c/o The Wellness Center at Packard Manse
583 Plain Street
Stoughton, MA 02072
Tel: (617) 344-9634

This newsletter was first published in April 1992. It provides an informational support structure for the thousands of Americans who have been infected with HIV through transfusions or the use of blood products, as well as for their friends and families. The publication is associated with the Hemophilia Treatment Centers. Subscriptions are free, although contributions are accepted and encouraged. Published quarterly.

Critical Path AIDS Project Newsletter
Critical Path AIDS Project
2062 Lombard Street
Philadelphia, PA 19146
Tel: (212) 545-2212; E-mail: kiyoshi@critpath.org

This is one of the best PWA newsletters in print; it is well researched, thoroughly referenced, and up to date. Subscriptions are free for those with HIV/AIDS; all others $50/year. Published monthly.

The Hopkins HIV Report
Johns Hopkins University AIDS Service
Carnegie 290, 600 North Wolfe Street
Baltimore, MD 21287-6220
(no telephone)

This report, published six times a year, is perhaps the most informative newsletter on AIDS treatment issues currently in print. It contains no activist rhetoric and has the patient's welfare as its primary focus. Separate versions are available for patients and care providers. Subscriptions are free for Maryland residents, $25/year for other U.S. residents, U.S.$45/year outside the United States.

Medical Alert
National Association of People with AIDS
1413 K Street, NW
Washington, DC 20005
Tel: (202) 898-0414; Fax: (202) 898-0435

This bimonthly newsletter features the latest medical news

involving HIV/AIDS. Some material is given in Spanish. Donation requested.

Notes from the Underground
PWA Health Group
150 West 26th Street, Suite 201
New York, NY 10001
Tel: (212) 255-0520

Subscriptions are $35/individuals, $75/institutions and doctors, sliding scale for low-income persons.

PI Perspectives
Project Inform
1965 Market Street, Suite 220
San Francisco, CA 94103
Tel: (415) 558-9051, (800) 334-7422, or (800) 822-7422

This newsletter is an excellent source of detailed information written in easy-to-understand language. A donation is requested, although no one is denied a subscription for lack of ability to pay. Published as frequently as possible.

Positive Health News
Keep Hope Alive
P.O. Box 27041
West Allis, WI 53227
Tel: (414) 548-4344

This source provides information on alternative medical treatments for AIDS/HIV. Subscriptions are $10.00/year. Published three times a year.

Positive Living
AIDS Project Los Angeles
1313 North Vine Street
Los Angeles, CA 90028
Tel: (213) 993-1362; Fax: (213) 993-1592

This publication features news and treatment briefs, with excellent firsthand reports on alternative therapies as they appear in Los Angeles. Donation requested, otherwise free. Published monthly.

The Positive Woman
P.O. Box 34372
Washington, DC 20043

Tel: (202) 898-0372

This is a good source for information on HIV/AIDS in women. Sliding-scale subscriptions: $12–$75. Published bimonthly.

Positively Aware
Test Positive Aware Network
1258 West Belmont Avenue
Chicago, IL 60657-329
Tel: (312) 472-6397; Fax: 472-7505

This publication is a good source of basic information that is very well presented. It is funded in part by Burroughs Wellcome in cooperation with local U.S. PWA coalitions. Free. Published quarterly.

Poz
P.O. Box 1279, Old Chelsea Station
New York, NY 10113
Tel: (800) 973-2376 or (212) 242-2163; Fax: (212) 851-1938

This is a slick, glossy publication, but its columns and feature articles are not slanted. Personal profiles of PWAs are balanced with articles on advocacy and treatment information. Subscriptions required; $19.95/year. Published bimonthly.

PWAlive
PWA Alive
P.O. Box 80216
Minneapolis, MN 55408

This lively, eminently readable community newsletter is "by, for, and about persons affected by AIDS" and provides good information on conventional and unconventional treatment approaches, as well as opinions on the politics and social impact of AIDS. The publication includes art, photography, and literature geared to the PWA community. Subscriptions $10/year. Published quarterly.

PWA Rag
Prisoners with AIDS Rights Advocacy Group
P.O. Box 2161
Jonesboro, GA 30327
Tel: (404) 946-9346

This newsletter for PWAs in prison provides an important service; it includes articles, treatment news, and prisoner resources. Donations are appreciated. Published sporadically.

PWAC-NY Newsline
PWA Coalition of New York
50 West 17th Street, 8th floor
New York, NY 10011
Tel: (212) 647-1419; hot line: (212) 647-1420 or (800) 828-3280

The articles in this newsletter are not always well researched, and details are sometimes imprecise, but the publication tries—often successfully—to convey a sense of what it is like to live with HIV. Subscriptions are $35/year, free to PWA/HIVs who cannot afford to pay. Published monthly.

The SEARCHlight
(Re)SEARCH Alliance
7461 Beverly Boulevard, Suite 304
Los Angeles, CA 90036
Tel: (213) 930-8820

This newsletter is published by a community-based research group. Subscriptions are free, although donations of $25 are encouraged. Published bimonthly.

STEP Perspective
Seattle Treatment Education Project
127 Broadway East, Suite 200
Seattle, WA 98102
Tel: (800) 869-7837

Subscriptions are free, although donations are encouraged. Published three times a year.

TAGline
Treatment Action Group (TAG)
200 East 10th Street, Suite 601
New York, NY 10003
Tel: (212) 260-0300; Fax: (212) 260-8561

TAGLine presents sophisticated insider information on clinical trials, experimental protocols, and NIH research policy issues, as well as breaking news on experimental drug development. Some Spanish sections. Subscriptions: individuals $30/year; institutions $50/year. Published monthly.

Treatment Issues
Gay Men's Health Crisis, Treatment Information
129 West 20th Street
New York, NY 10011
Tel: (212) 807-6664; Fax: (212) 337-3565

This PWA newsletter is carefully researched and referenced and is an excellent information resource for patients and care providers. Suggested donation: $30 for individuals, $50 for physicians and institutions, free to those unable to pay. Published 10 times a year.

Treatment Review
AIDS Treatment Data Network
611 Broadway, Suite 613
New York, NY 10012
Tel: (212) 260-8868 or (800) 734-7104; E-mail: network@atdn.org

This excellent newsletter, written in plain English, carefully explains complex medical treatments so they are easy to understand. $16.00/year suggested donation, but free to those unable to pay. Published eight times a year.

Treatment Update
Community AIDS Treatment Information Exchange
517 College Street, Suite 324
Toronto, Ontario, Canada M6G 4A2
Tel: (416) 944-1916

This newsletter provides a well-presented accounting of current treatments for AIDS, some of which are unavailable in the United States. English and French versions are available. Free for Canadian citizens; U.S. citizens, $15/year; sliding-scale subscriptions are available. Published 10 times a year.

VA AIDS Information
Veteran's Administration (San Francisco)

This publication seems to be available only on-line at present. Also at NIH gopher site. Published monthly.

Women Alive
Women Alive Women's Services
Being Alive/People with HIV/AIDS Action
Coalition of Los Angeles
1566 South Burnside Avenue

Los Angeles, CA 90019
Tel: (213) 965-1564; Fax: (213) 965-9886

This publication is produced by and for HIV-infected women.
Cost: $12/year; free to those unable to pay. Published quarterly.

WORLD (Women Organized to Respond to Life-Threatening Diseases)
Rebecca Denison
P.O. Box 11535
Oakland, CA 94611
Tel: (510) 658-6930

This is a good source of information on HIV/AIDS in women.
English and Spanish versions are available. Subscriptions:
$50–$100/year; low-income: $0–$20/year; no one is denied a
subscription for lack of ability to pay. Back issues/resources: $1
each. Published monthly.

The listings below include more technical newsletters for
those who need such information. These newsletters are not free.
Most are geared toward professionals or semiprofessionals who
need scientific information, but they provide some useful information for PWAs as well. Some are available on-line, although
some organizations only post summaries or abstracts of their articles on-line or even demand a fee to access their information.

AIDS Clinical Care
Publishing Division of the Massachusetts Medical Society
P.O. Box 9085
Waltham, MA 02254
Tel: (617) 893-3800 (ext 1199) or (800) 843-6356; Fax: (617) 893-0413

This publication includes well-documented cases of AIDS treat-
ments and is geared to the professional. It is published by the or-
ganization that publishes the *New England Journal of Medicine*.
Only briefs and abstracts are available at no cost. Subscriptions:
U.S.—$8.50/issue, $89/year; Canada/international—$117/year.
Published monthly.

AIDS Weekly and AIDS Weekly Plus
P.O. Box 830409
Birmingham, AL 35283
Tel: (404) 377-8895; Fax: (404) 378-5411; E-mail: info@henderson-
net.ati.ga.us

This newsletter comes in several editions and provides exhaustive coverage of all aspects of the pandemic. For scanning the field, it is a major resource. Subscriptions: U.S. $995/year; $1,195 a year for other countries. No discounts for people with HIV/AIDS. Only summaries are available on-line, although a selection of full-text AIDS Weekly Plus articles is available at the AEGIS Website archives.

Antiviral Agents Bulletin
Biotechnology Information Institute
1700 Rockville Pike, Suite 400
Rockville, MD 20852
Tel: (301) 424-0255; Fax: (301) 424-0257; E-mail: biotect@clark.net

This excellent site offers industry-based pharmaceutical information and a beautifully designed website. Subscriptions: $350/year (North America); $410 (outside North America, air mail).

**Journal of the International Association
of Physicians in AIDS Care**
Medical Publications Corporation
225 West Washington Street, Suite 2200
Chicago, IL, 60606-3418
Tel: (312) 419-7074; Fax: (312) 419-7079

This journal is an excellent source for professionals and informed patients. Subscriptions: $60/year. Published monthly.

A number of other medical journals are going on-line: *British Medical Journal, Cell, Emerging Infectious Diseases, Immunology News* (gopher), *Immunology Today, Journal of Immunology, Journal of Molecular Biology* (UK), *Nature, New England Journal of Medicine,* and *Science*. A few, like the *New England Journal of Medicine,* post full-text articles rather than abstracts and summaries. Most also offer convenient on-line subscriptions.

Anthologies

ACT UP New York Women and AIDS Book Group. *Women, AIDS, and Activism.* Boston: South End Press, 1990. 295p. ISBN 0-89608-394-2.

This anthology of articles by the activist ACT UP focuses on the often neglected issues facing women with HIV/AIDS. Articles cover safe sex, HIV testing, drug treatment and drug trials, public policy, and activism.

Alyson, Sasha. *You Can Do Something about AIDS.* Boston: Stop AIDS Project, 1988. 126p. ISBN 0-945-97200-8.

Contributors ranging from Abigail van Buren to Whoopi Goldberg to former White House Press Secretary Jody Powell wrote short essays for this project. The contents cover many viewpoints on personal involvement in AIDS issues, as well as educational and service projects for schools, congregations, and workplace groups.

Brickner, Philip W., et al. *Under the Safety Net: The Health and Social Welfare of the Homeless in the United States.* New York: W. W. Norton, 1990. 439p. ISBN 0-393-02885-2.

This anthology of more than two dozen articles on health care for the homeless is the result of national street and shelter outreach programs to the homeless. The book includes useful articles on the health problems of homeless people with HIV/AIDS, tuberculosis, and substance abuse difficulties.

Brown, Lawrence D., ed. *Health Policy and the Disadvantaged.* Durham, N.C.: Duke University Press, 1991. 212p. ISBN 0-8223-1142-9.

As more and more poor people are affected by the HIV/AIDS epidemic—through IV drug use, sex with an infected partner, or perinatal transmission—their lack of access to necessary health care is easily highlighted. This anthology of readings focuses on the juncture of specific disadvantaged groups—the homeless, people with HIV/AIDS, the uninsured, substance users—and the need to implement adequate health care policies.

Clarke, Loren K., and Malcolm Potts, eds. *The AIDS Reader: Documentary History of a Modern Epidemic.* Boston: Branden, 1988. 350p. ISBN 0-8283-1918-9.

All aspects of the AIDS epidemic are covered in this first volume of a planned series. More than 50 articles are reprinted.

Crimp, Douglas, with Adam Rolston. *AIDS Demographics.* Seattle: Bay Press, 1990. 141p. ISBN 0-941920-16-x.

ACT UP has been an influential activist force in the fight against HIV/AIDS. To make its point, the organization has frequently drawn on the skilled resources of artists and writers, who have created its forceful and sometimes controversial graphic statements. This book reproduces some of ACT UP's best art and essays.

Fee, Elizabeth, and Daniel M. Fox, eds. *AIDS: The Burdens of History.* Berkeley: University of California Press, 1988. 362p. ISBN 0-520-06396-1.

AIDS has caused enormous suffering and death in a relatively short period, but the epidemic can also be viewed by its impact on society. This book examines the historical issues of quarantine and plague, physician responsibility, and disease as punishment for sin.

Graubard, Stephen R., ed. *Living with AIDS.* Cambridge, MA: MIT Press, 1989. 463p. ISBN 0-262-57079-3.

This collection of 20 essays focuses on the social history and impact of the AIDS epidemic, as well as its public policy implications. A section is devoted to the international aspects of HIV/AIDS.

Klein, Michael, ed. *Poets for Life: Seventy-Six Poets Respond to AIDS.* New York: Crown Publishers, 1989. 244p. ISBN 0-517-5724-7.

Poet Michael Klein contacted over 500 U.S. poets to gather material on HIV/AIDS—much of which had never before appeared in print—for this volume. Included are works by June Jordan, Adrienne Rich, Brad Gooch, Paul Monette, Joe Papp, and Bishop Paul Moore.

McKenzie, Nancy F., ed. *The AIDS Reader: Social, Political, Ethical Issues.* New York: Meridian/Penguin, 1991. 597p. ISBN 0-452-01072-1.

Just as HIV illness seeks out the body's vulnerabilities, the epidemic itself has highlighted social prejudices, unresponsive institutions, and a flawed health care system. This anthology brings together more than 30 articles by leading researchers, scholars, and scientists to explore these issues.

Osborn, M. Elizabeth, ed. *The Way We Live Now: American Plays and the AIDS Crisis.* New York: Theatre Communications Group, 1990. 282p. ISBN 1-55936-005-4.

This anthology of plays with HIV/AIDS as their protagonist includes works by William M. Hoffman, Lanford Wilson, Harvey Fierstein, Susan Sontag, and Terence McNally.

Russell, Letty M. *The Church with AIDS: Renewal in Time of Crisis.* Louisville: Westminster/John Knox Press, 1990. 223p. ISBN 0-664-25111-0.

Although religious belief about sexual practices, homosexuality, and other issues has been a controversial source of criticism of people with HIV/AIDS, all communities of faith contain PWAs. This anthology of articles by both ordained clergy and academics reflects the efforts of the Church of Christ to address the spiritual needs of all members in the age of AIDS.

Siegel, Larry, M.D. *AIDS and Substance Abuse.* New York: Harrington Park Press, 1988. 206p. ISBN 0-918393-59-0.

A variety of researchers and clinical experts contributed to this anthology, which explores basic questions of the connection between substance use and HIV infection and progression. Essays ask whether drug and alcohol use depresses the immune system, increases the risk of primary infection with HIV, and contributes to the progression of HIV to AIDS.

Sontag, Susan. *Illness as Metaphor and AIDS and Its Metaphors.* New York: Anchor/Doubleday, 1989. 183p. ISBN 0-385-26705-3.

This volume combines Sontag's two famous essays that address the punitive meaning attached to illness in U.S. society. In the first, written in 1978, Sontag reveals the social stigma attached to cancer. She wrote about AIDS in 1989 to examine the thinking behind the "plague" title given to the illness.

Personal Accounts

Arenas, Reinaldo; Doris Koch, tr. *Before Night Falls: A Memoir.* New York: Viking, 1993. ISBN 0-670-84078-5.

Arenas was an internationally renowned Cuban author who died of AIDS in 1990. In this book—his autobiography—he recounts his life in Cuba, the persecution he experienced under Castro as a creative thinker and a homosexual, and his disappointment in the United States. The specter of his death from AIDS and the impact of his realization of death's approach crystallize the devastation of an extraordinary life cut short by an amoral virus better than many more elaborate accounts of the disease.

Baxter, Daniel. *The Least of These My Brethren.* New York: Harmony Books, 1997. ISBN 362-1969-B.

This book is the firsthand account of a doctor who treats destitute AIDS patients at the Spellman Center, an AIDS unit at Saint Claire's Hospital in New York City. The stories portray both the patients and the humanity of the doctor who cares for them.

Callen, Michael. *Surviving AIDS.* New York: HarperCollins, 1991. 256p. ISBN 0-06-092125-0.

The late Michael Callen achieved prominence as a long-term survivor of HIV. He testified before Congress, wrote a popular song, recorded an album, and self-published a PWA magazine. In addition, he cofounded the People with AIDS Coalition and the Community Research Initiative.

Cox, Elizabeth. *Thanksgiving: An AIDS Journal.* New York: Harper Perennial, 1990. 230p. ISBN 0-06-092041-6.

Cox kept this journal during the years 1985–1987, while her husband, Keith Avedon, fought HIV/AIDS. Avedon died in 1990.

DePrince, Elaine, *Cry Bloody Murder: A Tale of Tainted Blood.* New York: Random House, 1997. ISBN: 0-679-45676-7.

This book is a poignant firsthand account of a mother who lost her two hemophiliac sons to AIDS after they received tainted blood-clotting factors. The book reflects the extent of the author's loss and gives testament to the way the hemophiliac community as a whole fell victim to mistakes by the Federal Food and Drug Administration, the blood industry, and the U.S. government.

Fortunato, John E. *AIDS: The Spiritual Dilemma.* San Francisco: Harper and Row, 1987. 156p. ISBN 0-06-250338-3.

Psychotherapist Fortunato has written widely on AIDS and gay issues. Here, he discusses his own experiences of listening to the stories of those with HIV/AIDS and exploring the spiritual impact the epidemic has had on him.

Fumia, Molly. *Honor Thy Children: One Family's Journey to Wholeness.* Berkeley: Conari Press, 1997. 350p. ISBN 1-57324-077-X

This book chronicles the way a Japanese family weighs the value of its cultural traditions against its love for its sons when it is revealed that the sons are gay. Eventually, AIDS forces the family to decide.

Glaser, Elizabeth, and Laura Palmer. *In the Absence of Angels.* New York: G.P. Putnam's Sons, 1991. 304p. ISBN 0-399-13577-4.

Elizabeth Glaser, wife of a popular television star, received a contaminated blood transfusion that infected her and two of her children with HIV. This memoir tells of her family's struggle with that reality and of her work to establish the Pediatric AIDS Foundation.

Hoffman, Amy. *Hospital Time.* Durham, NC: Duke University Press, 1997. 144p. ISBN 0-8223-1920-9.

The responsibility as primary caregiver for someone with a terminal disease can be as emotionally devastating as being ill oneself. In this book, Hoffman describes caring for her friend Mike Riegle during the final stages of his life, chronicling both of their experiences.

Kincaid, Jamaica. *My Brother.* New York: Farrar, Strauss, and Giroux, 1997. ISBN 0-14-086737-6.

This account balances the weight of the death of Kincaid's brother from AIDS with the weight of a culture deeply vested in ignorance, denial, and indifference toward the epidemic.

Klitzman, Robert. *Being Positive: The Lives of Men and Women with HIV.* Chicago: Ivan R. Dee, 1997. ISBN 362.1969-K.

In this collection of narratives about HIV-positive New Yorkers from diverse backgrounds, a doctor analyzes how people cope with the disease.

Koop, C. Everett. *Koop: The Memoirs of America's Family Doctor.* New York: Random House, 1991. 342p. ISBN 0-394-57626-8.

In 1981, Dr. C. Everett Koop was one of the nation's leading pediatric surgeons when he was nominated by President Ronald Reagan to be the U.S. surgeon general. His vigorous work to educate Americans about HIV/AIDS and the need for sex education in the schools gave him a reputation as an effective surgeon general.

Kramer, Larry. *Reports from the Holocaust: The Making of an AIDS Activist.* New York: St. Martin's Press, 1989. 291p. ISBN 0-312-03921-2.

Kramer is a well-known writer who helped start the Gay Men's Health Crisis in early 1982. He has been a controversial figure in the gay community for advising that men stop having sex to halt the AIDS epidemic. *Reports from the Holocaust* contains collected letters, speeches, columns, and other personal documents Kramer has written on the epidemic.

Mehl-Madrona, Lewis. *Coyote Medicine.* New York: Scribner, 1997. ISBN 0-684-80271.

Mehl-Madrona draws on his Native American background to integrate shamanism with traditional Western medicine to create a new holistic model of treating patients in which the client plays a role in healing. The chapter "AIDS and the Spirit of Illness" specifically applies this model to HIV/AIDS.

Monette, Paul. *Borrowed Time: An AIDS Memoir.* New York: Avon Books, 1988. 342p. ISBN 0-380-70779-9.

Nominated for the 1988 National Book Critics Circle Award, this book dramatically offers a personal account of Monette's 19-month struggle with AIDS.

Peavey, Fran. *A Shallow Pool of Time.* Philadelphia: New Society, 1991. 168p. ISBN 0-317-93395-7.

This account of an HIV-positive woman facing her diagnosis raises many of the questions all women must address during the HIV/AIDS epidemic.

Schwartzberg, Steven. *A Crisis of Meaning: How Gay Men Are Making Sense of AIDS.* New York: Oxford University Press, 1996. 240p. ISBN 0-19-509627-4.

A psychotherapist interviews 19 gay men living with HIV, exploring ways to find meaning amid trauma and uncertainty about the future with an emphasis on the enduring power of the human spirit.

Tilleraas, Penny. *Circle of Hope: Our Stories of AIDS, Addiction, and Recovery.* New York: Harper and Row, 1990. 364p. ISBN 0-06-255412-3.

Issues of continuing substance use and its influence on the immune system are important for the general health of all HIV-infected people. Many exclusively gay and lesbian recovery programs have begun to help people progress in an environment that supports their identity. A product of the Hazelden recovery program in Minnesota, this book offers the stories of two dozen PWAs who became part of that recovery community.

White, Ryan, and Ann Marie Cunningham. *Ryan White: My Own Story.* New York: Dial Books, 1991. 277p. ISBN 0-8037-0977-3.

Ryan White, a hemophiliac, was diagnosed with HIV at age 13 after he had received a contaminated transfusion of the clotting agent Factor VIII. He was refused permission to return to his school, and he and his family undertook a very public court battle that ultimately proved successful. Ryan's battle and his educational work in schools and with AIDS groups attracted the attention of celebrities. Here, he tells his story, accompanied by family photos.

Wyatt-Morley, Catherine. *AIDS Memoir: Journal of an HIV-Positive Mother.* West Hartford, CT: Kumarian Press, 1997. 216p. ISBN: 1-56549-067-3.

This book offers a firsthand journal by a mother who began to record her daily experiences and feelings shortly after finding out she had AIDS. Her experiences include hospital stays and her struggle with both her disease and trying to keep her family together.

Photographic Works

Huston, River, with photographs by Mary Berridge. *A Positive Life: Portraits of Women Living with HIV.* Philadelphia: Running Press, 1997. 128p. ISBN 0-7624-0244-X.

This book incorporates a series of interviews and photographic portraits of 31 HIV-positive women who discuss the unique issues that affect their lives, including discrimination and dealing with the medical bureaucracy.

Nixon, Nicholas, photographer, with text by Bebe Nixon. *People with AIDS.* Boston: David R. Godine, 1991. 160p. ISBN 0-87923-886-0.

Fifteen individuals with AIDS and their family members and friends volunteered to work with photographer Nicholas Nixon as he chronicled their life-and-death struggles with the disease.

Photographers + Friends United against AIDS. *The Indomitable Spirit.* New York: Harry N. Abrams, 1990. 96p. ISBN 0-801-09245-52.

In 1990, the photography exhibit "The Indomitable Spirit" was assembled to celebrate human strength, compassion, and endurance in the face of challenge and adversity. The show was produced by the organization Photographers + Friends, which unites the diverse elements of the photographic community—commercial art, fashion, sports photographers, and photojournalists—with artists and scientists who use photography in their work.

Ruskin, Cindy. *The Quilt: Stories from the NAMES Project.* New York: Simon and Schuster, 1988. 160p. ISBN 0-671-66597-9.

This book of photos, with images by Matt Herron, tells the story of the NAMES Project Quilt.

Nonprint Materials

Films and Videos

Acting Up for Prisoners
1992: 27 minutes

This documentary film depicts AIDS activists forcing U.S. authorities to take action in a prison where HIV-positive women are being abused.

Adolescents: At Risk for HIV Infection
Child Welfare League of America
1991: 21 minutes

The film discusses HIV prevention and care for U.S. adolescents.

AIDS: A Decision for Life
Health Visions, American College Health Association
1988: 20 minutes, color

This educational films is designed to provoke a dialogue among teens and young adults on HIV prevention. The narrative centers on a female college freshman at a large East Coast university who tests positive for HIV following a casual sexual relationship.

AIDS in the Nineties: From Science to Policy
University of California, San Francisco
1990: 84 minutes, color

This film documents the opening ceremony of the Sixth International Conference on AIDS.

AIDS Is about Secrets
Research Foundation for Mental Health, HIV Center, New York
1988: 38 minutes, color

This educational film uses short vignettes to illustrate particular behaviors that place women in danger of becoming infected with HIV.

AIDS: Me and My Baby
Research Foundation for Mental Health, HIV Center, New York
1988: 22 minutes

This educational film uses a series of vignettes, each focusing on a specific issue pertaining to the prevention of HIV infection and decisions relating to pregnancy.

AIDS: No Second Chance
Vista Communications
1991: 25 minutes

Four young people discuss AIDS in this film directed primarily to teenagers.

AIDS, Not Us
Research Foundation for Mental Health, HIV Center, New York
1989: 36 minutes

A series of vignettes focus on sexual risk taking and decision-making, attitudes toward AIDS, risk reduction, and the use of condoms among African American and Hispanic adolescent males.

AIDS: The Second Decade
Cable News Network (CNN), Turner Home Entertainment
30 minutes, color

This series of CNN presentations on AIDS from the early 1990s, hosted by Dan Rutz, contains 10 segments: Cuba: AIDS Quarantine; National Policy; HIV; AIDS Treatment, Part 1; AIDS Treatment, Part 2; AIDS and Women, Part 1; AIDS and Women, Part 2; Living with AIDS; Civil Liberties; and AIDS Education.

The AIDS Show: Artists Involved with Death and Survival
Adair Films, Direct Cinema Limited
1987: 58 minutes

The show explores the anger of gays and their families and friends over AIDS through a series of comic, dramatic, and musical sketches.

And the Band Played On
Home Box Office
1993: 140 minutes

Based on Randy Shilts's history of the early years of the AIDS epidemic, this dramatic story focuses on the struggle of a small group of strong-willed men and women who took on the fight to save lives in the face of the mysterious illness now called AIDS.

As Is
Brandman Productions, Lorimar Home Video
1985: 85 minutes

This adaptation of William Hoffman's drama focuses on two gay New York men whose long-time relationship is tested when one discovers he has contracted AIDS.

Born in Africa
WGBH Educational Foundation
1990: 88 minutes

This documentary tells the story of a prominent Ugandan who publicly acknowledges that he has AIDS.

Caring about AIDS: The Common Ground
Planned Parenthood
1989: 39 minutes

This is a documentary about the global AIDS epidemic that profiles the responses of four different communities from around the world. The film illustrates how fear has fostered discrimination against infected people and how education and caring can change that situation.

Caring for Infants and Toddlers with HIV Infection and **Caring for School-Age Children with HIV Infection**
Child Welfare League of America
Both 1991: 21 minutes

These two films explore the daily lives of three families caring for infants and toddlers with HIV.

Christmas at Starcross
Elfstrom-Hilmer Productions, Villon Films
1990: 52 minutes

This documentary focuses on a monastery-like community of people who raise Christmas trees and provide homes and families for babies with HIV. The film focuses on the spiritual and emotional aspects of these tragic early deaths.

Common Threads: Stories from the Quilt
Names Foundation
1991: 79 minutes

This documentary features random stories of people represented by panels on the AIDS Memorial Quilt.

DiAna's Hair Ego: AIDS Info up Front
Women Make Movies
1990: 30 minutes

This documentary examines the growth of the South Carolina AIDS Education Network, which operates out of DiAna's Hair Ego, a beauty salon.

Dying for Sex
British Broadcasting Company (BBC Lionhart Television)
1993: 47 minutes

This documentary explores the role of the commercial sex industry in Thailand in the spread of HIV/AIDS.

An Early Frost
NBC (RCAA/Columbia Home Video)
1985: 100 minutes

This is one of the first U.S. television movies about AIDS. Its story focuses on a traditional American family trying to cope with the fact that their son is homosexual and is dying of AIDS.

Forrester Church
Public Affairs Television (from the "World of Ideas with Bill Moyers" series)
1988: 28 minutes

The focus of this film is on Forrester Church, a liberal Unitarian minister who ministers to the poor, the homeless, and AIDS sufferers.

Longtime Companion
American Playhouse, Vidmark Entertainment
1990: 100 minutes

This is one of the first commercial films dealing with AIDS to receive wide distribution. Set in New York City in the 1980s, the film focuses on a group of homosexual friends who are alternately affected by and infected with HIV.

Medicine in the 90s: Women and HIV Infection
Kaiser Permanente
1991: 55 minutes

This film discusses the increasing risk of HIV infection and AIDS for women and their children.

Non, Je Ne Regrette Rien (No Regret)
Frameline Home Video
1992: 38 minutes

This groundbreaking documentary explores the lives of five gay African American men who are HIV positive. Through music, poetry, and confession, they reveal how they are battling the double social stigmas surrounding their infection and their homosexuality.

One Foot on a Banana Peel, the Other in the Grave (Secrets From the Dolly Madison Room)
Juan Botas and Lucas Platt
1993: 83 minutes

A doctor's office becomes a most unlikely salon in this moving film produced by Jonathan Demme. Banana Peel documents the poignant relationships formed among a group of AIDS patients as they confront their illness while exchanging humorous anecdotes and sexy stories.

Philadelphia
Tri-Star Pictures, Columbia Tri-Star Home Video
1993: 125 minutes

This major motion picture by Jonathan Demme deals with the plight of an AIDS-afflicted lawyer who is fired by his firm and seeks retribution in court.

The Pilgrim Must Embark: Living in Community
Cut and Run Films, Terre Nova Films
1991: 25 minutes

This film documents Chicago's Bonaventura House, a communal home for 26 people with AIDS run by Catholic Alexian Brothers.

Political Funerals
DIVA (Damned Interfering Video Activists—ACT UP New York)
1995: 29 minutes

This forceful and moving documentary depicts a bold new movement within AIDS activism that rejects the notion that one should die of AIDS quietly and peacefully.

Ray Navarro Memorial Tape
DIVA (Damned Interfering Video Activists—ACT UP New York)
1990: 30 minutes

The tape is a tribute to AIDS activist and videographer Ray Navarro, who died while making a film on Latino gay male assimilation into the white gay culture.

Savage Nights [Les Nuits Fauves]
Gramercy Pictures
1993: 126 minutes

This autobiographical French film depicts Cyril Collard's life as an HIV-positive bisexual man and his sexual encounters with both male and female lovers. Collard died before the film garnered him the French equivalent of an Academy Award for Best Director. The film gained notoriety when it was revealed that Collard had infected a number of female partners with whom he had engaged in unprotected sex.

Science of Hope with Jonas Salk
Public Affairs Television (from the "World of Ideas with Bill Moyers" series)
1990: 28 minutes

Jonas Salk, developer of the polio vaccine and founder of the Salk Institute in La Jolla, California, discusses AIDS research.

Sex, Drugs, and AIDS
O.D.N. Productions
1986: 19 minutes

This film dispels the myths around how AIDS is transmitted and gives young people ways to safeguard against being infected with the virus.

Silverlake Life: The View from Here
Tom Joslin and Peter Friedman
1993: 99 minutes

This film is essentially a video diary of Tom Joslin and Mark Massi's life together, their love for and commitment to each other, and their losing battles against AIDS.

Tongues Untied
Frameline Home Video
1989: 55 minutes

Director Marlon Riggs uses poetry, rap, interviews, and dramatic situations to express the oppression faced by black gay men in America today.

Who Pays for AIDS?
Documentary Consortium, PBS Video (from the "Frontline" series)
1988: 60 minutes

Who Pays? examines the predicament of people with AIDS who face not only social ostracism but also exorbitant medical bills.

CD-ROMS

The following list of CD-ROMS was prepared by the Centers for Disease Control. The list is indicative of the growing number of unique information sources available on HIV/AIDS.

Abstracts: XI International Conference on AIDS
Vancouver, July 7–12, 1996
Marathon Multimedia Group
P.O. Box 409

Northfield, MN 55057
Tel: (507) 645-2705
1996

This CD-ROM provides an electronic text version of the abstracts presented at the Eleventh International Conference on AIDS in Vancouver, July 7–12, 1996. The abstracts include new information reported on such topics as disease etiology, treatment issues, and prevention of HIV disease. The software offers a Boolean logic-based search tool for locating specific topics or abstracts and contains 5,254 abstracts. The program also offers a system for tagging certain entries so printing can be done at a later time.

IWAX HIV Glossary
Cambridge Center for Clinical Informatics
Institute of Public Health
University of Cambridge
Cambridge CB2 2SR, UK
http//www.mediainfo.cam.ac/uk/wax
(011) 44-1223-330303
1998

This CD-ROM provides an intelligent searchable version of AIDS Research Information Center's *Encyclopedic AIDS Medical Glossary* (see description under Reference Books).

IWAX HIV Manual
Cambridge Center for Clinical Informatics
Institute of Public Health
University of Cambridge
Cambridge CB2 2SR, UK
http//www.mediainfo.cam.ac/uk/wax
(011) 44-1223-330303
1998

This comprehensive medical resource provides up-to-date information on the treatment of HIV and its related infections using an intelligent searchable interface.

KISS: HIV/AIDS Interactive Nights Out
World Institute of Leadership and Learning
12404 Beall Mountain Lane
Potomac, MD 20854-1121
Tel: (301) 983-6006
1996

This CD-ROM is an interactive virtual experience that addresses issues related to risky behaviors. Viewers are presented with a protagonist and are allowed to choose from a variety of "paths" of behavior ranging from high to low risk, each with a different outcome. The paths involve choices pertaining to safer sex, ethical and fidelity issues, sex and substance use, peer pressure, and personal responsibility in decisionmaking. The CD-ROM was created primarily to engage and educate adolescents, young adults, teachers, and parents, but it also offers a valuable learning experience for other members of the community. A supplemental manual with further information and assistance is included.

Primary Care of the HIV/AIDS Patient
Interactive Media Laboratory, Dartmouth Medical School, and Columbia University School of Nursing
Order from Appleton and Lange New Media
P.O. Box 120041
Stamford, CT 06912-0041
Tel: (800) 423-1359

Dr. John G. Bartlett, chief of the Division of Infectious Disease at Johns Hopkins, hosts this CD-ROM, which provides an interactive continuing education experience for primary care providers (including physicians, nurse practitioners, and physician assistants). Participants learn about HIV and AIDS in a variety of ways: They can manage a simulated patient over a span of several years, each visit accompanied by case discussions by Dr. Bartlett. They can visit a learning resources area to attend minilectures given by two experts in HIV care, do computer-based activities and puzzles to learn about various aspects of HIV, and "interview" real HIV/AIDS patients. Health care providers learn the most up-to-date care methods in an immersive, easy-to-use environment.

3TC
Produced by Glaxo Wellcome, Advocacy Relations
5 Moore Drive
Research Triangle Park, NC 27709
Tel: (919) 248-3000
1996

This interactive CD-ROM, available in English and French, takes an in-depth look at the drug 3TC. Various sections offer detailed information on the characteristics of 3TC, the structure of the drug, 3TC/ZDV susceptibility, the role of 3TC/AZT, and 3TC/AZT rationale. In addition, a number of video clips feature medical professionals who draw conclusions from individual studies, explain the benefits of the drugs, and answer commonly asked questions. The CD-ROM also includes new information reported on various protocols, including NUCA 3001, NUCA 3002, NUCB 3001, and NUCB 3002.

Websites

The Access Project: http://www.aidsnyc.org/network/access

AIDS Action Council:
http://www.thebody.com/aac/aacpage.html

AIDS Clinical Trials Information Service: http://www.actis.org

AIDS Education Global Information System:
http://www.aegis.com

AIDS Research Information Center:
http://www.critpath.org/aric/; for ARIC's on-line AIDS medical encyclopedia, http://www.aricinc.org

American Association for World Health: http://aaworld-health.org

The Body: http://www.thebody.org

CDC National AIDS Clearinghouse: http://www.cdcnac.org

Centers for Disease Control and Prevention:
http://www.cdc.gov

Community Research Initiative on AIDS: http://www.aidsinfonyc.org/cria

Critical Path AIDS Project: http://critpath.org

Food and Drug Administration: http://www.fda.gov

Gay Men's Health Crisis: http://www.aidsinfonyc.org/gmhc

The Hopkins HIV Report: http://www.hopkins-aids.edu
Human Rights Campaign Fund: http://www.hrc.org

Joint United Nations Programme on HIV/AIDS (UNAIDS):
http://www.unaids.org

Journal of the American Medical Association HIV/AIDS Information: http://www.ama-assn.org/special/hiv/hivhome.htm

Mothers' Voices: http://www.mvoices.org

NAMES Project Foundation: http://www.aidsquilt.org/names

National AIDS Treatment Advocacy Project:
http://www.natap.org

National Association of People with AIDS:
http://www.napwa.org

National Institutes of Allergies and Infectious Diseases:
http://www.niaid.nih.gov

National Minority AIDS Council:
http:///www.thebody.com/nmac/nmacpage.html

Project Inform: http://www.projinf.org

Test Positive Aware Network: http://www.tpan.com

University of California at San Francisco: http://www.hivinsite.ucsf.edu

Glossary

A wide array of medical, scientific, and public health terms is used in the discussion of HIV/AIDS. Some of these terms involve sexual practices or drug use; some describe testing procedures, drug trials, or legal issues. These terms are basic to understanding HIV/AIDS as discussed in much of the literature. The glossary contains commonly used terms. Many are used in this book, but others will be found in the resources described. Many of the scientific terms in this section are taken from *HIV Vaccine Glossary*, a public domain fact sheet published by the National Institute of Allergy and Infectious Diseases/National Institutes of Health.

abstinence Refraining from, as in abstinence from sexual activity or from the use of drugs.

Acquired Immune Deficiency Syndrome (AIDS)
The final stage of a series of specific health conditions and problems and opportunistic infections caused by a virus (HIV) that can be passed from person to person chiefly through sexual contact, the sharing of syringes used for intravenous drug injection, or transmission from an infected mother to her unborn child. In AIDS, the body's natural immune system is suppressed, which allows for the active presence of microorganisms that would otherwise be fought off by the immune system. The acronym AIDS was first used by the Centers for Disease Control in late 1982 to name cases of illness first reported in 1981.

acyclovir An antiviral agent approved to treat herpes simplex and varicella-zoster infections. It is also under investigation for use against cytomegalovirus.

adjuvant   A substance sometimes included in a vaccine formulation to enhance or modify the immune-stimulating properties of a vaccine.

aerosolized Pentamidine   A drug, administered by inhalation of a fine mist, approved for use against one of the primary fatal infections of AIDS, *Pneumocystis carinii* pneumonia. Injectable Pentamidine is also used.

AIDS Clinical Trial Group (ACTG)   Medical centers taking part in the evaluation of treatments for HIV-related infections; the sites are sponsored by the National Institute of Allergy and Infectious Disease.

AIDS Related Complex (ARC)   A now antiquated term, once used frequently in the literature to describe symptoms found in some persons with HIV and to describe symptomatic HIV infection. Symptoms include recurring fever, weight loss, fungal infection in the mouth and throat, and swollen lymph nodes.

AIDS virus   A popular and widely used but inaccurate term for the Human Immunodeficiency Virus (HIV), the virus that leads to AIDS.

AL 721 (Active Lipid)   An antiviral drug used to treat conditions related to AIDS. The drug was developed from an egg-based compound and affects membrane fluidity without being toxic. It was popular as a self-administered therapy in the mid-1980s but did not meet with institutional success once AZT became available.

alpha interferon   The body makes small amounts of this hormonelike protein. It is produced in laboratory settings to treat Kaposi's sarcoma and infection with amoebas, including Entamoeba histolytica. Such infections are common among PWAs.

ALVAC-HIV™   A genetically engineered HIV vaccine composed of a live, weakened canarypox virus (ALVAC™) into which parts of genes for noninfectious components of HIV have been inserted.

amino acid   Any of the 26 chemical building blocks of proteins.

Amphotericin B   An antifungal medication used to treat cryptococcal meningitis.

Ampligen   A drug still in trials that may be an immunomodulator and an antiviral.

anal intercourse   The sexual practice in which a man inserts his penis into his partner's rectum.

anamnestic response   The heightened immunologic reaction elicited by a second or subsequent exposure to a particular pathogenic microorganism (for example, bacterium, fungus, virus), toxin, or antigen.

anemia   A condition in which a person has a reduced number of red blood cells.

anergy   The loss or weakening of immune response to an irritating agent or antigen. Anergy can be thought of as the opposite of allergy, which is an overreaction to a substance.

anorexia   A loss of appetite that is a neuropsychological disorder; commonly referred to as an eating disorder.

antibiotic   A type of drug used to fight bacterial infection.

antibody   The body's immune system develops this special protein in the blood as a defense against illness when a foreign substance is present. Specific antibodies are developed to fight various infections.

antibody positive   The result of a blood test that shows that a person has been exposed to a particular infection at some time and has developed antibodies to it.

antigen   This substance, when introduced into the body, provokes the production of an antibody that will specifically react to it.

antiviral drug   A medication that will halt the work of a virus before it multiplies or damages other cells.

anus   The opening of the lower end of the bowel.

apoptosis   Cellular suicide, also known as programmed cell death. A possible mechanism used by HIV to suppress the immune system. HIV may cause apoptosis in both HIV-infected and HIV-uninfected immune system cells.

arm   A group of participants in a clinical trial, all of whom receive the same treatment, intervention, or placebo.

asymptomatic   Having no symptoms. Persons infected with HIV may not have symptoms for years.

attenuated   Weakened. Attenuated viruses are often used as vaccines because they can no longer produce disease but still stimulate a strong immune response, such as that to the natural virus.

autologous   Having to do with the same organism or its parts. An autologous blood transfusion involves a person donating his or her own blood for later transfusion back into his or her own body.

AZT (Retrovir)   An antiviral and the first prescription drug approved by the Food and Drug Administration in 1987 for use in prolonging life. The drug was approved before testing was completed; testing was done only on male subjects. AZT and another drug, ddT, are members of the same nucleoside analogue family. AZT is expensive and has shown toxicity in a small number of patients, as well as a loss of effectiveness over time. Although research released in early 1992 showed that the drug did not prolong the lives of users, it has since been proven to dramatically reduce the rate of vertical transmission from mother to child and the seroconversion of health care workers exposed through needle prick incidents.

Bactrim   An antibiotic effective in treating *Pneumocystis carinii* pneumonia.

barebacking   The practice in which an HIV-infected man engages in sex, particularly anal sex, with another man (who may be HIV infected or not) without using condoms.

biopsy   A surgical procedure in which a sample of tissue is removed for examination.

bisexual   A person who is sexually attracted to both males and females.

blinded study   A clinical trial in which participants are unaware of whether they are in the experimental or the control arm of the study.

blood count   A laboratory test to determine the number of red blood cells, white blood cells, and platelets in the blood at a given time.

B lymphocyte (B cell)   One of the two major classes of lymphocytes, B lymphocytes are white blood cells of the immune system that are derived from bone marrow and the spleen. B cells develop into plasma cells, which produce antibodies.

boarder baby   An infant who is medically able to go home but lives in a hospital because he or she has no place to go. The number of boarder babies has risen with the increase of HIV/AIDS. Many boarder babies contracted HIV from their mothers. In some cases, a baby's mother has died; in other cases, because of the mother's drug use, homelessness, or illness, the baby cannot go home. In some communities, litigation compels a search for a foster home so the baby does not remain in the hospital.

body or bodily fluids   A euphemism to describe semen, blood, saliva, urine, and other fluids found in the body and central to the discussion of HIV transmission.

bone marrow   Soft material at the center of the bone that serves as the site of red blood cell production.

booster   A second or later vaccine dose given after the primary dose(s) to increase the immune response to the original vaccine antigen(s).

campylobacter   A bacterial infection caused by contact with infected animals or contaminated food or water.

canarypox   A virus that infects birds and is used as a live vector for HIV vaccines. The virus can carry a large quantity of foreign genes. Canarypox virus cannot grow in human cells, an important safety feature.

cancer   Several diseases in which abnormal cells grow out of control in the body, destroy surrounding tissues, and may spread to other parts of the body.

candidiasis (*Candida albicans*)   Also known as thrush in the mouth, this treatable yeast infection is common in persons with immune suppression and causes a funguslike growth in the mouth, sinus cavity, esophagus, and vagina.

carcinogen   Any substance that produces cancer.

case control study   An epidemiological study that uses persons with a particular problem (cases) with others who do not have that problem (controls). The two groups may be matched for other factors, such as age, race, and occupation.

case definition   The official Centers for Disease Control definition of AIDS.

casual contact   Ordinary daily activity. For instance, HIV cannot be transmitted by shaking hands with someone who has it, by using a telephone touched by a person with HIV, or by sitting in a classroom with a child who has HIV.

catheter   A line installed in the body semipermanently to inject or remove fluids.

CD4   Also known as T4, CD4 is a protein in T lymphocyte helper cells. HIV first infects cells by becoming attached to CD4 molecules. HIV destroys T4 cells, and a T4 cell count is one laboratory means of assessing the status of the immune system.

CD8   Also known as T8, CD8 is a protein in T lymphocyte suppressor cells. The ratio between CD4 and CD8 cells is an important means of judging the viability of a person's immune system.

Centers for Disease Control (CDC)   A federal government agency responsible for infectious disease control. The agency is located in Atlanta, Georgia, and operates under the U.S. Public Health Services, a part of the U.S. Department of Health and Human Services.

cervical cancer   The second most common malignancy of the reproductive organs in women. This cancer is seen at higher rates among poor women, women who have their first sexual experience at a relatively early age, and women with multiple sex partners. Cervical cancer has been characterized as a common component of HIV/AIDS in women.

cervix   The neck of the uterus.

chemotherapy   Treatment of the body with drugs that fight cancer.

clean needles   Usually refers to syringes used for injecting drugs. Clean needles reduce the chance of passing HIV through blood that accumulates in the syringe. A clean needle is also one that has been sterilized with bleach after a previous use.

clinical trial   A research study in which new therapies are tested in humans after they have been tried in animals and laboratory studies.

cofactors   Scientific, medical, psychosocial, or other conditions that exist simultaneously with, and influence the progress or likelihood of, a disease or condition.

cohort   In any research study, a group of subjects that has a common statistical factor.

colitis   Inflammation of the colon.

Combivir (zidovudine/iamivudine)   A combination of AZT and 3TC in one pill.

communicable disease   A disease that can be spread from one person to another.

Community-Based Clinical Trial A situation in which primary care physicians work closely with patients as an accompaniment to conventional research studies.

compassionate use A means of using an investigational new drug, following FDA approval, before much established data exist on its capacity to produce results. Drugs must generally be distributed to patients at no charge by the companies manufacturing them.

condom A shield placed over the penis during sexual intercourse. Condoms can be made of latex or sheep's intestine, although only latex condoms prevent the spread of HIV and other sexually transmitted diseases. Condoms are also known as gloves, French letters, and rubbers.

contact tracing A public health measure used in cases of sexually transmitted diseases. Current and previous sex partners are contacted by public health officials, who may or may not identify the other partner.

contagious disease An illness that can be spread through casual contact.

crack A very addictive smokable drug derived from cocaine. Crack is frequently traded for sex, making its use an indicator of frequent and multiple sexual partners, as well as a likely source of unsafe sexual practices. Crack use is the behavioral factor most likely to identify a female as HIV positive.

cross-resistance Resistance of HIV to more than one drug at the same time; usually applies to a particular class of drugs as a whole.

cryptococcosis (*Cryptococcus neoformans*) A yeastlike fungus that ordinarily attacks the brain and lungs and is very life threatening.

cryptosporidiosis A parasitic infection based in the intestines that causes chronic, severe diarrhea. The parasite is transmitted through direct contact with an infected animal or through contaminated food or water.

cunnilingus The use of the tongue or mouth on a woman's genitals during sexual activity.

cytokine A soluble, hormonelike protein produced by white blood cells that acts as a messenger between cells. Cytokines can stimulate or inhibit the growth and activity of various immune cells. They are essential for a coordinated immune response and can also be used as immunologic adjuvants. HIV replication is regulated by a delicate balance among cytokines.

cytomegalovirus (CMV) A pathogen that is a member of the herpes virus family. Almost all AIDS patients have been infected with CMV, and it is being investigated as a cofactor in the sequence of events that leads to AIDS. Infection occurs directly through the mucous membranes or through tissue or blood. Sites of infection are widespread in the body but frequently include the retina and the colon.

cytotoxic T lymphocyte (CTL) Immune system cell that can destroy cancer cells and cells infected with viruses, fungi, or certain bacteria.

CTLs, also known as killer T cells, carry the CD8 marker. CTLs kill virus-infected cells, whereas antibodies generally target free-floating viruses in the blood. CTL responses are a proposed but unproven correlate of HIV immunity.

Delavirdine (Rescriptor)　A reverse transcriptase inhibitor.

dementia　A loss of mental ability, which is one of the symptomatic illnesses of AIDS. Dementia is characterized by decreased concentration, loss of interest, and slowed motor abilities. At its end stage, it can result in a nearly vegetative state.

dental dam　A latex square that can protect against the transmission of HIV when placed over the vagina, clitoris, or anus during sexual activity.

Deoxyribonucleic acid (DNA)　The protein that carries genetic information in a cell. HIV can enter the DNA of a cell and use its structure to reproduce itself.

D4T (Zerit)　A nucleoside analogue drug.

diagnosis　An analysis of a patient's medical history.

Didanosine (ddI) (Videx)　A nucleoside analogue, like AZT, approved for use in 1991. ddI was the second drug approved by the FDA to fight HIV, and it is administered only to patients who cannot take, or who do not improve while taking, the first approved drug (AZT). As part of the process to speed the development of new drugs, ddI was approved before all of the research studies were completed.

Dideoxycytidine (ddC) (Hivid)　A nucleoside analogue.

directly observed therapy　A practice in the management of tuberculosis care in which a health care provider witnesses the patient taking medication.

DNA vaccine (nucleic acid vaccine)　Direct injection of a gene(s) coding for a specific antigenic protein(s), resulting in direct production of such antigen(s) within the vaccine recipient to trigger an appropriate immune response.

domain　A region of a gene or gene product.

dose-ranging study　A clinical trial in which two or more doses (starting at a lower dose and proceeding to higher doses) of a treatment drug or vaccine are tested against each other to determine which dose works best and has acceptable side effects.

double-blind study　A clinical trial in which neither the study staff nor the participants know which participants are receiving the experimental drug and which are receiving a placebo or another therapy.

drug-resistant tuberculosis　Recent strains of tuberculosis that are impervious to one or more of the 13 commonly used antibiotics employed to treat the disease.

efficacy　Ability to produce results. Investigational drugs are assessed for their efficacy in treating specific infections, for example.

ejaculation   The discharge of semen from the penis during sexual intercourse or other stimulation.

encephalitis   Inflammation of the brain.

endemic   Disease found in certain areas or groups of people.

end point   The results of an intervention compared among different study groups in a clinical trial. In early vaccine trials, common end points are safety and specific types and intensities of immune responses.

enteritis   Inflammation of the intestine.

envelope   Outer surface of a virus, also called the coat. Not all viruses have an envelope.

enzyme   A kind of protein that causes chemical changes inside cells.

Enzyme-Linked Immunosorbent Assay (ELISA)   A simple blood test that can measure antibodies to HIV. This test can produce false positive results, so it is repeated when positive and is confirmed with a more sophisticated test, the Western blot test.

epidemiology   The scientific and medical study of the incidence, distribution, and control of disease.

Epstein-Barr virus   A virus found in the nose and throat that causes mononucleosis and may cause chronic fatigue syndrome. It has been seen in lymphadenopathy, Kaposi's sarcoma, and other opportunistic infections.

erythrocytes   Red blood cells that carry oxygen to the other cells of the body.

Erythropoietin   A drug approved for treatment of severe anemia, which can accompany AZT use. The drug is based on a naturally occurring compound and stimulates red blood cell production.

etiology   The study of factors that cause disease.

expanded access   A system through which experimental drugs are distributed to some HIV-infected people who cannot participate in clinical drug trials and may lack other opportunities for treatment.

Factor VIII   A component of the blood system that causes it to clot. A shortage of this element is the source of hemophilia.

false negative   The result of a blood test in which a blood sample contains too few antibodies or antigens to show a positive result. A person with this test result could be thought not to carry the virus that causes AIDS even though it is present.

fellatio   The act of stimulating a male penis with the tongue or mouth during sexual activity.

fisting   The insertion of the hand into the rectum or vagina during sexual activity.

fluconazole   A drug approved for use against candidiasis and cryptococcal meningitis.

Food and Drug Administration (FDA)   The federal agency charged with approving new drug treatments for use by the public.

foscavir   An antiviral agent approved for use against CMV retinitis, CMV colitis, and strains of herpes simplex and zoster.

full-blown AIDS   A case of HIV infection that meets the requirements of the CDC case definition.

fungus   A class of microbes that includes mushrooms, yeasts, and molds. PWAs are vulnerable to a host of fungi that are usually fought off by the body.

ganciclovir   An antiviral drug approved for treatment of CMV retinitis.

gay   Specifically refers to a man who finds other men sexually attractive. The term is also used to refer generally to gay men and lesbians as a group.

genetic   Having to do with genes, tiny segments of chemicals inside all viruses and cells that carry the information needed to make proteins that perform basic functions (such as the replication of viruses).

genitalia   The external sex organs of the body. In the female, these include the vulva, the inner and outer lips of the vagina, and the clitoris. In the male, the penis, scrotum, and testicles are included.

giardiasis   An infection of the small intestine caused by a common protozoan passed through person-to-person contact or contaminated food or water.

glycoprotein (gp)   A protein molecule that is glycosylated—that is, coated with a carbohydrate, or sugar. The outer coat proteins of HIV are glycoproteins. The number after the gp (for example, gp120, gp160) is its molecular weight.

glycoprotein 120 (gp120)   One of the proteins that forms the envelope of HIV; gp120 projects from the surface of HIV and binds to the CD4 molecule on helper T cells. gp120 has been a logical experimental HIV vaccine because the outer envelope is the first part of the virus that encounters an antibody.

gonorrhea   A sexually transmitted disease.

hairy leukoplakia   A white lesion that shows on the side of the tongue. It may be related to Epstein-Barr viral infection.

harm reduction   Strategies aimed at assisting people who use drugs to do so more safely by helping them manage their drug use and their personal health and by placing abstinence from drugs at one end of a continuum of behaviors. The acceptance of harm reduction strategies has grown with the spread of HIV and the realization by some health care providers that services are needed for active drug users and for people seeking to end drug use.

helper T cells   Also known as T4 and CD4, this set of T cells (helper, killer, and suppressor cells) prompts antibody response and stimulates other immune functions.

hemoglobin   The component of red blood cells that carries oxygen.

hemophilia   A disorder of the blood system found in some people in which they lack a sufficient amount of clotting factor.

hepatitis   An illness causing inflammation of the liver, accompanied by fever and jaundice.

Herpes Simplex Virus I (HSV I)   A virus that causes sores or blisters around the mouth that can be transmitted to the genitals. The virus can be set into action by trauma, stress, infection, or immune suppression.

Herpes Simplex Virus II (HSV II)   A virus that causes sores or blisters on the anus or genitals. The virus may be in a latent state in nerve tissue, become active, and produce symptoms. HSV II can be transmitted to an infant from an infected mother at birth.

Herpes Varicella-Zoster Virus (HVZ)   The virus that causes chicken pox in children and may manifest in adults as herpes zoster, also called shingles. Shingles are painful blisters that pattern themselves on the skin along nerve paths, frequently on the face and trunk of the body.

heterosexual intercourse   Sexual activity between a male and a female.

high-risk behavior   The preferred term for referring to actions that place one in danger of being exposed to HIV. In the early years of the epidemic, high-risk groups included gay men, IV drug users, their sexual partners, and others, but the evolution of language has placed the emphasis on behavior that can be changed or influenced rather than on groups of people whose sexuality or drug use makes them a target of other discrimination. High-risk behavior includes unprotected sexual intercourse and sharing of needles in IV drug use.

HIV antibody screening test   Refers to the two tests for the HIV antibody—ELISA and the Western blot.

HIV negative   A test result that shows no antibodies to HIV. This result does not necessarily mean a person does not have HIV, however, because it may take as long as six months for the body to produce antibodies. During that period, the person can still transmit the virus to others.

HIV positive   A test result that shows the presence of antibodies to HIV. This result does not mean the person has AIDS or will develop AIDS.

homophobia   A bias against homosexuals and homosexuality.

horizontal transmission   The passing of HIV through blood or semen.

host   A cell or an organism that provides a home for the growth of a virus or a parasite.

Human Immunodeficiency Virus (HIV)   The retrovirus that causes AIDS.

Human T-Lymphotropic Virus Type III (HTLV III)   Term first used by U.S. scientists to refer to the virus that causes AIDS.

Human T-Lymphotropic Virus Type III/Lymphadenopathy-Associated Virus (HTLV III/LAV)   Two very similar viruses that are considered a primary cause of AIDS.

humoral immunity   Immunity that results from the activity of antibodies in blood and lymphoid tissue.

iatrogenic   Caused by the activities of a physician.

immune   Resistant to a disease, possibly because of the presence of antibodies.

immune boosters or immune modulators   Substances that enhance the body's natural defenses against infection and disease.

immune system   System through which the body fights off infections, viruses, bacteria, and other foreign matter. The body uses these defenses again when called on to fight the same threat.

immunity   Natural or acquired resistance provided by the immune system to a specific disease.

immunocompetent   Capable of developing an immune response; possessing a normal immune system.

immunodeficient   An immune system that is not functioning or that is suppressed in some way, making one vulnerable to infection and disease.

immunogen   A substance capable of provoking an immune response.

immunoglobulin   A general term for antibodies that bind to invading organisms, which leads to their destruction.

incidence   The number of cases of a disease occurring in a particular period of time.

inclusion/exclusion criteria   The medical or social reasons a person may or may not qualify for participation in a clinical trial. For example, some trials may exclude people with chronic liver disease or certain drug allergies; others may include only people with a low CD4+ T cell count.

incubation period   The period of time it takes for something, such as a disease, to develop in the body after infection or exposure has taken place.

Indinavir (Crixivan)   The most widely prescribed protease inhibitor.

infection   A bodily condition in which an infectious agent enters, multiplies, and produces a negative effect.

infectious   Can be transmitted by infection.

informed consent   A method of protecting people who are, for instance, being tested for HIV or entering a drug trial. Participants must indicate that they understand some basic information about the procedure by signing a consent form.

institutional review board   A group of doctors, scientists, and people with HIV/AIDS that ensures that a clinical drug trial or research program is safe and that the rights of participants are protected.

intercourse   Sexual activity in which a man places his penis into a woman's vagina (heterosexual activity) or into another person's (male or female) rectum (homosexual or heterosexual activity).

interleukin-2   A lymphokine that is important to immune response and results in the expansion and proliferation of T lymphocytes.

intravenous drugs   Chemical substances used in the body by inserting a needle into a vein.

investigational new drug (IND)   The status of an experimental drug after the FDA agrees it can be tested in people.

in vitro   A scientific study conducted in an artificial environment, such as one created in a test tube.

in vivo   A scientific study conducted in a living organism, such as an animal or a human being.

Kaposi's sarcoma (KS)   A rare form of cancer usually found in older men prior to the onset of the HIV epidemic. The cancer is most widely recognized by the appearance of purple spots on the skin, resulting from tumors in the walls of blood vessels. The lesions can occur inside the body as well.

Kaposi's sarcoma (KS) and opportunistic infections   An early name CDC officials used to describe what was eventually called AIDS.

latency   A period during which an organism is present in the body but is causing no apparent effect.

LAV-HTLV III   Another of the names used for the virus that causes AIDS.

lesbian   A woman who finds other women sexually attractive.

lesion   A term used to refer to the infected part or sore in a skin disease.

leukocytes   White blood cells.

leukopenia   A low level of leukocytes in the blood.

lymph   A yellowish fluid carrying lymphocytes. Lymph comes from fluids in tissues and is collected from all parts of the body and put back into the blood system.

lymph nodes   The specific sites of the immune system throughout the body. The nodes are small organs where lymphocytes are found and they filter lymph fluid. Antigens in the body are filtered by the lymph system or the spleen and are attacked by the immune system.

lymphadenopathy   Swollen lymph nodes caused by an infection. Influenza, mononucleosis, lymphoma, or HIV may be the cause.

Lymphadenopathy-Associated Virus (LAV) A retrovirus in a person with enlarged lymph nodes who may have engaged in high-risk behavior. LAV is believed to be the same virus as HTLV-III.

Lymphadenopathy Syndrome Chronically enlarged lymph nodes often found in HIV infection.

lymphatic system A network running throughout the body to transport lymph to the immune system and into the blood system.

lymphocytes Cells produced in the lymph tissue.

lymphokines Substances released into the bloodstream by the T cells to direct immune response.

lymphoma Cancer of the lymph nodes.

macrophage A cell that scavenges particulate matter in the system, especially in the form of infectious bacteria. These cells stimulate other cells to develop immune response by presenting them with small particles of invader cells. Macrophages are reservoir sites for HIV.

Magnetic Resonance Imaging (MRI) A diagnostic procedure that reveals information about the internal tissues and organs of the body.

malabsorption Deficient intake of nutrients from the intestinal tract. HIV infection can cause the absorbing villi lining of the intestines to atrophy. Malabsorption can lead to malnutrition, causing further immune suppression.

malaise A nonspecific condition of discomfort.

malignant Cancerous.

mandatory testing Required HIV antibody testing.

meningitis Infection of the membranes that surround the brain.

metastasis The spread of cancer in the body.

microbe Living organisms of microscopic size. Microbes includes fungus, protozoa, and bacteria.

molecule The smallest particle of a substance that can exist on its own.

monogamy A continuing sexual relationship with one partner.

morbidity Frequency with which a disease is appearing in a population.

mucosal immunity Resistance to infection across the mucous membranes. Mucosal immunity depends on immune cells and antibodies present in the linings of the reproductive tract, gastrointestinal tract, and other moist surfaces of the body exposed to the outside world.

multidrug-resistant tuberculosis Recent strains of tuberculosis that are impervious to 2 or more of the 13 commonly used antibiotics employed to treat the disease.

Mycobacterium Avium Intracellulare (MAI) A bacillus that causes infection of the internal organs. About 50 percent of PWAs show signs of MAI at the time of death.

natural killer cell   A nonspecific lymphocyte that attacks and kills cancer cells and cells infected by microorganisms. Natural killers do not need to recognize a specific antigen to attack and kill.

needle exchange   The practice of providing clean syringes to intravenous drug users in an effort to reduce the incidence of transmission of HIV.

Nelfinavir (Viracept)   A protease inhibitor that seems to cause fewer toxicities and have fewer dietary restrictions associated with it than many other drugs in its class.

neonatal   The period of the first few weeks of life after birth.

neutralizing antibody   An antibody that keeps a virus from infecting a cell, usually by blocking receptors on the cells or the virus.

Nevirapine (Viramune)   A reverse transcriptase inhibitor approved by the FDA in June 1996.

nonoxynol-9   A chemical in some spermicides, lubricants, and condoms that reduces the risk of HIV infection.

oil-based lubricants   Ordinary hand lotions, baby oil, Crisco, Vaseline, and mineral oil are oil-based lubricants that may be used in sexual intercourse but that can cause condoms to break.

open-label trial   A clinical trial in which doctors and participants know what drug or vaccine is being administered to all participants.

opportunistic infections   A general term for the variety of diseases and infections that can surface and become problematic when the immune system is depressed as the result of HIV infection. These infections would not affect a healthy person.

oral-anal sex   The use of the tongue or mouth to stimulate the anus of a sexual partner.

oral sex   Stimulation of a sex partner's genitals with the mouth or tongue.

orphan drug   A medication indicated for a rare disease. The Orphan Drug Act of 1983 gives tax breaks, as well as a monopoly, to pharmaceutical companies as an incentive to develop drugs useful for up to 200,000 people.

pandemic   An epidemic disease of widespread proportions.

parallel track   A method of providing experimental drugs to patients who cannot participate in regular drug trials and have no other opportunities for treatment.

parasite   A plant or animal that feeds off another living thing. Not all parasites cause disease, but some (especially food-borne parasites) can be life threatening to people with HIV/AIDS.

partner notification   A public health practice of notifying the sexual partners of a person infected with an STD of their own risk of transmitted infection.

passive immunotherapy A treatment in which blood from an HIV-positive asymptomatic person is processed to deactivate the virus and is then transfused to HIV-infected recipients.

pathogen Any microorganism or material that produces disease.

Patient Zero A term that refers to Air Canada steward Gaetan Dugas, established by public health researchers as the person who had sex with many of the first gay men diagnosed with what eventually became known as AIDS.

Pelvic Inflammatory Disease (PID) Painful infection of a woman's fallopian tubes, commonly transmitted by sexual intercourse and sometimes following an abortion. PID is not part of the CDC diagnostic framework for AIDS but has been characterized as a common component of HIV/AIDS in women.

perinatal Any event that takes places at or around the time of birth.

Persistent Generalized Lymphadenopathy Chronic noncancerous lymph node enlargement.

phagocyte A type of cell that destroys foreign matter in the system, including bacteria.

pharmacokinetics The processes of absorption, distribution, metabolism, and excretion of a drug or vaccine.

placebo A substance administered in a drug investigation to measure the efficiency of a specific drug. A placebo is inactive and can cause a change in a patient, called the placebo effect, as a result of the patient's expectations.

platelets Cellular fragments that circulate and play an important role in blood clotting.

Pneumocystis carinii **pneumonia (PCP)** A parasitic, fungal pneumonia common in persons with AIDS. PCP is the most life threatening of the opportunistic infections.

polymerase An enzyme that creates genetic material, either ribonucleic acid (RNA) or dioxynucleic acid (DNA), from building blocks.

polyvalent vaccine A vaccine produced from, or made to induce immune responses against, multiple viral strains.

prevalence The number of cases of a disease at a given time.

prognosis Medical outlook.

prophylaxis Any treatment intended to prevent disease and preserve health.

protease An enzyme HIV uses to make new copies of itself inside infected cells.

protease inhibitors A class of drugs that stop protease from making new copies of HIV that can infect other cells. When a protease inhibitor is used in combination with two nucleoside analogues in treatment, it can reduce levels of HIV in the blood to undetectable levels.

proteins   One of the major components of cells, made up of amino acids.

protocol   A set of rules for a clinical trial. The protocol describes what types of patients will participate, the schedule of tests and procedures, drugs and dosages, and the length of time the study will be conducted.

protozoa   One-celled animals, some of which cause disease in humans.

p24   A protein in HIV's inner core. The p24 antigen test looks for the presence of this protein in a person's blood.

quarantine   The often involuntary isolation of persons with infection. Cuba has quarantined persons with HIV infection.

radiation   A form of treatment for cancer using high-level radiation such as X-rays.

randomized trial   A study in which participants are assigned by chance to one of two or more intervention arms or regimens. Randomization minimizes the differences among groups by equally distributing people with particular characteristics among all the trial arms.

recombinant DNA technology   The technique by which genetic material from one organism is inserted into a foreign cell to mass-produce the protein encoded by the inserted genes.

recombinant human alpha interferon   A drug approved for use against Kaposi's sarcoma.

rectum   The end of the intestinal tract; the section of the intestine through which bowel movements, or stools, pass. It is also the interior site of anal intercourse.

red blood cells   The component of the blood that carries oxygen to the cells.

retinitis   Inflammation of the retina that can lead to blindness. In AIDS, it is caused by infection with CMV.

retrovirus   Group of viruses that contain the genetic material RNA and copy it into DNA inside an infected cell. The DNA that results from this process is then included in the genetic structure of the cell as a provirus, which is then passed to each infected cell's offspring cells. In the case of HIV, the problem this presents is that to kill the virus, the cell must also be killed.

reverse transcriptase   An enzyme in retroviruses that can copy RNA into DNA. This process is necessary for the life cycle of HIV.

reverse transcriptase inhibitor   A drug that stops reverse transcriptase from doing its job efficiently inside infected cells.

rimming   Stimulation of the anus with the tongue.

risk factors   Generally refers to behaviors or practices that place one at risk for HIV transmission. The most common risk factors are IV drug use and unprotected sexual intercourse. Previously, use of blood or blood products was also a risk factor.

Ritonavir (Norvir)   A protease inhibitor.

rubber   A common term for a condom.

safer sex   A general term to describe sexual practices and attitudes that protect a person from transmitting or receiving HIV. Also describes any sexual activity that does not involve the exchange of body fluids.

Salk Immunogen   A therapeutic vaccine developed under the direction of Jonas Salk (developer of one of the key polio vaccines in the 1950s) and Dennis Carlo. The vaccine is unique in two ways: First, it was developed as a treatment for those already infected, and second, it is made from whole killed HIV to which the body responds when exposed by producing antibodies to all of the core proteins (p24, p17, and others) and by developing massive cellular immunity. Early clinical trials showed the vaccine is both safe and effective, but large-scale efficacy trials may be indefinitely delayed.

salmonella   A bacterial infection about 20 times more common in persons with immune system deficiencies than in those with healthy immune systems; recurrent incidences in HIV-positive people are grounds for a diagnosis of AIDS.

salmonellosis (*Salmonellae*)   Bacteria that are usually food or water borne and multiply in the small intestine.

saquinavir (Fortovase)   A more powerful iteration of saquinavir mesylate that is better absorbed and, when used with two nucleoside analogues, produces more substantial decreases in the amount of HIV in the blood.

saquinavir mesylate (Invirase)   The first protease inhibitor available to people with HIV/AIDS.

semen   The fluid a male ejaculates from the penis during orgasm.

seroconversion   Change of a person's antibody status (seronegative) to positive.

serologic test   A class of laboratory tests performed on the serum (clear liquid) portion of the blood.

seronegative   Test result that reflects a negative result for the HIV antibody test.

seropositive   Test result that reflects a positive result for the HIV antibody test.

seroprevalence   A number that expresses the frequency or absolute number of people in a given group (city, state, clinic) with positive results for the HIV antibody test.

serum   The clear, fluid portion of the blood that contains antibodies.

sexually transmitted disease (STD)   A disease transmitted through sexual contact. More than 25 different infections are classified as STDs, including gonorrhea, syphilis, and herpes simplex. Most STDs can be treated.

sharing needles   Using a needle to inject drugs after it has been used by someone else, or passing it to another person after using it oneself. A small amount of blood accumulates in the syringe when it is used, and, if infected, that blood can transmit HIV to another user.

shigellosis (Shigella)   An acute infection of the bowel, caused by the Shigella organism, that is very common in persons with immune system problems.

shingles   See Herpes Varicella-Zoster Virus.

SIDA   The acronym for AIDS in Spanish and French.

side effects   Unwanted or unexpected actions or responses caused by a drug. Experimental drugs are studied for both short-term and long-term side effects.

Simian Immunodeficiency Virus   An HIV-like virus that infects and causes an AIDS-like disease in some species of monkeys.

spermicide   A chemical that kills sperm and other organisms on contact. Spermicides are used on condoms, in lubricants, and in contraceptive jellies and foams.

spleen   An organ in the abdomen that plays an important role in the functioning of the immune system.

straight   A heterosexual person.

subcutaneous   Beneath the skin, as in a subcutaneous injection.

sulfonamides   A type of antibiotic drug.

suppressor T cells   A type of T cell that stops antibody production and some other immune responses.

symptoms   Changes in the body or body functions that indicate disease.

T4   See CD4.

T cells, T helper cells, or T lymphocytes   White blood cells used by the immune system to fight infection. There are three types of cells helper, killer, and suppressor. They are found mainly in the blood and the lymph system and are targeted by HIV. When a patient experiences a T cell count of 200 or less, he or she is considered to have AIDs according to the most recent CDC surveillance case definition. AIDS-linked infections and deaths typically occur at levels below 50.

3TC (lamivuddine)   A nucleoside analogue frequently used in combination with AZT to prevent HIV from developing resistance.

thrush   An infection in the throat, mouth, or esophagus caused by the fungus candida. Thrush manifests as white patches.

thymus   An organ in the chest cavity in which T cells develop. The thymus is inert in adults.

titer   A measurement used in a laboratory to find the concentration of a particular component in a solution.

toxicity   The extent to which a substance is harmful or poisonous to the body.

toxoplasmosis   A disease caused by infection with the protozoan *Toxoplasma gondii,* passed in the feces of infected cats. Inflammation of the brain is a frequent result.

treatment IND (investigational new drug)   A program that offers experimental treatment to patients who lack satisfactory alternative treatments.

tuberculosis (TB)   An acute or chronic infection seen more frequently in HIV-positive people and poor people. It is caused by an airborne pathogen passed through inhalation, thus contributing to its spread in crowded physical situations, such as overcrowded housing and shelters. Although TB was once believed to be virtually extinct in the United States, case numbers have risen in recent years.

underground   A general term to refer to self-help activities by PWAs and HIV-positive people that bring untested or unapproved drugs into the country from other sources or manufacture them outside official laboratory environments.

unprotected sex   Sexual activity without a condom or dental dam.

vaccine   A substance made of the antigenic components of an infectious organism. The resulting substance prompts an immune response but not the disease itself when put into the body. A person is subsequently protected against infection by that organism.

vaccinia   A cowpox virus, formerly used in human smallpox vaccines. Employed as a vector in HIV vaccines to transport HIV genes into the body.

vagina   The organ in females that leads from the vulva to the uterus.

vaginal intercourse   The insertion of the penis into the vagina.

vaginal secretions   Fluids found in the vagina.

vaginitis   Infectious and inflammatory diseases of the vagina, usually caused by bacteria. Although not part of the CDC diagnostic framework for AIDS, vaginitis has been characterized as a common component of HIV/AIDS in women.

vertical transmission   The passing of disease or infection to a child through infection of the placenta.

viral culture   A method for growing viruses in the laboratory.

viral load   The numbers of viruses present in the blood or tissues.

viremia   The presence of virus in the bloodstream.

virology   The study of viruses.

virus   An organism that causes infectious disease and needs living cells (a host) to reproduce. A virus may take over a cell's normal functioning and cause it to behave in ways determined by the virus.

vulva   The inner and outer lips of the vagina and the clitoris in a female.

wasting   Involuntary weight loss, a common symptom of HIV infection.

water-based lubricant   A substance without oil or grease used in sexual intercourse because it does not weaken a condom.

weight loss   Indicates progression of HIV disease and can occur at any stage of the infection. It can result from malabsorption of nutrients and is thus associated with malnutrition, which can contribute to immune suppression.

Western blot   A laboratory procedure that detects antibodies to HIV. The Western blot test is more sensitive than the ELISA test and is used as a backup for positive ELISA results.

works   A slang expression for syringes used for injecting drugs.

zoster   See Herpes Varicella-Zoster Virus.

Index

Aaron Diamond AIDS Research
    Center, 75
Abstinence, 88, 136, 281
*Abstracts: XI International
    Conference on AIDS* (CD-
    ROM), 289–290
ACT UP (AIDS Coalition to
    Unleash Power), 25–26, 28,
    29, 50, 51–52, 53, 54, 55, 56,
    58, 64, 65, 73, 76, 247, 276–277
Acting Up for Prisoners (video), 283
Activism, 26, 43, 50, 52, 53, 54, 55,
    56, 60, 64, 65, 68
Adolescents, 61, 102, 132,
    148–149, 263
*Adolescents: At Risk for HIV
    Infection* (video), 283
Aerosolized Pentamidine, 10, 53
Africa, sub-Saharan, 4, 39, 79, 107,
    108–111
African Americans, 3, 11–12, 13,
    14, 67, 73, 152–154
    in demographic study, 132, 138,
    144, 148, 159
AIDS (Acquired Immune
    Deficiency Syndrome), 6, 7–8,
    26, 175, 262, 278–282. *See also
    under* Centers for Disease
    Control and Prevention
    epidemic onset, 1–2, 9, 169–182
    long-term survival of, 64, 65,
    72, 76, 83–84
    morbidity, by state, 119, 122
    morbidity/mortality, by year, 3,
    4, 11, 31, 34, 39–40, 41, 42, 43,
    44, 45, 46, 49, 50, 51, 52, 54,
    56, 58, 61, 64, 65, 67, 72, 76,
    77, 78, 79, 106, 107, 116.
    See also HIV (Human
    Immunodeficiency Virus);
    Primary immune deficiency
AIDS: A Decision for Life (video),
    283
AIDS Action Council, 238
AIDS Drug Assistance Program
    (ADAP), 18, 21, 24–25,
    125–130
AIDS Housing Opportunities Act
    (1990), 15, 209
*AIDS in the Nineties: From Science
    to Policy* (video), 284
AIDS Is about Secrets (video), 284
AIDS: Me and My Baby (video),
    284
AIDS: No Second Chance (video),
    284
AIDS Related Complex (ARC),
    8
AIDS Research Information
    Center (ARIC), 13, 238–239
AIDS services, 12–14, 17, 20–25,
    32, 41, 56, 60, 64, 65, 70, 71
    organizations for, 214, 247–251
The AIDS Show: Artists Involved
    (video), 285
AIDS: The Second Decade (video),
    284–285
AIDS Treatment Data Network,
    239
AIDS Treatment News, 49, 247
AL 721 (Active Lipid), 49
Alpha interferon, 153
Alternative medical treatment, 4,
    156, 270, 271

American Association for World Health, 152, 160, 161

American Civil Liberties Union (ACLU), 239

American Foundation for AIDS Research (AmFAR), 52, 239–240

American Red Cross, 42, 43, 71, 240–241

American Social Health Association (ASHA), 241

Americans with Disabilities Act (ADA) (1990), 15, 208, 217–222

An Early Frost (video), 286

Anal intercourse, 64. *See also* Male-to-male HIV transmission

And the Band Played On (video), 285

Animal testing, 72–73, 76

Antiviral drug, 30

As Is (video), 285

Asians, 111–112, 133–134, 159, 279–280

Asymptomatic individuals, 20, 22–23, 42, 45, 46, 71

Australia, 72, 80, 115

AZT (azidothymidine), 10, 18, 27, 47, 53, 58, 63, 64, 66, 74, 76
  monotherapy/combination therapy, 30, 71, 79, 142
  pricing of, 24, 26, 27–29, 53

Babalu-Aiye, 4

Baltimore, David, 40, 106

Barebacking, 137

Bartlett, John G., 8–9, 31, 82

Behavior modification, 48, 135–137

Behaviors, 34, 44, 45, 48, 88, 148–149, 264
  and individual responsibility, 212
  See also Heterosexual HIV transmission; Injection drugs; Male-to-male HIV transmission; Unprotected sex

Bergalis, Kimberly, 14, 61, 82–83

Biting, 222

Blood donations, 42, 43, 44, 46, 49, 67, 68, 70, 72

Blood/blood products, 77, 176–179, 269, 280
  clotting products, 45, 60, 66, 68, 137, 138, 139, 158
  transfusions, 41, 42, 44, 47, 55, 57, 107, 149

Bone marrow, 72

Born in Africa (video), 285

Buchanan, Patrick, 43

Buckley, Kathleen, 214

Burroughs Wellcome, 26, 27–29, 47, 53, 58, 66

Bush, George, 15, 50, 54, 60, 61

Callen, Michael, 83–84

Canada, 248, 268, 273

Candidiasis (*Candida albicans*), 96, 101, 138, 141

Caribbean, 114–115, 119

Caring about AIDS: The Common Ground (video), 285

Caring for Infants and Toddlers with HIV Infection (video), 286

Caring for School-Age Children with HIV Infection (video), 286

Carl Vogel Foundation, 241

Casual contact, 48, 49

CD4, 9, 68, 95–96, 142, 145

Centers for Disease Control and Prevention (CDC), 29, 46, 48, 55, 67, 68, 72, 73, 77, 78, 79, 235–236
  case definition of AIDS by, 7–8, 58, 61, 64, 95–97, 138
  recommendations by, 59, 60, 69
  reports of, 41, 42, 43, 71, 95–97, 148, 169–182

Cervical cancer, 7, 96, 138

Cervical intraepithelial neoplasia (CIN), 141–142

Chieze, François, 108, 109

Children, 11, 49, 77, 107, 114, 214, 216–217, 225–226, 260, 268
  HIV illness in, 7, 76, 97, 102, 144–148
  HIV testing of, 47, 49, 68
  See also Infants

Christmas at Starcross (video), 286

Clinical trials, 79, 141, 143–144, 207

Clinton, Bill, 16–20, 22–23, 70, 72, 73, 74, 75, 77, 79, 148

Cocktail therapy, 30–31. *See also* Combination therapy
Colitis, 303
Combination therapy, 10, 30–32, 71, 86
    triple, 74, 75, 78, 119
Combivir (zidovudine/ iamivudine), 10
Common Threads: Stories from the Quilt (video), 286
Community Programs for Clinical Research (CPCRA), 138, 141
Community Research Initiative on AIDS (CRIA), 241
Compassionate use programs, 25
Condoms, 56–57, 59, 62, 64, 75, 77, 110, 112
Conference of Mayors, U.S. (USCM), 237–238
Conference of State and Territorial Epidemiologists, 43
Confidentiality, 47, 66, 103, 104, 231, 232
Court cases, 34, 66, 67, 69, 73, 74, 76, 79, 211–214, 217–232
    on blood distribution, 57, 65, 68, 77
    on concealment of HIV status, 65, 68, 229
    on disability, 217–222
    on employment, 66, 222–225
Crixivan, 30, 73, 77
Cryptococcal meningitis (CM), 99–100
Cryptococcosis (*Cryptococcus neoformans*), 96, 99
Cryptosporidiosis, 31, 69, 96, 100–101
Cytomegalovirus (CMV), 31, 96, 98

Dana Farber Cancer Institute, 77
De Wit, John, 137
Deeks, Steven, 31
Dementia, 7
Dental practices, 14, 56, 59, 66, 83
Desrosiers, Ronald, 78
Diana (princess of Wales), 78
DiAna's Hair Ego: AIDS Info up Front (video), 286
Didanosine (ddI) (Videx), 59, 62
Dideoxycytidine (ddC) (Hivid), 62
Directly observed therapy, 62
Disability, determination of, 32–33, 65, 229–230. *See also* Americans with Disabilities Act
Discrimination, 14, 17, 46, 69, 70, 210–211
DNA (deoxyribonucleic acid), 40
Dole, Elizabeth, 71
Drug abuse, 54, 159, 278, 281–282. *See also* Injection drugs
Drug therapy, 3, 27–28, 30, 31
    approvals. *See under* Food and Drug Administration
    costs, 3, 9, 26, 27–29, 30, 32, 50, 53, 73, 158, 160
    print resources on, 262, 264, 265, 266, 267, 272, 273, 274, 275
    purchase programs for, 17, 18, 22, 24–25, 32–33, 255–257
    See also Combination therapy; Funding; Vaccine
Dying for Sex (video), 286

Education, 13–14, 26–27, 40, 54, 61, 87, 91, 136–137, 162, 212
    limitations on, 16, 20, 46, 55, 63, 71, 136, 208
    in minority communities, 152, 153, 154, 155, 157
Elderly, 3, 55, 149, 152
Employee rights, 66, 70, 204–205, 222–225
Encephalitis, toxoplasmic (TE), 98–99
Envelope, 6
Enzyme-Linked Immunosorbent Assay (ELISA), 6, 103
Europe, 71
    Western, 9, 107, 115–116
    Eastern, 115
Expanded access, defined, 62

Factor VIII, 45
Family Health International, 77
Federal Plan for Biomedical Research, 18
Financial planning, in end-of-life concerns, 214, 216
Fleming, Patricia, 116

Florida, 119, 122
Fluconazole, 141
Food and Drug Administration
    (FDA), 17, 25, 26, 62, 67, 71,
    236
    drug/test approvals, 10, 17, 18,
    25, 26, 48, 50, 53, 59, 62, 64,
    65, 66, 74, 76, 79
Forrester Church (video), 287
Forum for Collaborative HIV
    Research, 18
France, 10, 43, 44, 55
Francis, Don, 90
Funding, 12
    federal, 42, 44, 45, 46, 47–48, 74,
    116, 207, 208
    private, 12, 47–48, 52, 58, 60, 70,
    75, 78, 261–262
    state, 25, 125, 126, 243

Gallo, Robert C., 40, 44, 47, 55, 57,
    69, 84
Gates, Henry Louis, Jr., 154
Gay Men's Health Crisis, 12, 41,
    70
Geffen, David, 70
Gendin, Stephen, 31, 85, 212
Gonsiorek, John C., 135–137
Gore, Al, 22, 79
Government. *See* Legislation;
    individual presidents
Greenspan, Judy, 85
GRID (Gay Related Immune
    Deficiency), 2

Haitians, 2, 11, 26, 42, 43, 46, 64,
    152
Hardy, Lee, 13
Harrington, Imami, 86
Health and Human Services,
    Department of (DHHS), 40,
    43, 44, 46, 47, 79, 236
Health care, 4, 9–10, 16, 67, 69, 72,
    156, 214
    access to, 3, 20, 25, 32–33,
    46–47, 95
    print resources on, 260, 261,
    262, 265, 269, 276
    See also AIDS services; Drug
    therapy; Health care workers;
    Medicaid; Ryan White
    Comprehensive AIDS

    Resource Emergency Act
Health care workers, 2
    and HIV exposure, 54, 79, 161
    HIV status of, 49, 57, 58, 59, 60,
    63, 65, 68, 225
    print resources for, 260, 262,
    263, 264, 269, 274–275
    training for, 21, 42, 44
Health Insurance Portability Act
    (1996), 23–24, 30, 209–210
Health Resources and Services
    Administration (HRSA),
    236–237
Healy, Bernadine, 58
Heckler, Margaret, 43, 44, 46
Helms, Jesse, 58–59, 63, 69, 207, 208
Hemophilia, 11, 42, 45, 60, 66, 68,
    157–158, 176–179, 196–198,
    225–226, 279. *See also*
    Blood/blood products
Hepatitis, 158
Herpes simplex (HSV I, II), 96,
    102, 138, 141
Herpes Varicella-Zoster Virus
    (HVZ), 102
Herpes virus (CMV), 31
Heterosexual HIV transmission,
    3, 4, 41, 48, 49, 51, 179–180
    outside U.S., 107, 108, 112, 114
    and women, 12, 41, 42, 49, 137,
    139, 140, 155
High-risk behavior, defined, 48
Hispanic Americans, 3, 11–12, 13,
    14, 132, 144, 148, 154–156,
    159, 267, 268, 270, 274
HIV (Human Immunodeficiency
    Virus), 5–6, 74, 67, 77. *See also*
    HIV infection; Retrovirus
HIV antibody screening tests, 6,
    10, 44, 45, 46, 47, 65. *See also*
    HIV testing
HIV disclosure, 59, 63, 65, 68, 229.
    See also Confidentiality
HIV infection, 11–12, 74, 75, 80,
    122
    asymptomatic, 20, 22–23, 42, 45,
    46, 71
    classification of, 95–97
    individual awareness of, 60, 78,
    103, 106
    progression of, 6–9, 67, 68
    resistance to, 67, 68, 75, 78, 84

symptoms of, 6, 7, 67, 80, 138, 141–142
See also AIDS (Acquired Immune Deficiency Syndrome); Behaviors; HIV transmission; Opportunistic infections
HIV positive/negative, 15, 103
HIV reporting, 33–34, 43, 50, 78, 119, 122
HIV testing, 10, 34, 47, 49, 50, 64, 67, 68, 70, 103–104, 230–232
  in health care, 49, 58, 59, 60, 83, 89
  home, 68, 74, 78, 103
  mandatory, 15, 58, 209, 307
  oral, 65, 103
  in pregnancy/birth, 68–69, 71, 72, 73–74
  See also Confidentiality; HIV antibody screening tests
HIV transmission, 5, 40, 48, 49, 66, 67
  criminal prosecution for, 34, 74, 211–214
  in health care, 54, 57, 58, 59, 60, 63, 65, 68, 161, 225
  mother-to-infant (perinatal), 18, 45, 61, 74, 142–143, 144, 179
  See also Behaviors; Hemophilia; Heterosexual HIV transmission; Injection drugs; Male-to-male HIV transmission
Ho, David, 9, 30, 31, 39, 67, 75, 78
Hodgkin's disease, 102
Holding, Kimberly, 149
Homeless persons, 15, 61, 194–196, 276
Homophobia, 152, 155
Homosexuality, attitudes toward, 113, 152, 155, 157, 162, 208
Hot lines, 103, 251–254
Hotron, Meurig, 212
Housing, 13, 15, 17, 56, 64, 65, 76, 209, 227
HPA-23, 48
HTLV-III/LAV. *See* Human T-Lymphotropic Virus Type III/Lymphadenopathy-Associated Virus
Hudson, Rock, 14, 47, 48

Human papillomavirus (HPV), 141
Human Rights Campaign Fund, 21, 22, 162, 242
Human T cell leukemia virus type I (HTLV-I), 40
Human T-Lymphotropic Virus Type III, 44, 45
Human T-Lymphotropic Virus Type III/Lymphadenopathy-Associated Virus (HTLV III/LAV), 43, 46, 47

Immigration policy, 58, 64, 65, 68, 71, 76, 89, 208, 209
Immune system, 6, 263
India, 71, 112
Indinavir (Crixivan), 72
Infants, 2, 41
  HIV testing of, 68–69, 71, 73–74
  HIV transmission to, 7, 18, 45, 61, 72, 74, 142–143, 145, 179
Injection drugs, 3, 11–12, 42, 43, 45, 132, 149, 154, 159, 193–194
  outside U.S., 107, 112, 113, 114, 115
  women, 114, 137, 139
  See also Needle exchange
Insurance coverage, 23–24, 29–30, 32, 74
Interferon, 153
Interleukin–2, 40
International Conference on AIDS, 10, 50, 53, 58, 63, 74
Invirase, 69, 72
IWAX HIV Glossary, IWAX HIV Manual (CD-ROMs), 290

Jacobson, Jeffrey M., 77
James, John S., 22, 49
Johnson, Earvin "Magic," 14, 61, 63, 71, 86–87

Kaposi's sarcoma (KS), 7, 31, 41, 42, 65, 73, 96, 101, 138, 171–175
Kemron, 67, 153
Kennedy, Anthony, 218–219
Kennedy, Edward, 28
KISS: HIV/AIDS Interactive Nights Out (CD-ROM), 290–291
Kissing, 77
Koech, Davy, 153

Koop, C. Everett, 40, 50, 59, 87, 182–189, 280
Kramer, Larry, 2, 50, 65, 88, 281
Krim, Mathilde, 88–89

Lambert, Jack, 144
Lancet, 70, 112, 130
Latin America, 113–114
LAV-HTLV III. *See* Human T-Lymphotropic Virus Type III/Lymphadenopathy-Associated Virus
Legal planning, personal, 214–217, 261
Legal rights, print resources on, 264–265
Legislation, 15, 16, 17, 23–24, 207–210
Lesbians, 64, 65
Leukemia, 40, 43
Longtime Companion (video), 287
Louganis, Greg, 67
Lucey, Mary, 144
Lymphadenopathy, 7, 8, 42, 173
Lymphadenopathy-Associated Virus (LAV), 44

Macrophage, 6
Male-to-male HIV transmission, 3, 11–12, 41, 48, 107, 113, 115, 132–137, 154, 157. *See also* Unprotected sex
Mandatory testing, 15, 58, 78, 209
Marijuana use, 75, 76, 79
Mary Elizabeth, Sister, 91
Mason, Belinda, 61, 89
Medicaid, 16, 19, 20, 21–23, 61, 72, 69, 79
Medicine in the 90s: Women and HIV Infection (video), 287
Medicines. *See* Drug therapy
Mehl-Madrona, Lewis, 156, 281
Meningitis, cryptococcal (CM), 99–100
Meredith, Anne P., 109, 110
Mexico, 113
Microbicide, 18, 74
Military, 47, 49, 72
Mitzutani, Temin and S., 40
Montagnier, Luc, 10, 44, 57, 84

Morgan, D. A., 40
Mortality. *See* AIDS, morbidity/mortality
Mothers' Voices, 242
Mycobacterium, 96–97, 100
Mycobacterium avium complex (MAC), 100
Mycobacterium Avium Intracellulare (MAI), 100

NAMES Project AIDS Memorial Quilt, 51, 75, 242, 283
Natcher, William, 42
National AIDS Information Clearinghouse, 242–243
National AIDS Policy, Office of (ONAP), 18
National AIDS Research Foundation, 48
National AIDS Strategy, 16, 18, 21, 22, 104
National AIDS Treatment Advocacy Project (NATAP), 243
National Alliance of State/ Territorial AIDS Directors, 24, 243
National Association of People with AIDS (NAPWA), 190–192, 243–244
National Cancer Institute, 58, 76
National Commission on AIDS (NCOA), 1, 15, 53, 54, 63, 198–204
National Council of Churches/AIDS Task Force, 244
National Council of LaRaza AIDS Center, 244
National Gay and Lesbian Task Force (NGLTF), 244
National Hemophilia Foundation (NHF), 244
National Institute of Allergies and Infectious Diseases (NIAID), 138, 237
National Institute of Health and Human Development, 75
National Institutes of Health (NIH), 17, 54–55, 237
National Library of Medicine (NLM), 237

National Minority AIDS Council (NMAC), 245

National Native American AIDS Prevention Center, 157, 245

National Women's Health Network, 245

Native Americans, 20, 132, 156–157, 159

Needle exchange, 13, 50, 51, 52, 54, 57, 62, 71, 78, 131–132
and Clinton, 19, 74, 79, 159, 189–190

Needle sharing, 70, 160

Nevirapine (Viramune), 74

New England Journal of Medicine, 46, 63, 72, 77, 78–79, 80

New York, 41, 42, 43, 50, 51, 52, 54, 56–57, 62, 76, 116

New Zealand, 67, 115

Non, Je Ne Regrette Rien (No Regret) (video), 287

North American Syringe Exchange Network (NASEN), 131

Novello, Antonia Coello de, 155

Nutrition, 260–261, 264

One Foot on a Banana Peel, the Other in the Grave (video), 287

Opportunistic infections, 6, 31, 33, 42, 64, 65, 95–102, 170–175
health recommendations for, 69, 80
print resources on, 263, 266, 268

Orasure, 65

Orphan drugs, 27–28

Palo, Peter, 66

Parental rights, 227–228

Parents and Friends of Lesbians and Gays (PFLAG), 245

Patient assistance programs, 255–257

PCP. *See Pneumocystis carinii* pneumonia

Pelvic inflammatory disease (PID), 7, 142

People with AIDS (PWAs), 190–196, 243–244, 247–251

Pharmaceutical companies, 5, 25, 26, 27–29, 53, 79, 264

patient assistance programs, 255–257

Philadelphia (video), 288

Pierre, Laurinus, 152

The Pilgrim Must Embark: Living in Community (video), 288

Pneumocystis carinii pneumonia (PCP), 7, 9, 10, 31, 41, 42, 53, 97–98, 138, 145, 170–172, 173, 174–175, 176–177

Pneumonia, 2, 7, 96, 138

Poiesz, B. J., 40

Political Funerals (video), 288

Polls, 47, 48, 57, 68, 153–154, 162

Popovic, Mikulas, 47

Poz magazine, 26, 29, 73, 159, 271

Pregnancy, 18, 69, 72, 142–143

Prego, Veronica, 54

Presidential Advisory Council on AIDS (Clinton), 16, 18, 19, 51, 70, 79, 130–131, 189–190

Presidential Commission on the HIV Epidemic, 15, 51, 159

Prevention, 27, 54, 107, 110, 112, 162, 180–182
and behavior modification, 135–137
government policy on, 15, 16–17, 19, 46, 208
in minority communities, 153, 154, 155–156, 157
See also Education; Needle exchange; Vaccine

Primary Care of the HIV/AIDS Patient (CD-ROM), 291

Primary immune deficiency, 7, 145

Prisons, 85, 160–161, 180, 198–204, 228–229, 268, 271–272

Progressive multilocal leukoencephalopathy (PML), 97, 99

Project Inform (PI)/Treatment Action Network, 46, 246

Prostitution, 27, 49, 111

Protease inhibitors, 3, 9, 18, 29, 30, 31, 69, 72, 73, 76, 79, 86, 145, 158

Public Health Service, 44, 46, 48, 49, 142

Puerto Rico, 119, 155

PWAs. *See* People with AIDS

Quilt project, 51, 75, 283

Rape, 161, 213, 228
Ray Navarro Memorial Tape
    (video), 288
Reagan, Ronald, 14, 15, 45, 46, 48,
    50, 65
Religious belief, print resource on,
    278
Research funding. *See* Funding
Resistance. *See under* HIV
    infection
Retrovirus, 5–6, 10, 40, 43, 84
Reverse transcriptase, 40
Reverse transcriptase inhibitor,
    66, 74
Risk factors, 11. *See also* Behaviors
Ritonavir (Norvir), 29, 30, 72
Roman Catholic Church, 53, 55,
    56
Rubinstein, Arye, 2
Ruscetti, F. W., 40
Russia, 68, 75, 115
Ryan White Comprehensive AIDS
    Resource Emergency (CARE)
    Act (1990), 12, 15, 16, 17, 20,
    21, 25, 73, 125, 208–209

Safer sex, 71, 136, 212
Saliva, 65, 67
Salk, Jonas, 73, 90, 106
Salk Immunogen Vaccine, 10, 106
Salmonella, 97
San Francisco, 43, 44, 45, 46, 48,
    57, 75, 78, 137
Saquinavir (Fortovase, Invirase),
    79
Sarandon, Susan, 64
Sarngadharan, M. G., 47
Savage Nights (video), 288
School policies, 40, 47, 49, 50, 59,
    70
Science of Hope with Jonas Salk
    (video), 288–289
Seropositive/seronegative, 7, 103
Seroprevalence, 137
Serostatus, 60, 63, 68, 229
Sex, Drugs, and AIDS (video), 289
Sex education, 40, 50
Sexual practices. *See* Behaviors
Sexually transmitted disease
    (STD), 7, 70, 141, 148

Shalala, Donna, 19, 64, 74, 131
Shaw, George, 67
Shernoff, Michael, 135–137
Shilts, Randy, 2, 90–91, 265
Shingles. *See* Herpes Varicella-
    Zoster Virus
Silverlake Life: The View from Here
    (video), 289
Silverman, Mervyn, 44, 45
Social Security, and disability, 17,
    32–33, 229–230
Societal responsibility, 14–15,
    32–34, 51, 53, 277, 280
Sodomy, 34, 64
Spitting, 66, 211
Sports participation, 73, 79
States, AIDS in, 119, 122
    policy/funding for, 25, 43, 125,
    126, 130–132, 243
STD. *See* Sexually transmitted
    disease
Stigma, 4, 11, 14, 34, 69, 76, 89,
    278
Strub, Sean, 85
Substance Abuse and Mental
    Health Services (SAMHSA),
    237
Surgeon General's Report, 50,
    182–189
Syphilis, 70, 115, 152, 167(n110)
Syringes, 51, 57, 70, 71, 78, 131

T cell count, 7, 30, 64, 126, 142
T cell growth factor. *See*
    Interleukin–2
T cells/T helper cells/T
    lymphocytes, 40, 43, 44,
    97–96
TAT (HIV reproduction
    mechanism), 77
Taylor, Elizabeth, 48, 74
Test Positive Aware Network,
    246
T4 cells, 6, 47, 58, 102. *See also*
    CD4
Thalidomide, 70, 77, 141, 143
3TC (Iamivuddine, Zerit), 10, 30,
    66, 71
3TC (CD-ROM), 291–292
Thrush, 7, 101, 102
Tobacco, 65
Tongues Untied (video), 289

Toxoplasmosis (TE), 97, 98–99
Treatment Action Group, 246–247
Tuberculosis (TB), 7, 61–62, 69, 96

Ukraine, 72, 115
Ulcers, 77, 96, 141
UN AIDS (United Nations)
    program, 3, 71, 77, 79, 106
Unprotected sex, 51, 67, 73, 149,
    159, 213

Vaccine, 51, 63, 66, 71, 72, 73, 77,
    78, 80, 90, 104–106
Vaginal yeast infections, 141
Vaginitis, 7
Vertical transmission, 18, 72, 74
Viatical insurance firms, 29–30, 74
Violence Against Women Act
    (1994), 209, 231
Viral load, 30, 31, 68, 74, 103, 126
Visual AIDS, 247
Vitamin therapy, 79

Wasting syndrome, 70, 97
Waxman, Henry, 28
Western blot tests, 6, 44, 103
White House Conference on
    AIDS, 72
White, Ryan, 14, 47, 49, 51, 92,
    197–198, 226, 282

Who Pays for AIDS (video),
    289
Wilfert, Catherine M., 78
Wolfe, Maxine, 92–93
Women, 11, 55, 77, 86, 137–144,
    155, 158, 192–193
    and heterosexual HIV
        transmission, 12, 41, 42, 49,
        137, 139, 140, 154
    HIV disease in, 64, 65, 75, 138,
        141–144
    and injection drugs, 12, 42, 114,
        137, 138, 159, 160
    outside U.S., 107, 108, 110, 111,
        112, 113, 114, 115
    print resources on, 55, 261,
        270–271, 274, 275–276, 281,
        282
Women Organized to Respond
    (WORLD), 247
Women's International Health
    Study (WIHS), 141
Workplace policies. *See* Employee
    rights; Health care workers
World Health Organization, 55,
    60, 69, 71

Zingale, Daniel, 219
Zoster. *See* Herpes Varicella-
    Zoster Virus

Eric Lerner is a writer and graphic designer. Since 1982, he has written articles on different aspects of the AIDS epidemic for publications such as *The Washington Blade*, *The New York Native*, and *The Baltimore Alternative*. He has also produced educational materials on AIDS for numerous AIDS service providers, most recently the Baltimore American Indian Community Center. In 1996 and 1997, he coproduced AIDSWALK Maryland, the largest AIDS fundraiser in the state. Since 1992, he has served as volunteer Development Director for the AIDS Research Information Center, Inc. Currently, he serves as editor of *Santeria's New Aeon: Official Publication of the Orisha Consciousness Movement*. In July 1998 he was initiated as a priest of Obatala Ajaguna by Baba Raul Canizares.

Mary Ellen Hombs has long been an advocate for poor people. From 1971 to 1988 she lived and worked with homeless people in Washington, D.C.'s Community for Creative Non-Violence, helping create and operate emergency, medical, and housing services as well as being involved in national and local policy advocacy. She has worked with the National Coalition for the Homeless and the Legal Services Homelessness Task Force. She presently works in Boston. She is also the author of *American Homelessness* and *Welfare Reform*.